The Natural Trim
Principles and Practice

Wild stallion of the west surveying his kingdom . . .

With flowing tail, and flying mane,
Wide nostrils never stretched by pain,
Mouths bloodless to the bit or rein,
And feet that iron never shod,
And flanks unscarred by spur or rod,
A thousand horse, the wild, the free,
Like waves that follow o'er the sea.

George Gordon (Lord) Byron
From the poem, *Mazeppa* (1619)

The Natural Trim

Principles and Practice

Jaime Jackson

Author, *The Natural Horse: Lessons From The Wild*

The natural trim is a humane barefoot trim
method that mimics the natural wear patterns of
wild, free-roaming horses of the U.S. Great Basin.

Endorsed and Recommended by the

Association for the Advancement of
Natural Horse Care Practices

978-0-9848399-0-2 (Perfect bound)
978-0-9848399-1-9 (Comb bound)

Direct all inquiries to the author:
J. Jackson Publishing
P.O. Box 1432
Lompoc, CA 93438
www.jaimejackson.com

Natural hoof care is a sophisticated and highly technical process that should only be practiced by qualified natural hoof care practitioners trained and ideally certified in the principles and practices described in these instructions, or by persons under their immediate supervision.

Cover photos and design by Jill Willis.

This book was written to bring attention to horse owners and their professional service providers the many wonderful and proven benefits of genuine natural horse care (NHC), in particular, the "natural trim". Above all, it is my hope that its information will be studied closely, then taken immediately and directly to the horse and put into practice. There's an urgency to this! A vast (majority) population of horses worldwide continue to live miserable lives each day because of harmful, antiquated management traditions that just need to go. NHC — grounded in the laws of nature as demonstrated by America's wild, free-roaming horses — provides a way out and the means of ushering in a much needed Renaissance in humane equine care. *And it's time has come . . . .*

Contents

PART II: PRACTICE

Foreword

The hoof is a biodynamic and adaptive extension of the whole horse and his entire lifestyle, two concepts never divorced from one another. Hence, we do not "force" the hoof into anything, but, like the animal himself, stimulate and nurture it towards what nature intends it to be according to his specie's adaptation as *Equus ferus caballus*. And so, the master trims, the hoof "responds," and the master attunes — as two partners in an endless but concerted dance. The student, therefore, must learn to *sense* natural size, shape, and proportion in the hoof, and to distinguish its travails within a context of anti-holistic forces. And, finally to *see* with the mind's eye — sharpened by the most astute understanding of nature's healing pathway — the hoof's destination, though here and now, it is invisible to the naked and untrained eye. ~ Jaime Jackson

Nature is the source of all true knowledge. She has her own logic, her own laws. She has no effect without cause. She has no invention without necessity.
~ Leonardo da Vinci

If you are reading this foreword, then you may be among a growing population fortunate enough to be either already on, or at the precipice of, a remarkable journey into the healing powers of nature. If you are new to the holistic topic of Natural Horse/Hoof Care (NHC) or the work of Jaime Jackson, I congratulate you for reaching this point and encourage you to sit tight, stay on this largely untraveled road and enjoy the ride! Naturalizing the life of the horse is the only path leading to optimal health, happiness and wellness. Why it is not more widely understood, and practiced, is the subject of countless of hours of conversations between Jaime and I — and among a small group of people around the globe who use this information daily to improve the lives of horses in their care. But I've come to realize that some ideas, no matter how logical, sensible, factual or natural, do take time to be embraced by the masses. For example, many of Leonardo da Vinci's most significant contributions to the world today were not taken seriously at the time he was alive; instead, nearly 500 years passed before academics and scholars even paid attention to many of his groundbreaking studies.

I imagine there are some of you who already recognize that Jaime Jackson has few, if any, peers in his particular area of insights into and understanding of *Equus ferus caballus*. But if this is all news to you, I'm honored to introduce you to Jaime and his research and, encourage you to read *all* his books, and grapple with the information until you have achieved a solid acceptance and understanding of their contents. If you do, you will find it is easier to grasp all the instructions and guidelines published in The Natural Trim, in order to properly conduct this humane barefoot trimming method that he created as a result of the wild horse data he collected, his astute observations of nature and a keen understanding of physical laws.

Although the second half of the book focuses on the mechanics and methodology of natural trimming, the information covered in the first half, on the principles of NHC, are immeasurably relevant, even transformational, *to anyone with an interest in horses*. The characteristics of a healthy horse as well as the symptoms of the debilitating, but far too common, diseases and disorders can be easily seen in the hooves of horses. In fact, by the time you finish this book, you will have more education on the horse's foot than the vast majority of vet students are provided by the time they graduate (Jaime says more than most vets have in their lifetime). Not only will you know how to recognize a healthy, naturally shaped hoof but also what is needed to help your horse grow and maintain them. Because of this simplicity, you have an opportunity, and, I believe, a responsibility, to make a positive impact on the health of horses and on their future existence on this planet.

The Natural Trim is an attempt to explain, simplify and demystify the many complexities of the method itself as well as the principles of its foundation. But of course, you cannot simply sit down in one evening to read the book, and, upon finishing, know the information. It is to be studied and pondered. The hoof is not simply a "structure" to "shorten", but, as Jaime will explain, "a unique, biodynamic organism made up of a vast vascular network of intelligence that reacts, retreats, responds and remodels to numerous influences." One cannot simply 'trim' the hoof without understanding the characteristics of a naturally shaped hoof, its sensitivities and the laws of conservation of mass and energy. As you move through the following chapters, you will find a beautifully coherent, cohesive and comprehensive "how to" guide, stemming from his original research and findings, that can provide you with the key to having healthy domestic horses.

NHC is still a relatively new area of study and those who are already familiar with the topic realize it includes more than simply *trimming* the hoof. In fact, it is well understood by any competent NHC practitioner that as important as it is to be able to conduct a proper natural trim, it is useless to address the health of the hoof without also addressing the health of the horse, which relies upon naturalizing the diet, the boarding conditions and manner of riding. As a result, the terms *natural hoof care* and *natural horse care* are synonymous; they can and should be substituted for one another in your mind as you continue reading.

Jaime's research on wild horses and its application to the hooves of domestic horses was conducted from 1982 through 1986 in the U.S. Great Basin — mostly in Nevada, California and Oregon — both in the wild and at the holding corrals of the BLM (Bureau of Land Management). His experience — as well as his research, observations and findings — is chronicled in his first book, released in 1992 by Northland Publishing, *The Natural Horse*. I have to implore anyone interested in the health and longevity of horses to read it as well. At the time it was first published, traditional and popular magazines such as Horse Illustrated ("Truly spell-binding … a fine work worthy of attention") and Western Horseman ("Thought provoking and well-written") glowingly reviewed the book but much of the information published is still only trickling out into the mainstream.

The natural trim is, paradoxically, both simple and complex at once. I suspect its simplicity has been just as responsible as its complexity for throwing so many off the track while completely derailing others over the last few decades. Yet, the complexities are not so great to sufficiently fathom why so many have been unable to grasp, process and understand the information that Jaime first began sharing in the late 1980s. The application of the trim is a fairly simple, straightforward process of sequential steps aimed at mimicking the natural wear patterns of U.S. Great Basin wild horse hooves. It is critical that students and practitioners alike keep the naturally shaped hoof present in their mind's eye, accurately follow the guidelines and measure. The process of conducting a natural trim also requires understanding certain laws of nature that, if not violated, will always produce healthy, natural results once the technique is applied properly and incorporated with the other principles of NHC.

As a methodology, the natural trim works, but, on the surface, may appear to be much simpler to conduct than it actually is to master. Possibly because of the complexities of the process combined with too few truly understanding the underlying principles, making it impossible to apply with either precision or awareness. But those who have been able to discern the principles and master the techniques of the natural trim do so with great results. As more begin to follow in these footsteps, I firmly believe many more competent NHC practitioners will emerge with the ability to accurately conduct a natural trim on any hoof on any horse in any situation. But, as with any phenomenon governed by natural laws, certain conditions must be present in order for the natural trim method to work; it must be conducted properly and has to be integrated with the other "pillars" of NHC.

At the risk of redundancy, I have to empathize the importance of beginning with an understanding of the natural shape of a hoof. While this might sound fairly straightforward, it can actually be a bit murky because, as da Vinci rather poignantly stated, "There are those who see, those who see when they are shown, and those who do not see." This is, I think, what Jaime meant in the quote I used to open this *Foreword,* when he wrote, "And, finally to *see* with the mind's eye — sharpened by the most astute understanding of nature's healing pathway — the hoof's destination, though here and now, it is invisible to the naked and untrained eye." When and if you can "see", I believe you also have a responsibility to help to educate others. Even those of you armed with just the intellectual understanding will be able to see not only the natural shape of the hoof but also recognize those unnatural characteristics in the photos of hooves of those who use "natural" in their marketing materials but not in their methods. A fair number of people have built careers, companies and businesses as a result of Jaime's research but without any true understanding of the natural shape of the hoof — or the natural trim method. Many are associated with the "barefoot hoof care" world, but their photos, products, articles and publications consistently provide evidence that they do not know the basic characteristics of the natural shape of the hoof or how to "grow one", let alone understand the·data gathered in his research of the Great Basin wild horses. You do not have to dig far to uncover the fact that very few even seem to believe that nature, without the meddling of humans, has any particular innate wisdom.

Thus, at the same time I want to encourage you to "ignore all pathology" — one of Jaime's "Four Guiding Principles" when conducting the natural trim, I also want to warn you to be on the lookout for both intentional and unwitting imposters. When you come across those who claim to still be 'experimenting' with trimming methods or making statements about there being more than one natural method of trimming (besides the one that follows from nature), you would be wise to steer clear. Just as no one is still experimenting with the creation of the wheel, the natural trim method has been created and it works. Now, more just have to understand and learn the method for themselves. Then it will be clear that the only method better (as Jaime often tells his students), results when you put your horse in a trailer, head to an environment like the Great Basin and turn him loose with wild horses to develop rock hard, buffed & polished looking, short hooves as a normal consequence of natural wear.

But, I digress. I am hopeful that the most astute among you — even if it is a just a fraction of the readers — will study, ponder and absorb the information until you have mastered the information and concepts and understand every nuance, nook and cranny of this comprehensive foundational textbook and can recognize its brilliance, which is simply that of nature. We need an abrupt revolution in hoof care and in horse keeping practices and have the means to bring about a transformation in their overall health. But it is incumbent upon you to first truly understand this information in order to put it into practice and instigate an authentic paradigm shift in our approach to the species.

Most people shake their heads in disbelief, as I still do, when they discover the reality that a great majority of the products sold in this multi-billion dollar equestrian market were created without any knowledge of the actual needs of the species or an understanding of its natural habitat. In fact, far too many products appear to have been manufactured with a total disregard for the harmful effects of their ingredients, many of which have been determined to cause a metabolic break down in the horse, causing inflammation, immense suffering or death. Expensive "high-end" feeds and supplements sold at vet clinics, tack and feed stores are often just as perilous as those available in discount chain stores that are marketed as "All Livestock" feed for horses, goats, sheep, and cattle, clearly without concern to the biological or digestive differences of each species. The situation is further complicated by the fact that many medications and procedures for treating the symptoms of what are easily preventable medical conditions (metabolic disorders) are not only *not* successful, but often make things worse. Yet, they generate tremendous profits, and maybe this goes to the heart of the problem. Especially in those instances where there may be no equally profitable, alternative demand such as waste products like beet pulp or rice bran. If there is no other viable use for them, it is unlikely that sales to the equine food industry will be relinquished without a serious battle!

These easily preventable conditions (metabolic disorders), seem to just give rise to even more useless and harmful products marketed just to treat their symptoms without regard to causality. For example, a current trendy and profitable topic is insulin resistance. The horse appears to be an insulin resistant species, and yet the great majority of the most popular and widely available feeds, supplements, and medications often include high levels of sugars — whether in the form of sugar beets, cane molasses, high fructose corn syrup and/or artificial sweeteners. University researchers have demonstrated that laminitis can be induced in horses 100 percent of the time if given enough plant sugars to saturate their hind gut. Thus, if we naturalize the horses' lifestyles and diets, there is no need to for the test to determine insulin resistance. Further, horse owners might cease buying expensive medications such as *Pergolide mesylate*, whose side effects actually cause many of the very symptoms of the disorders the medication is prescribed to quell. Thanks to Jaime's research, we can bring greater health at less expense simply by naturalizing the diet and care of the horse.

Of course, the manufacturers of equine products don't have a corner on the market of ignorance. It can be found in abundance in a majority of the every day, acceptable traditions in the ways horses are fed, managed, and boarded. It appears the great majority of professionals working with horses — including vets, boarding facility managers, breeders, trainers, instructors and, even owners — either do not know, do not want to know or, do not care that the species cannot and will not be healthy, or sound, if they are managed, fed and housed in these commonplace, traditional manners that are completely contrary to what is found in their natural world — in an adaptive environment suited to their biological needs.

So, why is it that so many of these traditional practices are still used when they substantially contribute to the most common deadly diseases and disorders of the horse? I have to believe the infrastructure remains strong because there are not enough people who truly understand the species. Or, in a word, ignorance. Just as there is with humans, canines and felines, there is a huge industrial complex making and selling products which make horses sick, keep horses sick or even to provide them with a past-time while they are sick. Sugary feeds, cribbing collars, stall toys, paddock balls, blankets, tie-downs, hobbles, lubricants, ulcer medications — all useless products supporting an unhealthy, unnatural lifestyle through practices further perpetuated by books and magazines containing articles, ads or images with horses isolated from one another, confined in stalls, or turned out on lush grass pastures. Next time you are looking through any equine publication, if the hooves are even visible, look closely, and you will probably note the tell-tale rings circling the hoof wall, which are a symptom of metabolic distress known as laminitis.

As a result of Jaime Jackson's research — and others — we know what to do to keep horses healthy and thriving. Of course, Leonardo da Vinci discovered that the cause of heart disease was through a build up of cholesterol. He had worked out that a substance carried through the blood, produced by what we eat, imbeds itself into the arteries and blocks natural blood flow. But at the time he wrote of his discovery, it was not taken seriously. And it was not for nearly 500 more years.

Since I first began my own NHC education more than five years ago — and, especially in the last three and a half years since I began working along side of Jaime Jackson — I have heard countless stories from a number of horse owners who have either had a horse euthanized or were contemplating euthanasia because they were unaware of any other choices to cease the animal's suffering or symptoms causing lameness. It is actually quite common in the horse world for the euthanasia option to be kept close at hand. Traditional practices (grass pastures, sweet feeds, unnatural boarding practices, confinement, etc.) break down the horse and traditional treatments do not cure or "fix" these problems. The disconnect is that most do not seem to realize that "lameness" is not a random or natural occurrence. It is caused by things we do — usually a combination of those factors such as unnatural boarding practices (inability to move freely & naturally & engage in natural behaviors), insufficient conditioning of the horse, unnatural riding practices, poor diet or simply forcing the horse to perform in a manner that he or she is not prepared for or, possibly, ever capable of doing without risk of injury.

In fact, Jaime also writes about the testimony of Walt Taylor, co-founder of the American Farriers Association, in 2000, who said, "Of the 122 million equines found around the world, no more than 10 percent are clinically sound ... and could not pass a soundness evaluation or test." Because of Jaime's research of the Great Basin horses — as well as Dr. Ric Redden's that followed a few years later — we know that lameness is not natural. As Jaime points out, "It is almost always 'man-made'." The good news is that more and more people are finding their way to the truth. Jaime, myself and other NHC practitioners around the world have received numerous letters, emails or have been told directly about countless horses who have been saved just as a result of Jaime's book, *Founder: Prevention & Cure the Natural Way*. Even equine veterinarians — both from neighboring states as well as those practicing as far away as Russia, South Africa and Italy — have written to say that the typical, traditional methods they first tried did not work but they watched fast, healthy changes made after removing the shoes and following the lifestyle and dietary recommendations in *Founder*.

So, as I write, I wonder, just how many will take the time to fully grasp the information in this book? And of those who do, will they help spread the information in a responsible way? And, will their voices be louder than those who are threatened by the information and thus, do all they can to disparage it? I can only hope the positive changes in the equine industry and overall horse culture come soon. I would love to see, in Jaime's lifetime, major transformations such as large breeding operations and boarding facilities permanently turning horses out of their stalls and using the structures only for storage or for run-in shelters, dotting the tracks of Paddock Paradises where numerous horses live together.

So, I challenge you, the reader, to consider the followings: Many of Leonardo da Vinci's significant scientific studies, inventions and contributions, made during the 1400s, were not fully appreciated — some not even discovered — until the last 150 years or so. For the sake of horses, I hope that we can be smarter and that our society will fully appreciate Jaime Jackson's research, inventions, information and insights without having to wait hundreds of years.

But the parallels between the two men are vast and so, I am both optimistic and concerned. Like Jaime Jackson, many of Leonardo da Vinci's discoveries were a result of his astute observations of nature. Both men demonstrated the capacity to understand complex topics in science, art, physics, anatomy, engineering and invention. Da Vinci turned to science and nature to improve his artwork, and was the first artist to study the physical proportions of men, women and children and use these studies to determine the "ideal" human figure. Jaime Jackson turned to the natural world in order to see if there was an "ideal" natural shape for a hoof, and was the first farrier to study their natural proportions, angles, lengths, and wear patterns in these healthy, sound animals. Like Jaime, da Vinci was said to view the world as logical rather than mysterious; and both men used empirical methods to complete their studies.

To improve his art, Da Vinci spent hours in nature - just observing things and pondering universal truths. Jaime spent years in the U.S. Great Basin simply observing the lives of wild horses. Da Vinci locked himself away for endless hours cutting up human bodies to understand the exact characteristics, dimensions, locations and relationships of the parts. His work paved the way for remarkably accurate anatomical figures and sketches, which were not used at the time but are widely used today. Jaime's studies of the hoof's form and function, the natural gaits of the horse, the social hierarchy and band behavior alternated with spending years dissecting domestic cadaver hooves to study the anatomical relationship between the dermal and epidermal structures. Da Vinci's studies did not get published in his lifetime; Jaime received more than 150 rejection notices before Northland Publishing opted to publish *The Natural Horse: Lessons from the Wild.*

Jaime created the natural trim method and other concepts using the same resources that da Vinci used when he conceived of ideas vastly ahead of his own time — such as the helicopter, glider, calculator and parachute — just from pondering physical laws, making astute observations in nature and applying the ideas. Jaime began his initial experimentation by applying what he coined "mustang roll" on the bare hooves of domestic horses in his care and studied how their feet responded with more natural growth patterns that, in turn, generated more natural shapes. Like any good scientist, he simply observed what nature revealed. Da Vinci used sketches and sculpture to apply his ideas while Jaime applied his to hooves. Jaime conceived the idea of Paddock Paradise long before the first one was created, as a result of contrasting images of domestic horses housed in traditional boarding situations while reflecting upon behavior and movement of wild horses. Da Vinci used math and geometry to explain many of his theories. Jaime's research data was statistically evaluated (with the assistance of a university mathematician) and compiled into a "bell curve" from which Jaime created a new hoof gauge, the Hoof Meter Reader, so that anyone could measure their horse's hooves in a standardized manner and compare them with healthy wild horse hooves.

It is interesting to note that the pursuit of profits was clearly not the driving force behind the ideas, creations and inventions of either men. The natural trim is not a patented, licensed, registered or protected method that is "owned" by Jaime or any of the organizations he's created. It is a discovery that he has provided as a gift to the horse world just as many of his inventions and innovations have been made available to the public without regard for profits but to improve the lives of horses and horse owners. In fact, Jaime conceived the idea of a pastern strap as a means to better secure a hoof boot to the horse, publishing it as a suggestion along with a photo depicting his creation in an early edition of the book, *The Horse Owner's Guide to Natural Hoof Care*. Now, commonly referred to as the "gaiter", this hoof boot accessory has been freely used by a number of manufacturers and, ironically, is the subject of a patent infringement lawsuit between parties *not* including Jaime, who has never benefited monetarily from its creation or use.

I cannot help but wonder if the fact that material gain has never been his priority isn't also a contributing factor to the lack of widespread awareness of his significant contributions. Certainly there would be money and recognition pouring in if he chose to focus on, and market, his unique — and lesser known — talent and skill for communicating with these animals. There is probably no one better equipped to "train" horses or instruct people on true natural horsemanship, in my opinion, but the importance of their health and welfare (and, as a result, also their happiness) takes precedent even though it is a less popular subject. No one is advocating for the importance of naturalizing the horse's lifestyle like Jaime Jackson and those of us in the AANHCP. But there is no advertising budget for pointing to nature and its simplicity as the best source of information and so, I ask you to consider this: da Vinci derived little or no monetary benefit from the 13,000 pages of notes, sketches and diagrams he created that were later heralded as some of the most important contributions to society ever made. The only people who appear to recognize his progressive ideas and superior intelligence, while he was still alive, were those very close to him; it took hundred of years for everyone else to catch up. Thus, I want to stress that Jaime's somewhat "other worldly" insights should be carefully considered and put into practice —

now. Just because this information is not widespread does not mean it is not of colossal value. In fact, one final note on da Vinci is that his creation of the robot was another of his ideas not taken seriously by his contemporaries, but today, both his anatomical sketches and robotic designs serve as the basis for NASA's "anthrobots", designed to man the International Space Station.

It may just be that society does not tend to quickly embrace new, original or enlightened thought and, therein, lies the crux of my concern. The only way that Jaime's studies can truly make an impact is if the parallels between the men ends here. While it may not be the fault of the masses that too few have truly understood this visionary information to date, blame as to why it has not been widely practices is not the issue. Of paramount importance is that this should be widely practiced, can be and must be. I encourage anyone reading this to make a difference by helping to bring this information to the mainstream. I challenge anyone whose lives are touched by horses — through passion or profession — to read, study and ponder all of Jaime's published books and materials until you have reached a solid understanding of the guiding principles of Natural Hoof Care. At that point, I believe you will understand how much more is at stake than simply learning to trim hooves. It is my belief that then, and only then, can you master the application of the techniques, and do so responsibly, without doubts, excuses or experimentation. I encourage you all to work hard to understand his words — and mine here — with the goal of "doing good" in mind. With some guidance from Jaime, Nature has made this information freely available to anyone who wishes to use it.

Jill Willis

Preface

*T*he *Natural Trim: Principles and Practice* is largely based on the research I conducted in the U.S. Great Basin from 1982 to 1986. It is also tempered and shaped by my nearly 40 years as a hoof care professional, first as a farrier, later as an NHC practitioner and advocate. It was nearly ten years after I nailed on my first horse shoe that I found my way into wild horse country. I had been distressed by the realization that whatever good the shoe offered, it was far outweighed by the harm done. And distressed, too, that I was a big part of the problem, because I was a shoer who perpetuated it. During that early period in my career, I became increasingly haunted by the realization that I was causing harm to the horse by the mere act of shoeing him. In the introduction that follows this foreword, I will share the actual chain of events that led me into wild horse country, and forward from there into the NHC revolution. But suffice it to say, the long and short of it can be summarized in a flash — it was a wild horse that inspired me. Just captured, just purchased from the government by one of my clients, and with no more than a quick glance at her feet, I knew where I had to go.

My research, at first, centered on the hooves of wild horses, but quickly was expanded to include all facets of their lives, from habitat to behavior. Such are the holistic implications of naturally shaped feet as we've come to understand them in the horse's natural world. Vital "lessons from the wild" concerning their feet and life styles culminated in my first book, *The Natural Horse: Lessons From The Wild.* The natural trim instructions presented here are an extension of that book, but are expanded and detailed considerably to flesh out the nuances of trim mechanics.

For nearly 30 years — since the day I stepped into their world in 1982 — I have studied, applied and taught the principles of natural hoof care based on the wild horse model. This has been no small undertaking, requiring the authoring of five related books on the subject, numerous technical papers published by the American Farriers Journal, many magazine articles for horse owners, and, now, *The Natural Trim*. In addition, I have, at home and abroad, guest lectured at universities, scientific forums, farrier and veterinary conferences, and public seminars serving horse owners and their organizations. In the past decade, I have given to work with others in creating two advocacy and training organizations whose sole purposes have been to "spread the word" and train professionals. These are, respectively, the Association for the Advancement of Natural Horse Care Practices (AANHCP) and the Institute for the Study of Natural Horse Care Practices (ISNHCP).

After all these years, why write this book now? The reason is simple. We know much more now about how the process works. Our terminology, techniques, technologies, and our expectations have all evolved commensurately with our expanding knowledge and experience base. We have not stood still, because NHC is no more a passing fad than that naturally shaped hoof in wild horse country.

In my preceding comments, I have made reference to the harmful effects of the horse-shoe upon the horse's foot. In so doing, I have undoubtedly struck an unpleasant chord with some farriers of the world, who take their work seriously and with great pride. This is not my intention. I have no design to cast blame, lay guilt, or sit in judgment of anyone. These trimming guidelines are *not* an indictment of the professional farrier, whose hard labor and dedication is undeniable. To the contrary, NHC belongs equally to the farrier and the barefoot practitioner. Having practiced myself in both realms, I see the "natural trim" as a logical and necessary evolution in our professional understanding and work at the hoof, and the "hoof boot" as an equally logical and important evolution of the metal shoe. These coevolutions are inevitable, in my opinion, and as the massive gears of change continue to shift broadly across the hoof care profession, each will take their rightful place in the mainstream of modern hoof care.

The term "natural trim", now widely used among barefoot trimmers, and even farriers and some equine veterinarians, has, however, come to mean too many things, unfortunately. So, *The Natural Trim* is here to set the record straight as I see things. When applied according to the wild horse model, they bring soundness and relief to hooves suffering the injustices of human error, ignorance and antiquated technologies. Technically speaking, they delineate the necessary nuance that practitioners in the field will require to properly execute the natural trim. But as instructional guidelines, implicit is the understanding that, as in any serious profession, students of NHC should use them judiciously in conjunction with hands-on training under the supervision of qualified instructors. We have those in the world today, so there is no need for anyone to "go it alone".

Jaime Jackson
Lompoc, CA
June/2012

Special acknowledgment

This book is one I probably would not have written had it not been for my colleague and partner Jill Willis. Jill prodded me from the beginning to put in writing what it is that I do at the horse and at his feet, but which I have not either explained sufficiently in the past or simply did not mention at all. Possessing her own keen understanding of NHC as an AANHCP certified practitioner, and having worked at my side for the past three years, not to mention having also scoured all my previous books, technical articles, PowerPoint lectures, and unpublished papers, Jill would know more than anyone where I have been delinquent. This hasn't been easy for her, for, it may come as a surprise to the reader, and especially those who think they know me professionally, I am not one to welcome question after question about my work. But once I concede, which isn't often, I can be harsh and demanding that I am perfectly understood. Jill has bravely stood up to me in this task, and the reader should be as grateful to her as much as I am in awe of her tenacity.

Part I
Principles

I expect to pass through this world but once; any good thing there-
fore that I can do, or any kindness that I can show to any fellow
creature, let me do it now; let me not defer or neglect it, for I shall
not pass this way again.
    Étienne de Grellet du Mabillier (aka Stephen Grellet)

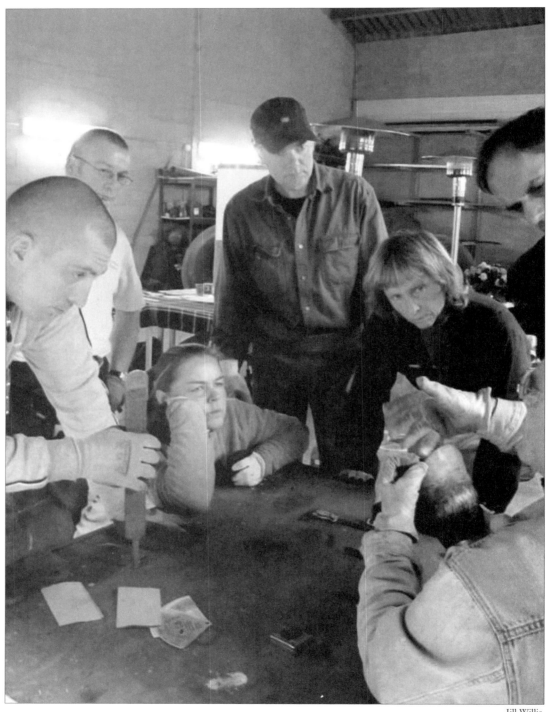

Jill Willis

What Is Natural Hoof Care (NHC)?

This concise and comprehensive guide to the natural trim was written with two objectives in mind. First, to serve as a training manual for professional hoof care practitioners wishing to master the artful science of natural hoof care. And second, to impress upon any horse owner who happens upon this guide to consider the merits of its contents and make the decision to give their horse the humane benefits of natural horse care that his species needs and deserves. The American Farriers Journal reported a decade ago that over 17 percent of all U.S. horses go without shoes.[1] Today, in the aftermath of an unprecedented barefoot revolution, that number is certainly greater and growing. Why do people shoe their horses? The answer is invariably the same: horse owners and their service providers assume that their horses' hooves are too weak and too sensitive to go unshod. That somehow, humans have, through selective breeding and other practices, "bred the foot off of the horse". Further, that soundness is only possible if the hooves are given the type of support that only horseshoes can provide. Many horse owners, aided by a new generation of NHC practitioners, have challenged and disproved this false assumption. They neither shoe their horses nor coddle their hooves once they are free of the horseshoe. To the contrary, unshod horses in their care are given natural trims and are ridden as before with one significant difference: their horses feet are healthier and sounder than ever before. How is this possible? The answer is *natural hoof care*.

What is Natural Hoof Care (NHC)?

Simply stated, natural hoof care (or NHC for short, and I will use this acronym throughout this text) is the holistic care of the horse's foot modeled after the horse's hooves and lifestyle of the U.S. Great Basin wild, free-roaming horse. This new realm of hoof care is founded upon the following facts:

- Nature — as a result of the evolutionary descent of *Equus ferus caballus* over 55 million years through natural selection — created a hoof that serves the horse perfectly well without the aid of horseshoes attached to it.

[1]Journal of the American Farriers Association (May edition, 1998).

(*Facing page*) Senior certified NHC practitioners of the AANHCP representative of Denmark, Italy, The Netherlands, Germany, and the UK meet with the author at lower right to discuss trim mechanics and coordination of future training in Europe.

- The unshod hoof, given reasonably natural care, is a hoof that is vastly superior to the same hoof shod. This belief is supported by a wealth of scientific and anecdotal evidence, largely ignored or denied altogether today by the farrier and veterinary establishments.
- Conventional horseshoeing, synergized by other unnatural care practices, is directly or indirectly responsible for lameness in horses. The "natural hoof", from both humanitarian and practical perspectives, is a sound alternative that always serves the best interests of the horse.
- Horseshoes preclude the hoof from functioning normally as nature intended. Horseshoeing causes hoof pain from errant nails, introduces pathogens through nail holes, affects the foot's homeostasis as nails act as temperature conduits from the environment to the hoof dermis, obstructs healthy circulation through the hoof, cuts off the hoof's ability to feel the ground, unbalances the horse as the hoof grows unchecked under the metal barrier, and, in conjunction with other unnatural practices, sends many horses to an early grave or lives characterized by perpetual unsoundness. Tens of thousands of unwitting riders also suffer serious trauma injuries as a result of shoeing and equally egregious horse care practices.

NHC demonstrates that there is no logical reason nor legitimate justification for this kind of carnage and suffering caused by shoeing (and other practices that violate the horse's biology and natural gaits). All arrows of hoof care intent should point towards the humane treatment of the horse, if for no other reason that horses, from a utilitarian standpoint, are no longer necessary in the world we live in today. And while this may be true, the fact is, NHC is simply the better way to go for all parties involved, horse and human.

Before beginning our brief journey into the world of NHC — as a prelude to learning how to do the natural trim — the reader may be wondering why I am emphasizing the term "NHC" instead of the "natural trim"? Aren't they the same? While related, they have different meanings, and the reader should know what these are. The natural trim refers specifically to trim mechanics, that is, how we physically trim the hoof. It is technically defined as *a humane barefoot trim method that mimics the natural wear patterns of wild horse feet exemplified by wild, free-roaming horses of the U.S. Great Basin.* NHC (natural hoof care), is much broader in meaning and is defined as *the holistic approach to hoof care based on the wild horse model, including natural boarding, natural horsemanship, a reasonably natural diet, and the natural trim itself.* I call these holistic practices the "Four Pillars of NHC", and they are the subject of Chapter 2. I think of NHC as being the most important thing for horse owners to understand, as how the horse is cared for can either help or hinder the effects of the natural trim. The trim, while not unimportant to know something about, is very much a highly technical skill whose nuances and undertaking is truly the providence and responsibility of the trained professional — the NHC Practitioner.

§

Roman "hipposandal" sans leather thong, c. 4th Century AD. Can you imagine strapping one of these to your horse's feet? I don't think so, and you don't need to. Modern hoof boots provide an excellent "contemporary" alternative!

NHC: A Historical Perspective

Until more recent centuries, the historical record shows that most horses have been ridden unshod since their domestication 8,000 or more years ago.[1] They and their owners lived relatively simple, Spartan lives, in fact, under conditions which favored strong, healthy, and naturally shaped hooves. Ancient peoples of Greece, Mesopotamia, Mongolia, and Rome, for example, all rode unshod horses — domesticated horses that lived the better part of their lives on the rugged mountain ranges, deserts, and semi-arid regions of the Old World. The Ancient Greek general Xenophon left us a vivid written accounting of natural hoof care used by his barefoot cavalry, 1,500 years before the dawn of horseshoeing.[2]

Eventually, and coinciding with the rise of modern civilization, the riding stock of these early horsed peoples found their way into the hands of Northern Europeans. Significantly, these horses were also passed into an alien habitat whose moist, lush grasses and cold winters contrasted sharply with the sparse bunch grasses and dry browse of the arid high desert type biome of their ancient homeland. There is credible evidence that this change in natural habitat may very well explain the epidemic numbers of horses that have succumbed to founder (laminitis) ever since. But another event soon occurred which, in the stream of creating the modern horse breeds, obscured this issue — and nearly buried for-

[1]The "Red Earth Peoples" of upper Mesopotamia are thought to be the first horsed society, ca. 5,000 BC. (See Francis Haines, Horses In America.) Other authorities place the peoples of ancient Susa in Southwest Asia as the first domesticators, ca 3,000 BC. Conceivably, however, North American tribes may have adapted horses to their cultures 10,000 years ago or earlier.
[2]See: *Art of Horsemanship* by Xenophon (c. 350 BC), trans. Morris Hicky Morgan, Harvard University, 1898.

XENOPHON

ON THE ART OF HORSEMANSHIP

"The same care which is given to the horse's food and exercise, to make his body grow strong, should also be devoted to keeping his feet in condition. Even naturally sound hoofs get spoiled in stalls with moist smooth floors. [A] place outside of the stall would be best suited to the purpose of strengthening the horse's feet if you threw down loosely four or five cartloads of round stones, each big enough to fill your hand and about a pound and a half in weight, surrounding the whole with an iron border to keep them from getting scattered. Standing on these would be as good for him as traveling a stony road for some part of every day."

Xenophon,
Greek General
c. 350 BC

Early 1st Millennium horseshoe unearthed in Europe. They actually nailed these crude things onto horses' feet, so desperate were the feudal kings of medieval Europe with their close confined horses!

ever our knowledge of the true natural hoof of the ancient Old World homeland.

By the early to mid-Middle Ages, 300-700 A.D., increasing numbers of European horses found themselves living in close confinement. This was a by-product of the new feudalism, an era ushered in by the conquest of the Western Roman Empire by "barbarian" Germanic tribes. Castles, complemented with armies and cavalries, were built by the victorious German tribal chiefs to give their subjects security from rival kingdoms. Horses were stabled in paddocks and stalls, where the hooves were subjected to the animal's own wastes, day in and day out. Moreover, so confined, the hooves could neither function naturally nor optimally. The result was that hooves began to deteriorate systematically across feudal Europe during this period.

It was thought that horseshoeing, still a primitive technology with obscure roots that may have originated with the pagan priests of ancient Gaul (France), could provide a remedy. Horseshoeing, or blacksmithing, henceforth, would evolve inexorably as a commonplace practice such that, by the Crusades (1096 - 1270), its lampblack roots were at last wedged firmly in medieval Europe for the reasons explained here.[1]

Feudalism, however, inevitably gave way to prosperous new economic conditions, and, along with the invention of gunpowder and the long bow, defending castles with knighted horsemen became ineffectual against cannons, harquebuses (an early forerunner of the rifle), long distance archery, and other "modern" contrivances of war. Kingdoms were then

---

[1]"Who Invented Horseshoeing?" by Henry Heymering, RJF, CJF. Published online by the Farrier and Hoof Care Resource Center.

replaced by thriving cities. Not surprisingly, however, the practices of close confinement and horseshoeing continued right on into the Renaissance. Horses were now put to more uses than just carrying soldiers and supplies into war, and the rationales for stalling horses and shoeing them were never called into question. Indeed, guilds were formed to advance the position of the blacksmith, now needed more than ever to meet the growing needs of a horse-dependent society.

With the advent of the Industrial Revolution in the late 18th century, most European, and later American, horses were routinely shod. By the mid-1800s machine-pressed horse-shoes began to replace the more time-consuming, and expensive hand-forged shoes, making shoeing more accessible and affordable to common horse owners. Horse owners were also now accustomed to the convenience of their horses "kept up" close at hand. Moreover, it was just assumed by most that horses needed shoes to "hold them together and provide support", and certainly such hooves, unshod, could not stand the rigors of "turn out" without causing injury. Astonishingly, this belief pervades the horse-using community to date! Now, as then, few questioned that shoeing and unnatural boarding conditions might be the cause of troubled hooves.

At least one veterinary authority, however, rose to challenge the status quo. Bracey Clark, a British equine surgeon, dared to write:

> For a period of more than a thousand years has the present mode of shoeing been in use, without the public being aware that there was anything wrong or injurious about it, if it was but properly executed; and though accidents, and unequivocal expressions of suffering accom-

19th Century horse sandal with wooden base and leather "upper" with straps. Although by now shoeing was entrenched across Europe (and much of the U.S.) early natural hoof care practitioners struggled with limited technology to create an alternative to a practice they knew was harmful. If you look closely at this forerunner of the modern hoof boot, you can see the single leather loop attached at the back of the base, through which was passed a buckled strap. The latter, fed through a reinforcement strap stitched to the toe wall of the boot, could be secured in three positions.

1800 horse boot. This one is beginning to take on the shape and utility characteristics of its modern descendents, including full front and back outer wall covering, adjustable keeper strap at coronet height, and a somewhat natural hoof shaped base. The belt at the neck of the boot, however, would tend to clash with the ascending and descending pastern, resulting in excessive friction and inflammation.

panied it continually, and were visible to the eye of every one, yet no one ventured to think upon a subject that appeared so abstruse; or if he did, was it likely to be received but with rebuff and insolence: and the mischief's arising from it were constantly evaded or denied, and were attempted to be overcome in every way but the proper and natural one—that of removing the cause—which cause also was, to the simple as to the more knowing ones, alike unperceived.[1]

Blacksmiths, as they were then called, were not entirely absent themselves in the early protestations, and some went so far as to manufacture the first modern hoof boots. Still, by 1900, most horse owners had no memory of the pre-horseshoeing days, such had become the convention of horseshoeing. After World War II, automobiles and tractors replaced horses for transportation, drayage, and farm work. Most horses then became "pleasure" animals, used recreationally for competition, trail, and companionship. The traditions of horseshoeing and keeping horses in stalls, nevertheless, continued without further thought or challenge. After all, history shows this has always been customary — who could honestly remember back to a time otherwise?

How Did This all Happen? — NHC in the Present and into the Future

This Guide reunites the NHC practitioner and the horse owner with the horse's forgotten ancient past and his natural world — and to the prospects of a healthier hoof with an unfettered horse attached to them. NHC has been slow in coming. A few words in this regard — how this all happened — are worth sharing.

The Natural Trim actually evolved from my earlier book, *The Natural Horse: Lessons From The Wild* (1992). *The Natural Horse* lays out a model for holistic horse care, including the feet, based on my extensive personal observations of numerous wild, free-roaming horses in the U.S. Great Basin from 1982 to 1986, including a systematic study of their hooves in U.S. government corrals during the same period. Readers should know that *The Natural Horse* provides the natural hoof care foundations discussed in this book. As of this writing (2012), I have been a professional hoof care provider — a traditional farrier until 20 years

[1]Clark, Bracey, F.L.S., . *Podophthora: Demonstration of a Pernicious Defect in the Principle of the Common shoe.* Royal Veterinary College Library, London, 1829, p. 2.

ago — for over 35 years.

At the time I wrote *The Natural Horse*, I confess that I was under a certain amount of "political" pressure from various colleagues to minimize any discussion of riding barefoot horses. The matter was simply too controversial (— not that it still isn't!), and the process too little understood at the time (early 1980s) to even consider asking horse owners to "de-shoe" their horses and go barefoot. I recall in the mid-1980s calling the president of the American Association of Equine Practitioners (the U.S.'s largest equine vet association) to tell them about my research and ask if their association would publish an article on NHC or have me speak at their annual conference. I was stunned by his response, "Mr. Jackson, I can't think of a single reason why one of our vets would want to hear anything about . . . what do you call it, 'NHC'?" But times have changed, and *The Natural Trim* now freely and unequivocally advocates both removing shoes from all horses and riding them either barefooted or with hoof boots — or both.

The "jump" to NHC did not occur overnight, however. It began rather slowly, and, admittedly, cautiously, with certain of my professional shoeing clients who seemed open-minded to the possibilities. I also began to take note of the (now and then) horses crossing my professional path in various barns that had been going unshod all along; thinking back, these were the horses with the least problem feet and who were invariably sound! This recognition, coupled with my many trips to wild horse country to see the natural hoof in action, gave me the confidence, and inspiration, to continue my experiments with developing the natural trim. One "experimental" venue was pivotal in this.

During the early 1980s, I was contracted to trim all the horses at a huge Peruvian Paso breeding and training ranch, whose owners — as well as the breed registry itself — did not want the horses shod. For six years, I had at my disposal a true experimental laboratory to test the forthcoming foundations for NHC. And that I did, keeping data records for each horse, and there were over 300 horses of every age — mares and their young, geldings, and stallions. I systematically compared my data with the measurements I collected for the wild horses.[1] Every effort was made to bring each hoof into the natural form, and as I was the only farrier working the premises, there was no "outside" interference to compromise my work. It was a great learning experience, and without going into the mass of details, the experiment was a great success.[2]

By 1990, I had de-shod many other horses and was now satisfied that barefootedness

---

[1] This successful cross-linking of data for wild horses and horses in my care led to the creation of the Hoof Meter Reader gauge discussed later in this book.

[2] Dr. John "Jack" Woolsey, the ranch's veterinarian, later penned a letter in 1988 on my behalf in an early effort of mine and Dr. Leslie Emery (co-author, *Horseshoeing Theory and Hoof Care*: Lea & Febiger, 1977), to form an advocacy organization based on the wild horse paradigm (see *The Natural Horse*, p. 154-155), writing, "I have never seen so many sound horses in one place in my entire career". Dr. Woolsey, with a long and distinguished career that included teaching at U.C. Davis, CA, passed away on March 23, 2011 at age 88.

was not only possible, and beneficial, but that horseshoeing wasn't the "necessary evil" history and convention in some quarters proclaimed it to be. I had by then also finished writing *The Natural Horse*, and pretty much decided that my career as a farrier was over. The future lay ahead, but I didn't know what it had exactly in store for me at the time.

§

History, it seems to me, never moves forward in a predictable straight timeline, and the evolution of NHC is no exception. My role in its recent incarnation and growth was equally unpredictable, yet things happened that, in retrospect, make sense. First came invitations to speak or contribute to professional journals as a result of either my research or the arrival of *The Natural Horse*: Annual Conference of the American Farriers Association, Lexington, KY (1988); Denver Area Veterinary Medical Association annual conference (1993); Arkansas Horse Council Annual Convention (1993, 1995); Bluegrass Laminitis Symposium, Louisville, KY (1995); Institute for Orthopedic Hoof Care, Tubingen, Germany (1999); Annual Student Educational Fair of the European Federation of Farriers, The Netherlands (2009); University of Teramo, School of Veterinary Medicine, Italy (2009); Sound Horse Conference, Louisville, KY (2011). Added to these venues were the series of articles published by the American Farriers Journal and the European Farriers Journal throughout the 1990s, and the many training clinics and camps operating from 2002 to the present run by the AANHCP and ISNHCP.[1] Then there were my private and smaller public horse owner clinics and speaking engagements, along with contributions to horse enthusiast magazines of all sorts. Virtually unknown to persons outside the NHC world was the secular newsletter, *The Hoof Care Advisor*, which I published briefly on either side of the 2000 millenium axis to encourage and support horse owners and early AANHCP practitioners who were grappling with the new hoof care revolution.[2] Of course, during the late 1990s, and right into the present, many others surfaced to push things along in their own right, if not always in the best interest of NHC, at least in the generic end of "barefoot hoof care".

Interest in NHC was never confined to the United States, indeed, from the outset, it arose simultaneously in Europe, the UK, countries of the Middle East, Australia, New Zealand, Mexico, Chile, and other places. More recently, interest has come from countries once held hostage behind the Iron Curtain of Soviet control. In fact, within a year or two of Soviet military withdrawal from Poland in the aftermath of Perestroika, Polish publishers attending the annual Berlin book publishers and distributors convention contacted me to request permission to translate and publish *The Natural Horse* in their native language. I agreed, and the first foreign translation of my written works emerged in Poland years

---

[1] Association for the Advancement of Natural Horse Care Practices, and, Institute for the Study of Natural Horse Care Practices.

[2] I terminated the *Advisor* in 2001 to concentrate on the demands upon me by the AANHCP. In 2012, I am publishing a new quarterly, the *NHC Journal*, a contemporary equivalent of the old *Advisor*.

before, I am sad to say, the American horse-using community every heard of the book! Since then, invitations to speak in the Balkans, the Republic of Kazakhstan, the Republic of Lithuania have come, all in the desire to learn more about NHC in countries once denied freedom of speech. Translations of my written works are now in different languages, a trend I see continuing into the future given the importance of NHC to horses anywhere on this planet.

By most accounts, the worldwide rise of NHC and the barefoot horse care movement in general is staggering. In the span of little more than one decade, most horse owners today have heard of NHC and many have taken their horses out of shoes to reap the benefits of NHC. Some advocates believe hundreds of thousands of horses have been taken into barefoot, but no one knows for sure. While farrier resistance has been strong, understandably so given the threats of competition by NHC practitioners, many have decided wisely to "cross over" and augment their shoeing practices with NHC. Some have done this out of necessity, with horse owners giving them the choice — "Take my horse barefoot, or I will find someone who will!" — or simply understand that it isn't a "hoax" and truly benefits the horse. Some farrier training schools have also appreciated the inevitable and now offer NHC as part of their curriculum. The Dutch Equestrian Center (Deurne), known as the Helicon, is such an example, and the head of its farrier instruction department, backed by the school's headmaster, is working with me to translate these NHC trimming guidelines and establish a curriculum. Other schools are sure to follow as burgeoning NHC demand continues among horse owners who ultimately have final say about what's going to happen to their horses' feet. An especially unique example of this "taking control" of one's horse is worth sharing here.

In the early 2000s, the Houston police department's mounted patrol became aware of the possibilities of NHC in their own ranks. Plagued by lameness issues, astronomical farrier and veterinary bills, senior officers in the department decided to look closer at options — NHC, in particular. Liking what they saw, several of their officers ultimately completed their training and

(*Above*) Conducting a 3 Day Continuing Education clinic in Texas, 2011, for AANHCP certified practitioners.

(*Below*) Demonstrating the natural trim with a hind hoof at the Helicon/Dutch Equestrian Center, as students, staff, and members of the European Federation of Farriers and Dutch Farrier Association look on.

With senior officers of the Houston Police Department's Mounted Patrol, the first such horse patrol unit in the United States to forsake shoeing and go entirely barefoot using NHC principles and practices. Lt. Randall Wallace (last officer on right), mounts stairs during tactical training. All three officers at rear are AANHCP trained.

certification with the AANHCP and began doing their own hoof work. The department's contracted farriers couldn't believe that such a thing could or would ever happen. It did, and today, half a decade later, the department now does all its own trimming, keeps all its horses barefoot (using hoof boots if needed), and has saved so much money due to fewer vet and shoeing bills that they were able to budget an entirely new barn facility with a forthcoming "natural boarding" adjunct in the near horizon. In 2010, fellow AANHCP board member Jill Willis, and I toured the new mounted patrol's headquarters, listened to their story and shared our own perspective on some of the "behind the scenes" things that happened to make it all possible.[1]

§

It is astonishing to me personally that so many quarters of the horse world are still unfamiliar with NHC, or fail to understand its actual value. I can account for this shortcoming as follows:

- *NHC is still relatively new to the horse-using community compared to the 800 year farrier tradition.* The Internet has really been the principal force in getting our message out there, and without it, would we be looking at another 800 years to make the change? Clearly, horse owners are leading the way today as they have from the beginning. Many have gone around the resistance and stood up against the ominous "health and soundness" warnings of their vets, farriers, trainers, instructors, fellow horse-owning friends and skeptics.

- *Farrier resistance is rigid, and determined to defend its turf.* There are thousands of farriers worldwide, so that's quite the opposition in terms of sheer numbers. But there is also

[1]"Houston Mounted Patrol Goes Barefoot", J. Willis, Equine Wellness Magazine, Aug/Sept., 2011.

Austin, Texas, Police Department's Mounted Patrol Unit line up for a photo shoot. Eleven of their thirteen horses are now barefoot and trimmed by an AANHCP certified practitioner. They credit the entirely barefoot Houston Police Mounted Patrol Unit (38 horses) with influencing their decision to remove the shoes and adopting the proven principles and practices of NHC for their hoof care.

the supply side of their industry, with heavy corporate marketing and manufacturers and distributors pushing product and shoeing-based technology to promote their culture.

- *Other "barefoot" trim methods have sprouted up competitively, if not opportunistically, all around the NHC matrix.* These are as varied as the many shoeing methods out there, and are championed by just about anyone who thinks they know what they are doing, but often without any credible training or experience. Some incorporate elements of NHC, others are simply "anything goes". In 2009, while conducting a demonstration on the natural trim, several Dutch farriers shared their anger and frustration with me that persons not trained in the farrier sciences were infringing on their professional turf and causing problems for horses. They were emphatic that NHC, if it is to be conducted at all, should be done by trained professional farriers. "You were a farrier, so you qualify and that is fine with us," they exclaimed, "but not those others." I countered, "NHC shouldn't be taught or practiced by anyone who doesn't really know what they're doing." That seemed to satisfy them, and before the day was over, 50 of their ranks watched closely as I worked the "natural trim" with my AANHCP colleagues (photo, page 21). That experience was truly history in the making!

Public NHC demonstration by senior AANHCP certified practitioners, Helsinge, Denmark, 2010. Several Danish farriers were present, exclaiming their interest in and support for the new NHC movement in their country. Horses line up quietly side-by-side to be trimmed, in what I call "sequencing". Learn about this in chapter 3.

Jill Willis

- *Veterinarians are not taught anything about NHC and very little about the foot at all in the university sector!* Consequently when they reach the field they fall back on the only thing they know anything remotely about — horseshoeing. Hence, vets are often in conflict with NHC principles and practices in the field through no fault of their own. But it isn't much better for the farrier. In fact, it is one of the supreme ironies of the horse world that vets, who receive virtually no training in the farrier sciences, are expected to advise on or direct corrective and orthopedic shoeing procedures to farriers, who, in turn, have little or no training at all in animal physiology, behavior, pathology and medicine that vets ostensibly receive. This discrepancy, in my opinion, has done little to serve the horse well, but much to cause him problems — with his feet, in particular! Further, I believe unequivocally that the import of NHC science, principles, and holistic practices into the mainstream curriculum of vet schools would serve demonstratively to mitigate the shortcomings perpetrated upon the horse by this vet/farrier conundrum. Farrier schools would be wise to follow suit too, if not lead the way — like the Helicon is in the process of doing in the Netherlands.

- *The horse boot industry.* While I personally welcome this burgeoning industry's contributions to getting horses out of shoes, I am dismayed by their negligence to embrace and import the science of NHC in their designs. What we have are boots that typically are neither naturally shaped nor sized, typically aggravate soft tissue structures above the hoof capsule, and obstruct or conflict with the natural gaits and the "hoof mechanism" — how the hoof naturally functions during its support (weight-bearing) phase (discussed at length in chapter 7). In my opinion, they certainly don't meld with the science of NHC and the genuinely naturally shaped foot. There is a rational explanation for this clash. Most have been designed by horse owners with no formal training at the hoof, or by hoof care professonals who are unfamiliar with or do not understand NHC or who do not embrace it for whatever reason. Given the growing barefoot revolution, I'm frankly surprised that horseshoe manufacturers haven't quietly scanned the horizon and begun to use their ingenuity and industrial capability to come up with their own boots.

§

Demonstrating balancing and placement of the hind hoof during an NHC advanced trimming clinic attended by over 30 AANHCP certified practitioners in Kentucky (USA), 2010. Women comprise over 60% of all AANHCP certified practitioners.

What all the foregoing means is that the transition of NHC from its peripheral position in the horse world to its center — inevitable, in my opinion — will require simply more innovations (e.g., better boots), education (e.g., this textbook, the ISNHCP and sanctioned training), and shifts in antiquated paradigms that fail the horse and his owner. I am hopeful though that my fellow humans will rise to the occasion. Here is my thinking on how I see the future unfolding in this regard . . .

Slowly, horse owners will be relieved of their burden to single-handedly "lead the way" to and through the doors of NHC. For sure, in the immediate years ahead, they will continue to press their farriers and vets to look into it. Failing there, they will use the internet to find NHC practitioners and advocates, and host grassroot clinics and seminars through which to educate themselves and fellow horse owners with open minds. This is the way it has happened in the past (and from the beginning) and will undoubtedly continue into the foreseeable future.

Horse owners, not their personal farriers, will continue to seek out NHC training to do the work themselves. This also is how it has happened from the beginning, and inevitably will continue to happen into the immediate future.

Farriers will begin to feel the economic pinch, as they are relieved of work by a new generation of NHC practitioners arising from the horse owner fold. Farriers will become more competitive among themselves with clients still holding out to shoe. The smarter ones will, initially, crossover to offer NHC services, even if mediocre by NHC standards. Most will discover

Before the cameras in a 2011 General Motors Corporation sponsored documentary to explain the science and value of NHC. Filmed at Return To Freedom wild horse sanctuary, Lompoc, CA).

Jill Willis

that there is more work available if they will simply educate themselves and augment their training with genuine NHC. They will also discover, much to their delight and surprise, that NHC pays well and is a thousand times easier on their bodies. They will discover that there is no longer a need to haul around heavy and expensive inventories of horseshoes and shoeing technology (much to the chagrin of manufacturers and suppliers). The smarter ones will also look to horse boots to replace the old metal stock. Above all, they will see and be humbled by the incredibly durable, naturally shaped, and healthy hooves made possible with NHC. Every honest farrier I know who has "crossed over" will tell you, "There's no turning back. NHC is just the right place to be." What ethical professional would choose a life fighting with nature, absorbed with pathology, and contending endlessly with lame horses? The farrier will also discover and embrace the camaraderie of fellow NHC practitioners. He or she will look back from whence they came, and, like myself years ago, sigh in relief.

It is inevitable, the horseshoe and horse nail manufacturers will sooner than later begin to feel the squeeze too and change. Demand, if it hasn't already begun to slacken, is going to dwindle and then disappear altogether. It will no longer be profitable. The smarter ones, as I've written, will (secretly, at first, so as not to alienate their culture) begin to think about creating the "horse boot of the future" and transition away from the medival techology that has caused so much harm. I suspect the wiser ones will seek out NHC experts to guide them and so spare themselves the folly of re-creating "white elephant" relics and parodies already flooding the marketplace instead of what is really needed. What is needed, in fact, are true innovative industrialists who will recognize the magnitude of the marketplace serving over 30 million horses worldwide.

Jill Willis

(*Left*) During the filming of a special program on "The Natural Horse: Lessons From the Wild" in Italy.

As the holistic healing effects of NHC on horses everywhere increasingly take hold, vets in the field will have to take notice sooner or later. Like the farrier feeling the sqeeze and looking further afield for scarcer and scarcer shoeing customers to keep themselves afloat, so will the vet have to compete harder for clients. This tighting noose will signal the arrival of the long awaited holistic vet trained in the science of NHC. And NHC advocates will point horse owners to them, away from the "old school" vets hopelessly mired in the self-perpetuating cycle of pathology, drugs, invasive procedures, and lameness. It is a fact that horse owners who embrace genuine NHC — not the artificial generic "barefoot rims" I alluded to above — rely less and less on their former vets, because their horses are healthier and have fewer problems.

Horse owners will demand health care products free of toxic chemicals and harmful drugs that upset the horse's sensitive biology, and more natural feeds. This is already happening, and, to some extent, the supply industries are cooperating — simply because there is demand.

Jill Willis

(Continued on page 29)

Clinics here and there.

(This page)
(Above) In Italy, demonstrating what I call the "elevator" — a way to position the hind leg effortlessly so that it goes up and down to receive the hoof stand (at my right).

(Below) In Kentucky (USA), introducing "sequencing" for the first time to CPs (certified practitioners) of the AANHCP. Sequencing, discussed at length in the introduction to Part II of this book, is a way to effectively manage the horse, conserve one's energy during trimming, and be efficient with tools and equipment

(Facing page)
(Above) AANHCP practitioners relax and amuse themselves with photos taken after a public clinic in Denmark, while I doze.

(Below) CPs and students from Europe gather to notch and probe cadavers. Always an interesting and important learning experience, notching is the subject of chapter 15.

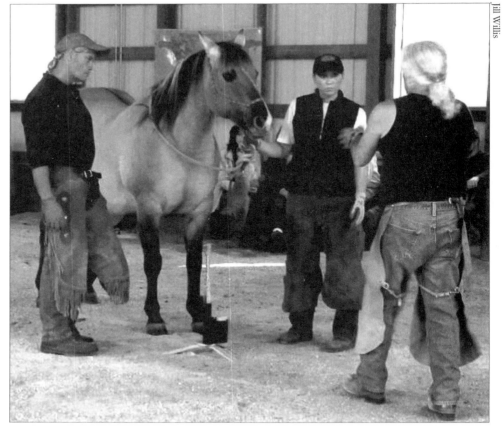

Edwin Siebers

Jill Willis

(Continued from page 27)

In conclusion, it seems to me that NHC has established its place in the mainstream horse-using community. From my vantage point, it appears to be a growing influence as people take its vital lessons from the wild to heart and make them work for their horses. I imagine that, one day, NHC practices will be simply assumed as mainstream practices, with no distinction made in the minds of horse owners and their professional care providers. While pioneers of this movement may be long forgotten, their legacies will surely live on for what they are . . . humane and natural, useful practices.

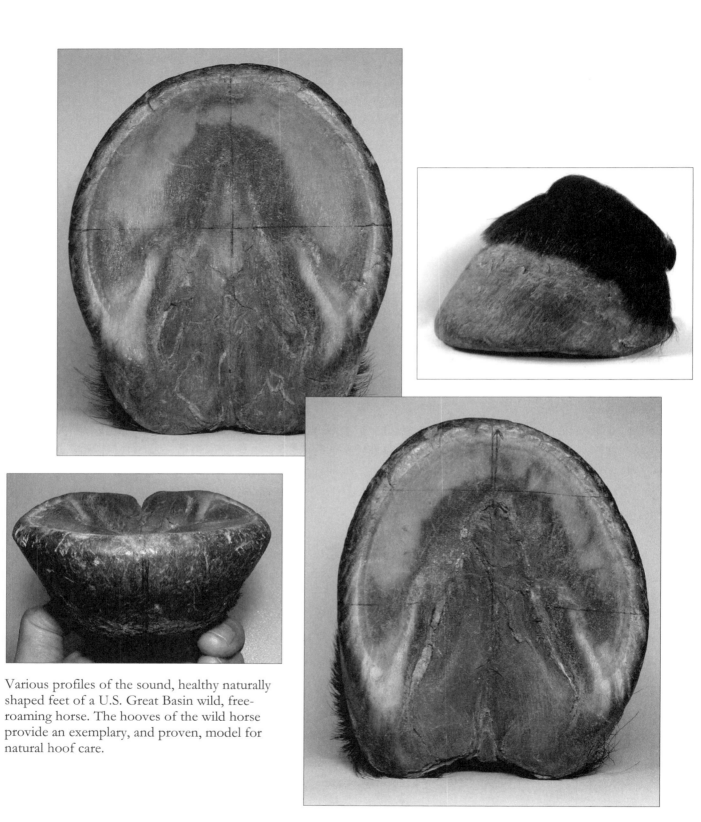

Various profiles of the sound, healthy naturally shaped feet of a U.S. Great Basin wild, free-roaming horse. The hooves of the wild horse provide an exemplary, and proven, model for natural hoof care.

The Perfectly Natural Hoof

"Thus it appears advisable to me to look back from the perfect animal and to inquire by what process it has arisen and grown to maturity, to retrace our steps as it were, from the goal to the starting place, so at last when we can retreat no further, we shall feel assured that we have attained to the principles." William Harvey, M.D. *Essays On The Generation of Animals (1651)*

This comprehensive guide to the natural trim has as its model the wild, free-roaming horse of the U.S. Great Basin. *The sound, healthy feet of the Great Basin wild horse define the natural state of the hoof and the foundations for natural hoof care.* Thus, any intelligent consideration of such a model must begin with a discussion of the meaning of "natural state" and why it is applicable and useful in the care of domesticated horses.

At first thought, there can be a tendency among horse owners (and their many service providers) to reject the wild horse hoof as a model worthy of emulation. At surface, this seems reasonable. What business does a "wild" hoof have being on a "domestic" horse? More often I hear, "What applies to wild horses doesn't apply to domestic horses, because domestic horses aren't wild and they don't live naturally."

Evolution, Adaptation, and the Horse's Foot

This type of logic, on closer inspection, is fraught with misunderstanding. While the science of how and when the horse as we know him today arrived on our planet lies somewhat beyond the scope of this text, it is the relevance of the wild horse to his domesticated cousin that necessarily draws us into the discussion. Paleontologists and other scientists using radiocarbon-dating and DNA techniques suggest strongly that the modern horse, *Equus caballus* arrived over a million years ago, the result of a complex evolutionary descent from *Hyracotherium* (also called Eohippus, the "dawn horse") spanning over 50 million years.[1] Of significance to NHC principles and practices is that the modern horse — technically *Equus*

---

[1] *Hyracotherium* is pronounced *HYE-rak-oh-THEER-ee-um,* The horse's evolutionary "tree" is extremely complex and certainly non-linear. Of the many scientific journals, papers, and Internet forums on the subject, Kathleen Hunt's website, "Horse Evolution", is one of the more interesting and fun, and also takes up the Evolution-Creation clash! http://www.talkorigins.org/faqs/horses/horse_evol.html#part2.

This is the only known photo (1884) of a live Tarpan (*Equus ferus ferus*), also known as the Eurasian wild horse. The last individual of this subspecies died in captivity in Russia in 1909. The evolutionary descent of *Equus ferus caballus* through natural selection spanned tens of millions of years. Scientists believe there were many branches of related species that became extinct along the way. Research continues to ravel the horse's family tree, deploying ever more sophisticated DNA tracking technology.

ferus caballus — and his wild, pre-domesticated antecedent, *Equus ferus ferus*,[1] form a single homogeneous group ("clade") and are genetically indistinguishable from each other.[2] This fact is foundational to our work because what we do for the horse is based on his biological adaptation. Hence, the entire battery of NHC practices, from natural boarding to feeding a reasonably natural diet to engaging natural horsemanship to diligently executing the natural trim, all follow from this premise.

So, when we say that a horse is "wild", all we're really saying is that it isn't domesticated. But it's the same animal, nonetheless. As I described in my book *The Natural Horse*, the modern horse emerged from the wild thousands of years ago as a result of domestication.[3] So rejecting the value of "wildness" in the horse, in a sense, is foolish because it means re-

[1] *Equus ferus ferus* was reclassified by scientists as *Equus ferus caballus* upon his earliest domestication, possibly in Kazhakstan during the Botai Culture. Ref. "The Earliest Horse Harnessing and Milking". http://www. sciencemag.org/content/323/5919/1332.abstract?sid=d021eb55-bcbd-4ebd-9eca-145ce25969b0.

[2] Weinstock, J.; *et al.* (2005). "Evolution, Systematics, and Phylogeography of Pleistocene horses in the New World: A Molecular Perspective". *PLoS Biology* 3 (8): e241. Orlando, L.; *et al.* (2008). "Ancient DNA Clarifies the Evolutionary History of American Late Pleistocene Equids". *Journal of Molecular Evolution* 66 (5): 533–538. Cai, Dawei; Zhuowei Tang, Lu Han, Camilla F. Speller, Dongya Y. Yang, Xiaolin Ma, Jian'en Cao, Hong Zhu, Hui Zhou (2009). "Ancient DNA Provides New Insights into the Origin of the Chinese Domestic Horse". *Journal of Archaeological Science* 36 (3): 835–842. Vilà, Carles; Jennifer A. Leonard, Anders Götherström, Stefan Marklund, Kaj Sandberg, Kerstin Lidén, Robert K. Wayne, Hans Ellegren (2001). [10.1126/science. 291.5503.474 "Widespread Origins of Domestic Horse Lineages"]. *Science* 291 (5503): 474–477.

[3] Scientists think the first equines were domesticated as early as 4000-3500 BC (~6,000 years ago) in the Eurasian Steppes and central Europe, i.e., the regions including the Ukraine and Kazakhstan today. See also: "What We Theorize – When and Where Did Domestication Occur". *International Museum of the Horse*. http:// imh.org/legacy-of-the-horse/what-we-theorize-when-and-where-did-domestication-occur/.

Museum replica of the earliest known ancestor of the horse, *Eohippus*. [Restoration of *Eurohippus parvulus*, Museum für Naturkunde, Berlin]

jecting the horse's biological roots. It blinds us to the essence of what it means to be a horse.

Another word that seems to throw people for a loop, adding to the storm of confusion over what is and isn't wild, is the term *feral*. Wild horses of the U.S. Great Basin are sometimes said to be "feral", which simply means that they were once domesticated but have returned to their wild state, or lifestyle. The term "feral" means *wild beast* (in Latin) and refers

(Continued from page 33)

to any animal that makes the transition from being domesticated to living naturally in the wild. Nevertheless, feral horses, like domesticated horses, genetically speaking, are all derived from the same wild animal, *Equus ferus ferus*. They are still the same species. This is really no different than with camels, llamas, and elephants, all of which have known feral, wild, and domesticated lifestyles too. So, if there is an issue here in differentiating what is wild, from what is feral, or from what is domesticated, it is really a question of the effects of lifestyle and environment, rather than inherited biology.

The difference, then, between wild horses at the dawn of domestication upon the Eurasian steppes thousands of years ago and all horses today, is not in variant species, but in the wilderness and domesticated *experiences*. The domestic experience is inseparable from the human influence ("meddling" is a term I often use); wildness, on the other hand, bears the untampered hand of species *adaptation*. And here is yet another word that invites confusion, given the wide overlap between its scientific and lay usages!

Most people think of adaptation as some one or some thing getting accustomed to something new or different in the short term. Scientists, in contrast, define adaptation as the evolutionary process by which a population becomes better suited to its environment over many generations and thousands of years. Adaptations occur through *natural selection.* Natural selection is the process by which those heritable traits (e.g., hair color serving as camouflage or sexual attraction) that make it more likely for an organism to survive and successfully reproduce become more common in a population over successive generations. Natural selection acts upon the *phenotype,* or observable characteristic of an organism; and so it goes that the heritable (genetic) basis of any phenotype that favors reproduction will become more common in a population. Scientists studying the genetic evolution of the horse believe that the modern horse, *Equus ferus caballus* evolved through natural selection over a stretch of 55 million years following the extinction of the last dinosaurs in the Cretatious Period,[1] arriving as we know him today (based on his DNA) approximately 1.4 million years ago, long before the dawn of humans.[2]

What the foregoing means is that the wild horse foot, like the wild horse himself, is, from an evolutionary standpoint of long term species stability, very much worth our while as a model to emulate. This certainly became clear to me as a result of my studies of the wild horses of the U.S. Great Basin — an animal reproductively prolific (a signature of

---

[1]Called the Cretaceous–Tertiary extinction event, or "K-T Extinction Event", forming the "K-T Boundary" between the demise of dinosaurs and the rise of mammals.

[2]As I mention at the front of this chapter, by no means did the evolution occur in a linear progression. Apparently many species and sub-species came and went along the way, such that the "family tree" of the horse had many branches with many extinctions.

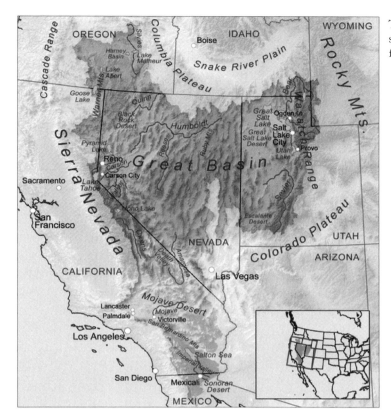

The United States Great Basin, home to America's wild, free-roaming horses.

successful adaptation), healthy, and sound. But I would like to point out that these wild horses did not technically adapt to that environment, as some might suggest. As I wrote in my first book, *The Natural Horse*, wild horses that I studied in the U.S. Great Basin came from run aways and deliberate turn-outs, the very first probably deriving from Spanish stock during the Age of Exploration and early colonization of the continent. Before the first Spanish explorers arrived from Europe,[1] there were no horses in the Great Basin or in North America ("New World"). Scientists believe that *Equus ferus ferus* became extinct across North America 10,000 years ago during the late Pleistocene Epoch. It is thought that unfavorable climate and vegetation changes caused the horse's extinction, possibly accelerated from over-hunting by early tribes of humans.[2] Over time, climactic and environmental conditions in North America reversed, once more favoring the adaptation of the horse. In fact, by the time the Spanish arrived in the American southwest, the region more closely resembled the semi-arid Eurasian steppes where *Equus ferus ferus* had long ago

[1]Garcés, Francisco. 1900. *On the Trail of a Spanish Pioneer: The Diary and Itinerary of Francisco Garcés*. Edited by Elliott Coues. Two vols. Francis P. Harper, New York, NY.; 1967. *A Record of Travels in Arizona and California, 1775–1776*. Edited by John Galvin. John Howell, San Francisco.

[2]Called the "prehistoric overkill hypothesis". Ref. "Prehistoric overkill" in *Pleistocene extinctions: The search for a cause* (1967, ed. P.S. Martin and H.E. Wright). New Haven: Yale Univ. Press

(*Right*) Although a different species of *Equus* than the horse, the Zebra is nevertheless a potentially valuable study subject for NHC. Never truly domesticated, his hooves bear the mark of a truly wild equine living in an adaptive environment similar to the Eurasian steppes in which *Equus ferus ferus* survived in the post-Pleistocene Epoch. I have seen one photo taken of a zebra hoof and it is remarkably similar to that of the donkey.

(*Facing page*)
(*Above*) Semi-feral horses of Dartmoor, southwestern England. Stress rings in outer wall are symptoms of laminitis (chapter
(*Below*) The Duelmener ponies of Germany, living in a lush "founder trap". Both the Duelmener and Dartmoor horses, as with many other feral horse populations in the world, are simply poor study groups for NHC practitioners due to their non-adaptative habitats.

survived, flourished, and became domesticated — at the same time members of his species perished in North America. Spanish and other European runaways (called "mustangs") now readily "re-occupied" the North American "pre-Pleistocene" niche and propagated — flourishing into the millions according to 19th century explorers. But my point is that these imported horses did not actually adapt to this environment, only that the Great Basin once more "fit" their specie's adaptation that occurred 1.4 million years earlier. Thus, the hoof we see in the Great Basin today, is the hoof representative of that adaptation — what I have come to appreciate as the perfectly natural hoof. This does raise the issue of the sorts of environments inhabited by feral horses are deemed useful to us as models for NHC practices.

As it turns out, not all wild horse or "feral" herds are suitable as models for NHC and the natural trim as they do not inhabit the high desert type *biome* (ecosystem) of their specie's ancient adaptation. In all other environments to which the horse did not adapt 1.4

million years ago, his feet will reflect the deleterious influences of those environments. NHC advocates and others have investigated the hooves of feral herds in such "non-adaptive" environments, including the Kaimanawa horses of New Zealand, Chincoteague ponies of Assateague Island (one of several U.S. coastal islands off of Virginia and Mary-

land), the feral horses of Cumberland Island National Seashore (Georgia/USA), Camargue ponies of France, and the Dartmoor Ponies of southwestern England, and, without exception, all demonstrated hoof issues ranging from extreme capsule overgrowth to chronic laminitis. The Duelmener ponies of Germany, for example, live in a moist, relatively swampy environment. NHC advocates have visited these herds and investigated their hooves; not surprisingly, they found them to be overgrown, suffering from diseases, and badly in need of natural hoof care. Like all feral horse herds today, they are managed for population control; according to one official, "To this day, the Duelmener wild horse project is merely breaking  even by selling off yearling colts every year and selling tickets for the event of gathering the herd and catching the yearling colts." The Dartmoor horses of southwestern England suffer a similar fate. The right front (RF) hoof of the mare in the photo above is covered with stress rings, a telltale symptom of chronic laminitis.

Jill Willis   Our four horses moving on track in our Paddock Paradise, a concept for natural horse boarding based on the wild horse model. Natural boarding is one of the four foundational pillars of NHC, upon which our principles and practices are premised.

The Four Pillars of NHC

My closest professional colleagues and I continue to query passionately among ourselves, often to the point of anguish, how can something so obvious and harmonious with the horse's innate biology — the paradigm of the natural horse — be so completely unknown or misunderstood in the Information Age? Have we as a species become so separated from nature that we cannot see the forest for the trees? Are we unable to appreciate another species for what it is, rather than what we wish for it to be under the misguiding delusions of anthropomorphism or commodity ownership and exploitation? And so it goes as we advocate for the humane care of the horse, waiting patiently for others to arrive and join us.

On the bright side, there appears to be hope as horse owners worldwide continue to flock in ever-increasing numbers to the new paradigm. Most arrive eagerly, entering our world through different doors, in the same way that one music lover reaches Mozart at a recital, another through a lullaby jingle ("Twinkle Twinkle Little Star"), and another who first takes up an instrument and then discovers the great composer. Once inside, however, all begin to see and appreciate the full vision of what it is. Sometimes the discovery, like the journey itself for some, is overwhelming. But with few exceptions, we all agree: once one arrives, there is no turning back.

The world of NHC is built upon four inseparable and defining foundational pillars: *natural boarding, a reasonably natural diet, natural horsemanship, and the natural trim.* By inseparable, I mean that each inescapably affects all the others. Hence, the pillars are intrinsically a part of a whole system and, and, therefore, interdependent. For this reason, NHC is a true holistic approach to horse care. Each pillar is defined by the natural horse paradigm. We would never attempt to say, for example, that riding a horse this way or that is natural to the horse, unless, of course, a reputable source has documented it in the wild. Nor would we conduct a natural trim, and then ignore all else in the management of the animal. Being insistent and reliant upon the natural horse paradigm is a necessity, or the doors to "anything goes" would be opened wide, and the horse's natural world — as a model — would be reduced to meaningless rubble.

While the tenets of NHC may seem purist and restrictive to some, they are also pragmatic and fair to both horse and rider. This is nowhere more evident than in the summary advice give in the opening pages of the *AANHCP Field Guide to NHC*[1]:

- Trim your horse's hooves very specifically to mimic the wear patterns of naturally shaped wild horse feet.
- Find ways to provide him with a more natural living environment that suits their specie's physical and mental needs.
- Discuss how to simplify his diet so that it works better for his digestive system and overall health, including laminitis prevention.
- Recommend riding methods that work with his natural gaits and do not cause harm.

The natural trim is the subject of this book and requires no further discussion at this point. While the natural diet of the horse is still unknown as that research has not yet taken place by qualified scientists, safe recommendations for a reasonably natural diet are given below. Natural boarding practices based on the wild horse model are now beginning to take hold and are showing up widely around the world following the publication of my book, *Paddock Paradise: A Guide to Natural Horse Boarding* (2006). With my colleague Jill Willis, I've finally put one together myself! Jill and I have made great progress in just two months since our four horses were put "on track". In the discussion below, I will share some thoughts and images about what we are doing. But I encourage you to read the book, and to visit the Paddock Paradise and Facebook websites for more information. There's a lot going on, and the thousands of horse owners who are now visiting the Facebook website are always eager to share with others good things they are doing for their horses. Finally, there is the matter of natural horsemanship. So far as I'm concerned, there is no good and reliable system of horsemanship based on our wild horse model. There are certainly elements of it taking place here and there, but as a whole, much — too much — is lacking. Instead of taking up the matter here, I will defer to Chapter 7, casting the discussion within the larger discussion of hoof biomechanics and the natural gaits.

Natural Boarding

Interest in natural boarding has paralleled interest in natural hoof care and diet for years, with hoof disease and lameness not too far in the background as self-propelling influences in their own right. But once discovered, natural boarding has become a force and focal point based on its own merit — and an avenue into NHC for many horse owners still oblivious to the broader natural care movement.

The principal objectives of natural boarding are:
- Provide an interesting life.
- Stimulate movement via the natural gaits.
- Stimulate movement along paths within "tracks" as seen in the wild and described in

[1] Jaime Jackson, *AANHCP Field Guide to NHC*, p. 3.

Wild ones hoofing it single file "on track" in central Nevada. Their well-worn paths criss-cross the rangelands as family bands move from one "activity" to the next. Photos: Luca Gandini.

Paddock Paradise.

- Enable and facilitate band behavior (as opposed to life in isolation).
- Provide a reasonably natural diet and facilitate natural feeding behavior.
- Prevent diseases caused by close confinement.
- Minimize lameness due to lack of nature-based exercise and subsequent equestrian demands.
- Strengthen hooves using NHC principles and the natural trim.

In late 2011, Jill and I began formulating our own plans for a Paddock Paradise (*Overleaf*). Raw acreage adjacent to Vandenberg Air Force Base and the small town of Lompoc, California, had become available for boarding our four horses, thereby setting the stage. The terrain there is steep to hilly, the soil gravelly everywhere, grass sparse, lots of coastal brush, and Oak forests in the canyon areas below the windy ridge where most of our useable land is situated. Paddock Paradise puts horses on well-defined "tracks" that go

(Continued on page 48)

Overleaf — Our Paddock Paradise

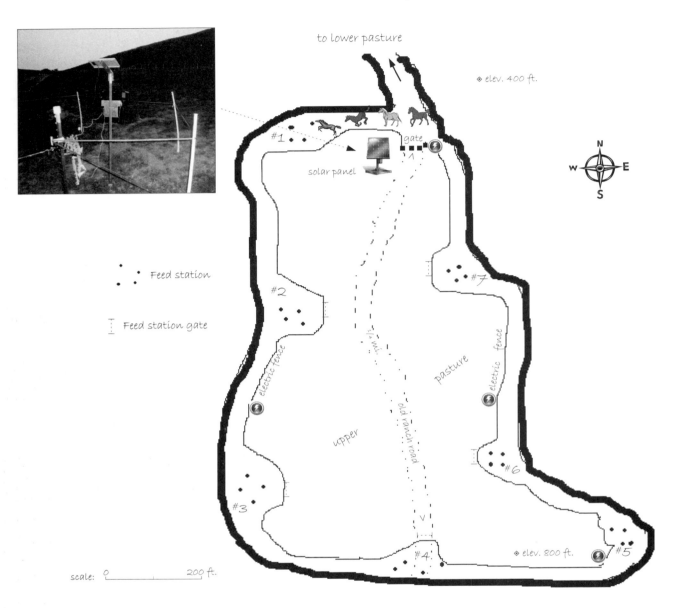

In this natural boarding system adapted from my book *Paddock Paradise*, horses travel together in a "track" that loops around two connected pastures. The outer perimeter of the track is formed from an old ranch fence line, bluffs, steep hillsides, dense forest and brush. The inner perimeter is a temporary electric fence. The width of the track varies widely. It extends half a mile (.8 km) long around an upper pasture that traverses a ridge, with seven feed stations positioned at intervals that include 4 feeding units per station with hay nets. The track leads also to a lower pasture where they get water. The horses must climb and descend a steep gravelly hill to go between the lower and upper tracks. You can't tell from drawing, but the track/field is not flat anywhere, rather a bumpy, sloping affair everywhere, with a 400 foot rise from front to back with hills and other convolutions in between. Inside the track, the horses have established "paths" going from feed station to feed station. The track from stations #2 to #3 is quite steep and rough in places, but the horses have establish 3 parallel paths. Each station has its own gate for easy access from the inner field. The fence is rendered "hot" by a solar panel-charger (*inset*) located within the upper pasture, out of reach of the horses. Now that we know what we are doing, a team of two could complete the whole set-up in less than a day.

Jill Willis

Jaime Jackson

Jaime Jackson

Jill Willis

Jill Willis

To feed the horses on track, and, hence, to keep them moving — an important objective of natural board-ing — we created a series of "feed stations" at intervals of several hundred yards. Each feed station consists one of one feeding unit per horse. Here's how they work:

(*Above, left thru right*) Since the ground is gravelly and difficult to set a wooden fence post, and there are no trees, we opted instead for 5 ft. metal t-posts. These are easy enough to drive and are sturdy standing alone. After the t-post is set, it is covered with a Schedule-40 PVC pipe just wide enough to slip over and swivel upon the t-post. The pipe extends all the way to the ground, so measure and cut to the length of the t-post set in the ground.

(*Below, left*) The pipe is fitted with a PVC cap, which isn't glued on. About 5 in. (12 cm) below the cap, drill a hole through the middle of the PVC pipe. Insert an eye-bolt, and secure it tightly with a washer and nut. Place over the t-post. The feeder unit's eye-bolt will rest and "spin" on the top of the t-post.

(*Below, right*) We then thread the draw-string of the hay net thru the eye-bolt, put several wraps around the PVP pipe, then thread it back down through the eye-bolt, and connect it to the hay net with a carbineer clip. Here, Chance is testing the first hay net, easily removing the hay with his prehensile lips.

At first, everything was done with a garden-type push cart — lots of good exercise, but that got old pretty quick moving along the half mile track over pretty steep and rough ground everyday. But, from the beginning, we wanted to keep things as quiet, low key, and natural as possible in our Paddock Paradise. But hay/tools are heavy. What were we to do?

[1,2] Going online, we discovered and purchased an electric cart made by a Japanese company. I then made a "hay crib" and bolted it to the cart's frame — immediate relief! Now we just walk alongside the cart, which does all the work. Chance, standing in wait in the background, makes a point of raiding the hay crib whenever we head up the hill to the upper track. The electric cart travels to each feed station, where hay is placed into the empty nets. We can cover all 7 stations in 40-50 minutes.

[3] Central command of the cart's nervous system — the electric controls. The battery is tucked under the deck, and easily removed to be charged (there's no power where our Paddock Paradise is — a mile from the area's power grid. Look at the payload on the steering column — 440 lbs (200 kg)! The cart is truly a tribute to Japanese technology and innovativeness.

[4] Looking to the east across Feed Station #6. The hardest part of being up on this section of the track is enduring the ocean wind that blows fiercely across the ridge. The horses don't mind, however, and the hay nets have eliminated virtually all hay waste that plagued us when we used to feed on the ground.

[5] View of track from #6 looking north. Station #7 is visible below at center. Jill has met the horses, who are curious to see what we've stocked in #6. They always stay together as a family unit, and we enjoy visiting them along their pathways just to say hello and watch their interesting interactions. We will soon be GPS-ing their movements just to see exactly where they go, when, and how far — important information for NHC practitioners like ourselves who are closely monitoring and studying hoof wear.

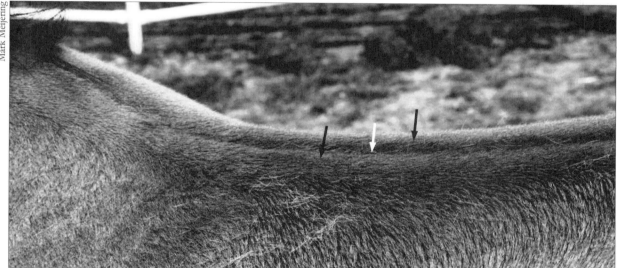

(*Above*) Chance browsing in the brush for forage on track, but "off path". The horses instinctively avoid certain plants while eating freely from others. Based on my observations of wild horses and our horses in PP, I am dubious of the scientific classification that horses are simply or predominantly "grazers" — grazer/browser, or "forager" seems more fitting. Long necks not only reach the ground, they also reach high in the brush.

(*Below*) This is an important close-up view of Chance's back. Black arrows point to two ridges of muscle separated by a deep furrow (white arrow). These muscle ridges (formed by the *Longissimus dorsi*) create the "double back" (or "double spine") described by Xenophon (p. 16, *Art of Horsemanship*, trans. by M.H. Morgan, 1962, London: J.A. Allen). They are the longest and strongest muscles in the horse's body, extending from the cervical vertebra to the sacrum. The nearby *Supraspinous ligament* extends from the poll to the croup, and supports the weaker thoracic and lumbar vertebra, above which the rider sits. The double-back is characteristic of a healthy, naturally shaped back, as opposed to one with a protruding spine. Horses ridden without double-backs are at risk of Navicular Syndrome (p. 238), since the spine is vulnerable to compressional trauma and fracture.

45

(This page)

(Above) Feed Station #6 is anything but level, as you can see here! We try to make track life as interesting and challenging as we can for them. After one month "on track," I am awed by the improvement of their hooves. They are bordering on "wildness", which speaks well for natural boarding.

(Below) Like in the wild, it's single file to the next grazing ground, counter-clockwise to station #5. Jill captured this great sundown silhouette.

(Facing page)

(Above) Our horses' hooves have entered into what I call a state of "biodynamic balance" with their environment. There is very little to trim, and what I trim must be carefully evaluated in relation to how the hoof is being worn through natural movement. The frog here has melded with the heel-buttresses, and during weight bearing, the heel bulbs are at ground level. Of course, these are terms I will define later in this book — so don't fret if you are new to NHC and don't know what they mean!

(Below) I've included this image as much to show the texture of the ground as the hoof itself. Constant wear over abrasive ground is natural to the horse's foot — necessary, in fact, if you want top quality hooves. They feel no pain at all. It is a sad fact that horses are shod because horse owners believe their feet "need protection". They don't need any protection, they need the shoes taken off and the hooves put to work! And they don't need to be standing around in stalls and small paddocks either — those just cripple movement and make for weak feet. The other thing they don't need is to be roaming around in green grass pastures, which are as bad for horses as a stall. This may come as a shock to newcomers in NHC — but read on and you'll know why!

(Continued from page 41)

here and there around the property. Within the tracks, which seldom are more than 15-20 feet (4 to 5 meters) wide, and sometimes just 6 feet (2 meters) wide, are paths which the horses create themselves. The concept is based upon my observations of well-worn pathways that wild horses use, typically in single file, to get from one activity (e.g., feeding) to another. Along our horses' paths, we created what we call feeding stations with hay nets. The horses seek these out for forage, along with some browsing for this and that in the brushy areas we included within the tracking system (page 45, *above*).

Almost immediately, the benefits of "life on track" became apparent to us. First, the feeding nets eliminated virtually all hay waste, typical of ground feeding horses. Spacing of the feed stations at intervals along the track meant they must move distances to eat, another characteristic of equine life in the wild. Within two weeks, I also found that track life was favorably impacting their feet and bodies. Muscles begin to tone and emerge in new places, due to the demands of moving up and down the steep hillside. Movement then favored their hooves, as we had predicted. Prior to life on track, I was trimming them at 4 week intervals. As of this writing (June, 2012), they are at 15 weeks on track without need of trimming — natural wear is checking excess growth. Our plan is to "step up" environmental pressure on track to maximize health and naturally shaped hooves. This means encouraging natural behaviors by introducing stimuli that enhance social interaction and movement. These are discussed in Chapter 7.

A Reasonably Natural Diet

Another core principle of NHC is feeding one's horse as natural a diet as possible. The table at right (*facing page*) is the recommended NHC diet for all equines. The percentages (%) recommended for forages are based on the total daily feed allotted per horse by weight.

My observations of wild horses revealed that high desert type bunch grasses are an important staple of the wild horse diet, and horse owners should make every effort to feed mixed grass hays such as Teff, Bermuda, Timothy, and mixed-meadow orchard grasses. These may be complemented with no more than 10-15% by weight of legume (e.g., Alfalfa, Lucerne and clover) or 15% grain hays (e.g., oat, wheat, and barley). These have been implicated as laminitis triggers by researchers; however, and should be avoided altogether for horses diagnosed with laminitis, or have a history of chronic laminitis. I recommend feeding at ground level or from low hanging "slow feed" hay nets (with holes too small for hooves to get snared) as described in the overleaf discussion of natural boarding (Paddock Paradise).

In addition to dry forage, feed cupful quantities at a time, per day, of whole or crimped oats or Timothy pellets. These should be free of sweeteners such as molasses, cane or beet sugar, sugar beet pulp, and high fructose corn syrup. It is recommended that these

NHC DAILY DIETARY RECOMMENDATIONS, PER HORSE		
Feed	**%**	**Description**
Grass hay staple	85-100	Mixed recommended, 20-30 lb.
Legume	5-10	No more than 10% of total diet (e,g., Alfalfa and clover).*
Grain hay	5-10	No more than 5%, alone or in 3-Way.*
Salt block	-	Salts with trace minerals (Redmond, Celtic & Himalayan).
Mineral block	-	Molasses-free; free choice.
Cereal grains	-	Whole/crimped oats only cupful up to 1 lb. am + 1 lb. pm.
Fresh fruits/vegetables	-	mixed, cupful, 3 x day.
Domestic green grass pasture	-	Avoid as they are all high risk for laminitis.
High desert pasture	-	Free choice x 24/7.
Safe supplements, particularly for hard keepers, laminitics and horses with other metabolic disorders	-	•ADM Stay Strong Metabolic Mineral Pellets (corn-alfalfa-molasses-free): one pound (½ lb. AM; ½ lb. PM). •Quiessence - a magnesium-based supplement that is a complimentary supplement with the ADM pellets listed above. •Ontario Dehy 100% Premium Timothy Cubes (low-NSC/low starch); useful also as a safe treat.
Hay pellets		Molasses and beet pulp free.
Water	-	free choice, at ground level

*Not recommended for overweight horses, or those sensitive to laminitis triggers.

grains be sprinkled into the hay mixes, rather than fed as separate concentrates. Recommendations for senior and weight-challenged horses are also given in in the table; as always, avoid formulations with sweeteners.

Avoid all grass pasture turnouts, except the natural Great Basin types foraged by wild, free-roaming horses. Managed and/or cultivated domestic grass pastures are potentially high risk forage environments for laminitis.[1] Many vitamin and mineral concentrates are also suspect for causing dietary/metabolic distress and are implicated triggers in colic and laminitis in equines; consequently, they should be used cautiously or avoided altogether. Instead, feed handful quantities at a time per day of chopped fresh vegetables and whole fruits. Salt and salt licks are provided free-choice. Water, too, should be available free-choice, 24/7, and, where possible, use natural resources (streams, ponds) instead of conventional wall mount fountains and ground troughs; it is very natural and preferable that horses be allowed to stand and bathe in the very bodies of water from which they drink.

There is considerable anecdotal evidence that chemical parasiticides and vaccinations may also be triggers for laminitis in horses. NHC practitioners regularly report the emer-

[1]C. Pollitt, K. Watts, "Equine Laminitis - Managing Pasture to Reduce the Risk", Publication No. 10/063, Project No. PRJ-000526, Australian Government: Rural Industries Research and Development Corporation.

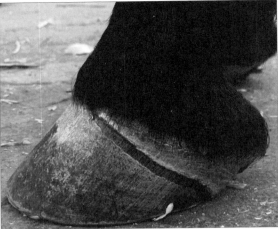

(*Above*) Hooves in distress. Look closely at the rings and grooves circumscribing these laminitic hooves. Laminitis, epidemic worldwide, is a diet-based life-threatening inflammation of the horse's foot that can be prevented entirely by natural boarding and a reasonably natural diet. Fancy shoes, pads, surgery and invasive trimming tactics are completely unnecessary and, in fact, just cause more harm. Get rid of them all and go with the 4 Pillars of NHC. I will take up how we trim such hooves in Chapters 9 and 10.

gence of lamellar stress rings and grooves in the outer walls of hooves, and pathological separation of the sole and hoof wall. This is something to discuss with your veterinarian and your NHC practitioner. Generally speaking, the more natural the horse's living environment, the less reliant we should be on these kinds of preventatives. This should be a goal, and the decision to use any chemical or pathogen to treat or prevent disease should be weighed carefully. I advise not giving multiple vaccinations all at once, instead spacing them out over weeks or months; and wormers only twice a year, if living conditions suggest their usage.

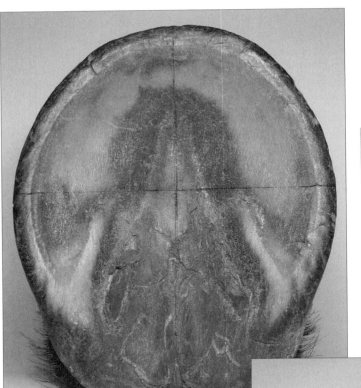

Various profiles of the sound, healthy naturally shaped feet of a U.S. Great Basin wild, free-roaming horse. The hooves of the wild horse provide an exemplary, and proven, model for natural hoof care.

Major Structures of the Horse's Foot

The horse's foot is, as with any complex structure in nature, a confluence of numerous parts that function optimally when in harmony with the evolutionary forces of adaptation discussed in Chapter 1. As logical as this may sound to the disciplined mind, it is largely a faint, if even existent, concern in the thoughts and methodology of many hoof care practitioners. The impact of this schism is reflected in the multitude of problems facing the domesticated horse's foot, if not the animal himself, as a consequence of human ignorance and meddling. Nonetheless, if one evaluates the parts and their functions according to nature's grand evolutionary plan, witnessed in the U.S. Great Basin's wild free-roaming horses, we can see and appreciate a great and miraculous system at work.

For our purposes, as NHC practitioners, the horse's foot can be divided into two parts: the horny protective covering and its contents. Technically, the outer covering is called the hoof, or "hoof capsule", or simply capsule (Latin: box), and throughout these guidelines, I will use "hoof" and "capsule" interchangeably. So, when I speak of the horse's foot, I am speaking inclusively of the capsule (or hoof) and all the contents within it. Conversely, when I speak of the capsule (or hoof), I am referring only to the foot's outer protective covering, and not of it's contents. As of this writing, we know quite a lot about the hoof of the wild horse, but very little about it's contents.[1] This is because qualified scientists have not yet conducted research of the wild horse foot's inner structures, including their physiology. This neglect and disinterest in the wild hoof is probably due to science's current preoccupation with the troubled domesticated hoof. Consequently, much of what we know about the horse's inner foot today is based on the domesticated hoof (i.e., human involvement or interference), and is tainted by pathology, rather than health and soundness as exemplified by nature's wild horse model. I mention this as a stern warning to students of NHC, who should be cautious about inferring anything about what is natural (healthy and

---

[1]There are many feral horse populations around the world; however, only those inhabiting the high desert type biomes similar to the ancient adaptive environment of the Eurasian Steppes are of value for modeling the natural trim and other natural care practices. Several have been studied closely with an eye to understanding their feet, diet, and behavior: my U.S. Great Basin studies conducted during 1982-1986 (*The Natural Horse: Lessons From the Wild*, Jaime Jackson, Northland Publishing, 1992); and Dr. Ric Redden's 2000 corroborative study in the same region (*The Wild Horse's Foot*, Bluegrass Laminitis Symposium Notes, written and presented January 2001 by R.F. Redden, DVM). The current ongoing study of Australian Brumbies under the direction of Professor Christopher Pollit's Australian Laminitis Research Unit (http://www.wildhorseresearch.com./Documents/newsletters-%20novt08.htm) is problematic, in my opinion, due to questionable research protocols in addition to studying horses in a non-adaptive environment. For critique, see: Bruce Nock, MS, PhD, "The Wild Horse Model—Worth Fighting For". Liberated Horsemanship Press, P.O. Box 546, Warrenton, MO 63383, Contribution #22 from Liberated Horsemanship.

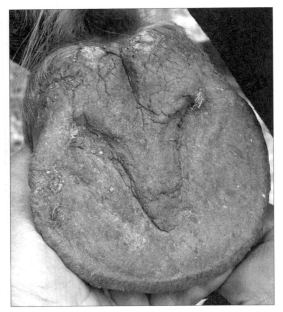

(*Above*) The Mongols of East-Central Asia use horses for their transportation, as they have for thousands of years. Their horses are neither trimmed nor shod, and their hooves are exemplary by NHC standards. These nomadic horsed peoples were visited by an AANHCP practitioner during the early 2000s, who naturally wanted to know who did the awesome hoof work. With a bewildered look, one of the tribal elders responded, "Mother Nature." As an exercise, contrast the major structures of this hoof with those of the wild horse feet in following pages.

[Photo credit: Paul Lutzen]

sound) from such an adulterated matrix of research findings. Ironically, as scientists delve ever deeper into the abyss of disease and lameness to somehow understand and conquer it, they move ever further away from the world of NHC with its bountiful lessons of health, soundness, and disease/lameness *prevention*. To my surprise and personal distress, many in the barefoot culture seem equally fascinated with and given to the science of pathology. I have watched time and again as they become stuck in its perilous academic quicksand and specious conclusions, seemingly blinded to the path of NHC. Why so much lopsided attention given to this negative vortex, when the obvious benefits of NHC justify little or no such attention in the first place?[1]

In the following pages are the principal structures of the hoof that NHC practitioners should familiarize themselves with and know by sight and name, since they are part of the language of our professional discipline. During the practical cadaver dissection exercises (chapter 15), some of the contents of the capsule will be visited in ways that will help the practitioner to understand the physical boundaries between the epidermal armor and the sensitive and vascular structures within which they are conformed to protect. These are never to be violated by any invasive means, or harm will be brought to the foot.

Finally, it might seem to some readers already experienced in trimming that I've not been sufficiently comprehensive in identifying the many other structures comprising the horse's foot — "What about all those other structures within the capsule? And what about the rest of the horse?". It is my opinion that NHC practitioners need not become experts at gross or micro (cellular and extracellular) equine anatomy. While interesting perhaps, we do not need to know all the bones, muscles, organs, their physiology, and so forth, to competently do our work. While some may protest this assertion, it has been my observation over many years that there are legions of those hoof care (and veterinary and research scientist) experts who profess to know all of this, and who clearly continue to bring harm to the horse, and his feet in particular. Wiser that they, and we, know instead hoof "basics" through nature's wild model and immerse our horses in the holistic practices of NHC — natural boarding, a reasonably natural diet, natural horsemanship, and the natural trim — where the adaptability of that model is now proven and beyond reproach.

[1]This recognition is foundational to one of the "Four Guiding Principles" (Chapter 5, p. 86) of the natural trim: *Ignore all pathology*.

Toe

Quarter

Heel

Coronary band

Mustang Roll

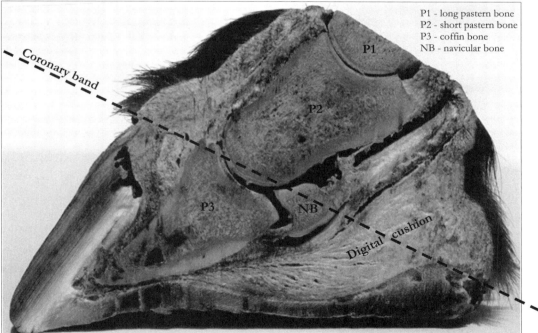

Coronary band

P1

P2

P3   NB

Digital cushion

P1 - long pastern bone
P2 - short pastern bone
P3 - coffin bone
NB - navicular bone

(*Above*) The *coronary band* is the soft tissue structure that forms a border between the hair above and hard hoof wall below. The outer wall is divided approximately into three parts: *toe*, *quarter*, and *heel*.

(*Below*) The hoof has been cut down the middle forming the *median plane*, and revealing the bones of the foot (*P1*, *P2*, *P3* and *NB*), and a massive fibro-fatty structure called the *digital cushion*.

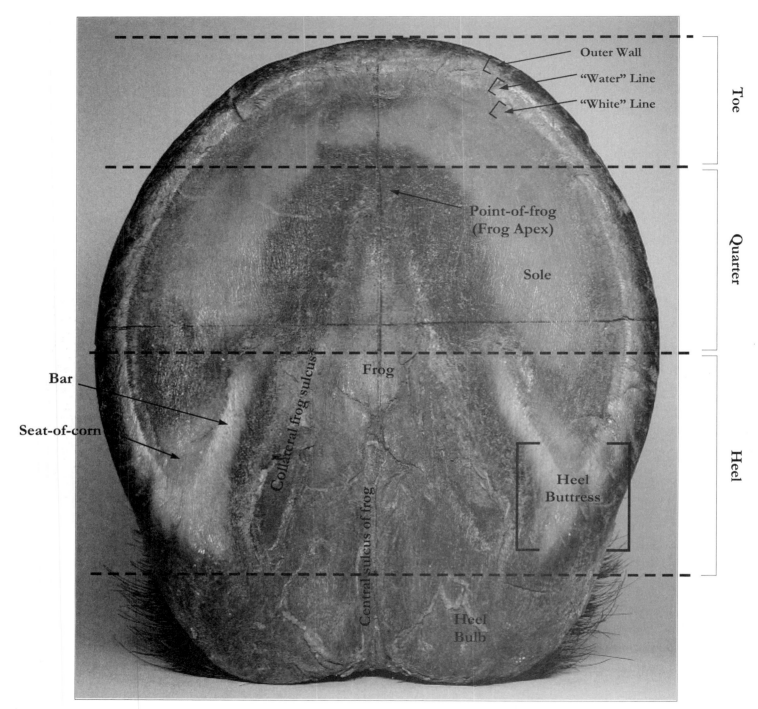

Outer Wall

"Water" Line

"White" Line

Toe

Point-of-frog
(Frog Apex)

Sole

Quarter

Bar

Seat-of-corn

Collateral frog sulcus*

Frog

Central sulcus of frog

Heel
Buttress

Heel

Heel
Bulb

Volar profile, front wild horse hoof.

*Also called the collateral grooves

(*Facing page*) A look at the bottom of a front wild horse hoof, called the volar profile [Latin: palm or sole], and all its parts. The median plane of the volar profile would pass through the line I've drawn down the middle of the hoof through the central sulcus of the frog. We'll have a lot more to say about the median plane and that line later! In the wild and in naturally worn hooves such as Jill and I see with our horses in our Paddock Paradise, the heel bulbs press against the ground. In shod hooves and unnaturally trimmed hooves with excessively long heels, they make no ground contact and, as a result, become soft and hypersensitive like the palms of your hands (and probably your feet if you never go barefoot yourself!). Memorize all of these as they are important navigational landmarks referenced during trimming.

(*This page*) View to the rear of a front wild horse foot, the heel-buttresses cut away. Note how the wall, bar, sole, and frog correlate to their relative positions seen on the facing page. The circles mark the ends of the "wings" of P3 (*inset*), called the "palmer processes of the distal phalanx". Attached to the proximal borders of the palmer processes are the cartilages (C), which are calcified to bone in the insert image. The digital cushion (DC) is situated between the cartilages, coffin bone, and heel bulbs (cut away in this cross-section); it also fills the grooves of the frog. Of interest also is how the frog and bars meld together. Right above the frog is the digital cushion.

White Line ————

Water Line ————

Outer Wall ————

We still use designated names borrowed from the farriery and veterinary anatomy texts to describe structures of the hoof. Often, these terms don't make any sense, as is the case here.

(*Above*) For example, the *white line* is not white but is normally yellowish in color. The *water line*, ironically, is unpigmented white horn when freshly nipped! It is also the driest and hardest part of the bottom of the hoof, and, further, protruding below the white line and outer wall as it does in naturally shaped hooves, and research has demonstrated it is the most distal structure of the volar profile.[1] [Distal > distant = situated away from the point of origin or attachment, as of a limb or bone.]

(*Below*) Note the relationship of each of these structures to each other in relation to the *volar plane (VP)*. The VP is an imaginary flat surface that supports the capsule. If the horse were standing on such a firm, flat surface, the water line would endure the most active contact, followed by the white line, sole, and outer wall. This ordering of active contact with the ground corresponds to the hoof's *relative concavity* — a matter we discuss at length later in the trimming guidelines. Everything is significant in nature!

[1] The Natural Horse, p.58.

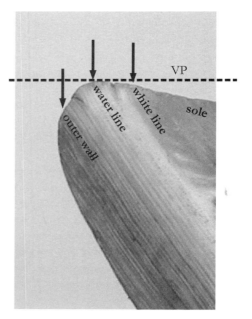

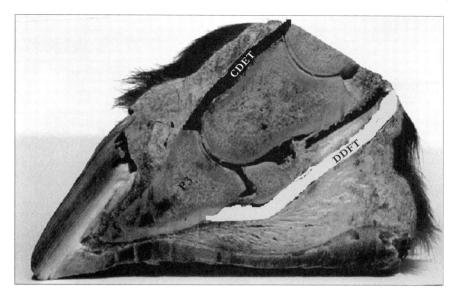

The hoof is moved to and fro by the action of two major tendons upon its bones.

(*Above*) The Common Digital Extensor Tendon (CDET) pulls the hoof forward (called "extension"); the Deep Digital Flexor Tendon (DDFT) pulls it back (called "flexion"). These tendons act upon P3.

(*Middle, left*) P3 sits at the bottom of the horse's lower leg, hence it is sometimes called the "coffin bone".

(*Lower, right*) Position of the CDET and DDFT on the bones of the lower leg. The DDFT is often the target of vets, who, unfortunately, and erroneously think it is necessary to sever in cases of laminitis so as to remove tugging pressure on P3. This is truly inhumane and something NHC practitioners advocate against, and I'll explain later why.

(*Lower left*) P1, P2, and P3 correspond to the toe bones in our own feet! And what we call the "knee" of the horse, is actually his wrist! And his hock is his ankle! I don't know how the mix-up got started!

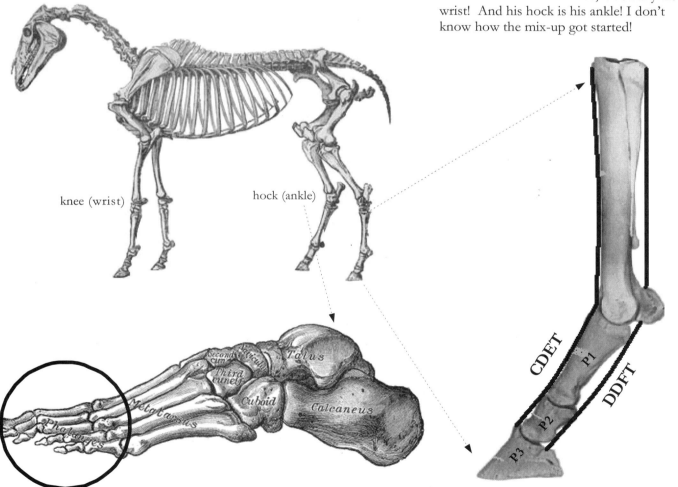

knee (wrist)

hock (ankle)

Growth Coria of the Hoof

This is an important part of our discussion of the horse's foot as they will come up again and again in your work as an NHC practitioner. We're going to identify the major dermal structures that are responsible for creating and maintaining the various epidermal structures of the hoof — collectively, what I think of as the Supercorium.

(Above) The capsule is removed and we're looking straight at the foot's dermis, which surrounds the bones, digital cushion, and tendons we discussed earlier.

(Below) CC marks the *coronary corium* out of which grows the entire hoof wall. It is situated behind and below the coronary band in what is called the coronary groove.

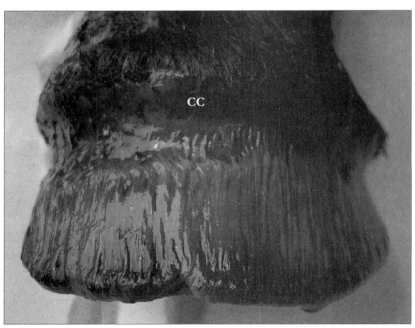

Growth Coria of the Hoof

(*Above*) The hoof wall is actually composed of minute hairs cemented together called "tubular horn". I've soaked the hooves here, which, in time, loosens the hairs. This propensity for the hoof to ravel in constant moisture is a clear message to manage horses in a dry environment. This is consistent with his specie's adaptation in a semi-arid biome.

(*Below*) Each hair, or tubule, has a hollow core called a medullae (M).

[Photo credit: C. Pollitt]

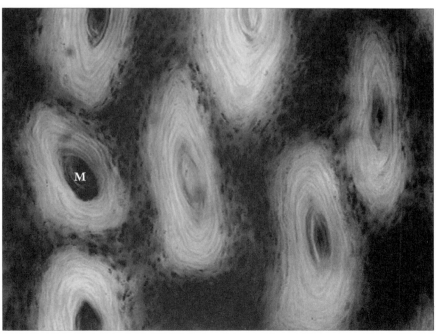

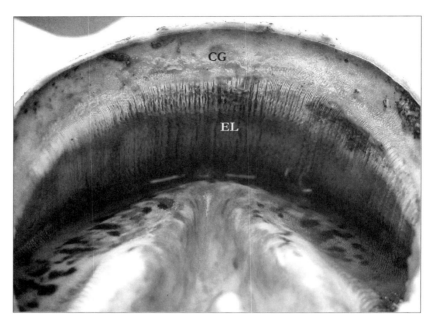

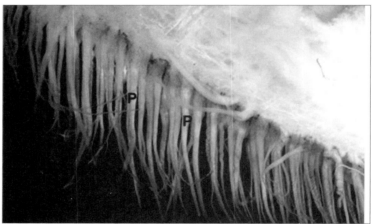

Growth Coria of the Hoof

(This page.)

(Above) This inner rim of hoof wall, called the *coronary groove* (CG), is where the coronary corium is situated. The coronary groove is pocked with countless minute sockets into which the coronary corium inserts itself.

(Below) The face of the coronary corium is actually covered with tiny hairs called dermal papilla (P). The papillae contains an artery, vein, and nerve. The role of the papillae is to produce and maintain its own tubule. It also receives information from the environment through its medullae, which is transmitted to the central nervous system of the horse. This information appears to be vital to sustaining bio-dynamic hoof balance and natural growth patterns. In my early research at the Paso ranch, I found that we can communicate with the Supercorium to help facilitate natural size, shape, and proportion by mimicking these natural wear patterns.

[Photo credit: C. Pollitt]

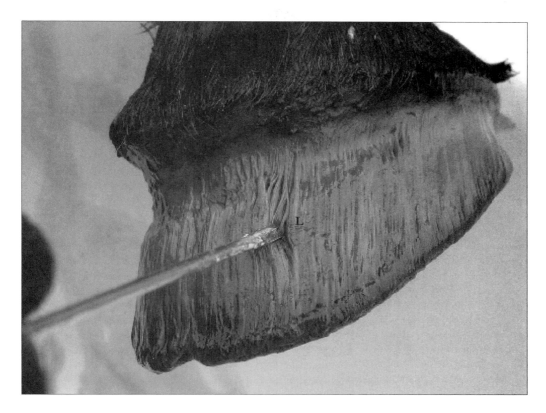

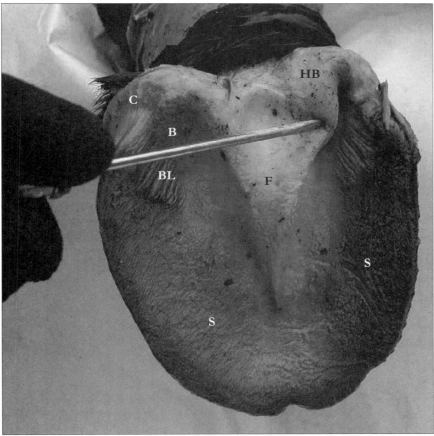

Growth Coria of the Hoof

(*Above*) I'm separating several dermal lamina (leaves) that coat the face of P3. Each dermal leaf (L) interdigitates (intermeshes) with a corresponding epidermal leaf (EL) which grows down from the lower shoulder of the coronary groove to the ground, where it is worn away (this page, *above*). Degradation of the dermal-epidermal lamellar (leaf like) bond is implicated in laminitis. I'll have a lot more to say about this later too!

(*Below*) Here, I'm poking at the frog corium (F), which is responsible for creating the frog. It is surrounded on all sides by the sole corium (S). Nearby are the bar lamina (BL), which interdigitate with the hoof wall as it lowers into the solar dome along the wings of the frog, forming the bars. The bar corium (B), which creates the bars, is an extension of the nearby coronary corium (C), which, together, create the heel-buttresses. The posterior dermal protrusions of the frog wings form the heel bulbs (HB).

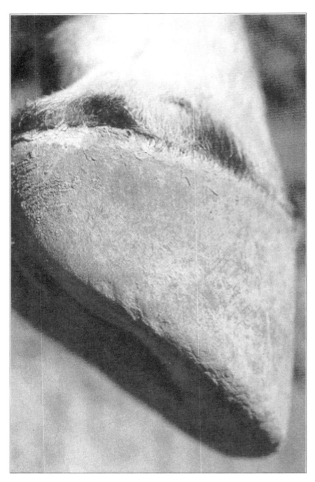

"Until I stepped into wild horse country, I had never seen anything like before in my professional life …" Jaime Jackson

Wear Characteristics of the Naturally Shaped Hoof

As with our own specie's feet, the natural hoof seen in the wild comes in different sizes, shapes, and proportions. The horse, however, must walk upon the ends of his "nails" (hooves) whereas we don't; hence, his "nail" must be worn into optimal size, shape, and proportion if it is to facilitate his survival. There are many social behaviors that, from the standpoint of movement, contribute to the shaping of his hoof in the wild.[1] But there is a less conspicuous force that drives all of these behaviors. This is his innate "prey awareness" rooted deeply in his specie's biology and evolutionary history; in fact, the horse is an animal of prey, something he is intensely aware of at all times. This is to say it is genetically encoded within his DNA and in his perceptions of the world around him. This is true whether he is living in the wild or isolated with humans in domestication. As such, he instinctively senses that he is vulnerable to predators if he cannot move soundly and unrestricted freedom to move. We see this same prey awareness in other wild ungulates such as the zebra, gazelle, and deer. This keen awareness also keeps him mentally and physically fit and "on alert" at all times — rendering him, in the wild, a limber equine athlete as a consequence. Hence, the import and importance of prey psychology into the shaping of his hooves cannot be ignored or underestimated. The white (unpigmented) hoof on the facing page, rock hard and impervious to abrasive forces that would tear our own shoes to smithereens in minutes, speaks to this composite of tough horn and rigorous, unrelenting behavior-driven wear, all turbo-charged by prey awareness. Until I stepped into wild horse country, I had never seen anything like it before in my professional life. It was a slap in the face and a wake-up call to look far beyond the confines of the shod hoof paradigm.

But the wear characteristics seen in the wild horse hoof turn out to be far more important and relevant to the natural trim than one might understand at first glance. As explained in much detail in the next chapter, they serve at the very foundation for the natural trim! In the following pages of the *Overleaf* we return to the major structures of the hoof, but this time with an astute eye to how those structures are worn in the wild in the horse's adaptative environment.

(Continued on page 74)

---

[1]These behaviors are identified and described in two of my books: *The Natural Horse: Lessons from the Wild (1992, Northland Publishing)* and *Paddock Paradise: A Guide to Natural Horse Boarding* (2006, Star Ridge Publishing).

Overleaf
Wear patterns of the naturally shaped hoof.

Angle of Growth

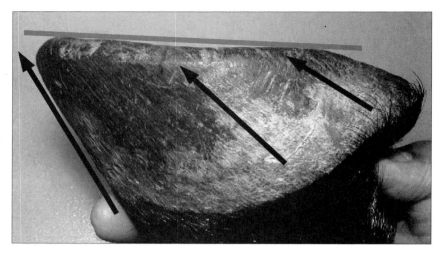

(*Above*) The toe wall of the hoof, when viewed from the side, should conform to a straight line, neither convex nor concave in conformation.

(*Center*) The grain of the hoof wall, when viewed from the front (the "mediolateral profile"), should be aligned nearly parallel to the vertical line drawn on the hoof at right angles (90 degrees) to the ground. The "grain" appears as tiny hair-like filaments embedded in the hoof wall; in fact, they are hairs bundled tightly together by glue-like substances during the formation of the hoof wall (called "keritinization").

(*Below*) The hoof's angle-of-growth from front to back ("anteroposterior" or AP) is extremely complex. At the toe, densely packed horn grows down from the hairline at a higher angle than at the heels, as depicted in the drawing here and as can be seen in the grain of the hoof wall in the upper photo on this page. This is true of all naturally worn hooves I have sampled, both in the wild and among my client horses.

To the limited extent that farriers and vets are aware of this growth peculiarity of the naturally shaped hoof (most believe the angle of growth is the same from front to back), all universally attempt to correct what they perceive as "run under" growth by letting the heels grow longer or wedging them up with shims, pads, or modified shoes. As I will explain later in this text, these measures actually have the opposite effect on the foot's future growth patterns and stability.

To further complicate the picture, not all parts of the hoof wall are worn the same in relation to a flat supporting surface. Which is to say the bottom of the hoof wall is not worn flat like a horseshoe. This can be seen in each of these images; for example, in the "arches" between the toe wall supports (called "pillars") in the center photo, and between the heel and toe in the upper and lower images. In this interpretation, both heels and the toe wall are said to be "active" support pillars. Arched structures in nature impart strength to resist weight-bearing forces from above.

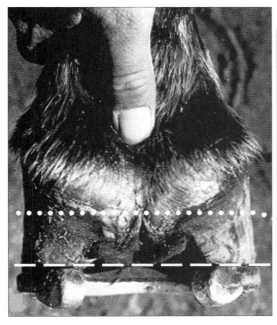 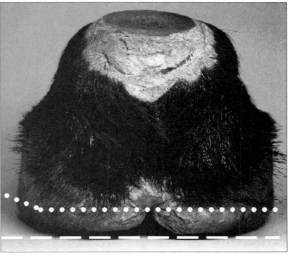

Angle of Growth and Conformation of Frog and Heels

Shoeing and generic unnatural trimming methods preclude the hoof wall, sole, and frog from wearing together naturally. This can be seen in the images here by contrasting a shod and wild horse foot.

(*Above, left*) The effect of the shoe, and generic trim methods for that matter, is to obstruct the hoof's angle of growth. Depending on the horse's upper body conformation, such hooves will then tend to grow either too far forward under the horse (called "run under syndrome") or too upright (called "club foot"). Both conditions destabilize the hoof and, as a consequence, obstruct the natural gaits. The door to lameness is then wide open.

(*Above, right*) I dare say that nearly 100% of the horse world today would say this naturally shaped wild horse hoof, seen from behind, possesses the pathological conformation and the shod mess to its left is a healthier specimen. Now that we've set the record straight follow the lines from one hoof to the other to see where things should and shouldn't be.

Overleaf continued
Wear patterns of the
naturally shaped hoof.

Conformation of the Frog

(*Above*) The naturally worn frog is typically flat, dry and leathery during the more arid times of the year, as can be seen in this close-up of a wild horse hoof I took in the summer of 1983. Note that the frog is well-ensconced and protected from more active wear by the sole, bars, and, generally speaking, the entire hoof's natural concavity. The frog takes its name from its physical resemblance to the amphibian. Note the "cleft" dividing it into two "wings" — accordingly, the ancient Greeks called it, not the frog, but the "swallow" after the bird.

(*Below*) Come winter rains and mud, the same frog swells and becomes less firm. The number 2 is on a sticker I used to correlate "hoof with horse" during my field research at the BLM's Litchfield, CA corrals.

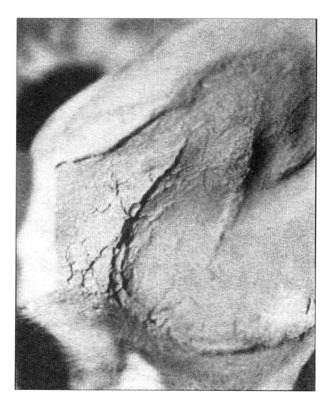

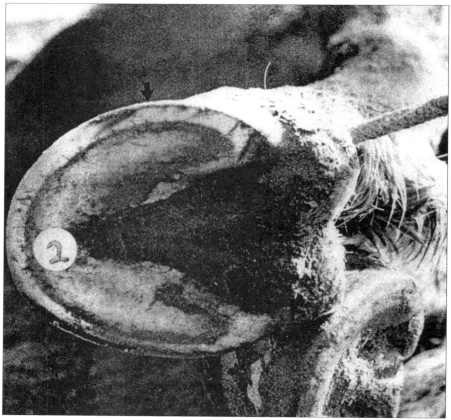

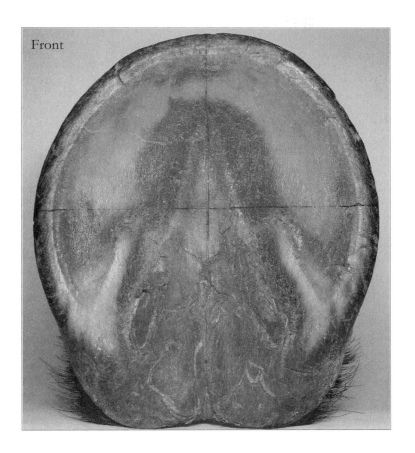

Front

Hind

Natural Thickness of Hoof Wall

(*Left, above* and *below*) It is commonly said in farrier circles and in their textbooks that the hoof wall is widest (thickest) at the toe. Heavily worn horseshoes over the toe are offered as evidence that greater wear occurs there, therefore, the wall is "naturally" thicker there to offset such wear. I was surprised to find this isn't the case at all in naturally worn hooves, where wall thickness is virtually the same all the way around — as seen with the front and hind hooves here, and the hind hoof on the previous page (below).

Overleaf continued
Wear patterns of the
naturally shaped hoof.

"Active" and "Passive" wear

In naturally shaped hooves, areas of greatest wear are those bearing surfaces of the hoof that endure most of the horse's body weight during the hoof's support phase. These "active" support "pillars" are analogous to the calluses on the bottom of your own feet, if you go barefoot often.

(*Above*) The "▼" arrows mark their locations along the wall of this front wild horse hoof. Read more about active/passive wear pillars and their locations on the facing page.

(*Below*) Active wear is also mirrored inversely on the "hoof side" of well-worn horseshoes, where the descending body weight — a compressional force that squeeze the hoof against the ground — quite literally gouges a depression into the horseshoe (marked by the arrows). Check this out the next time your local farrier removes a shoe.

[Photo credit: L. Emery]

toe wall

quarter (mid) wall

heel wall

▼ = active wear pillar

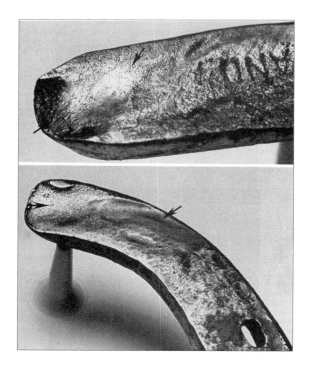

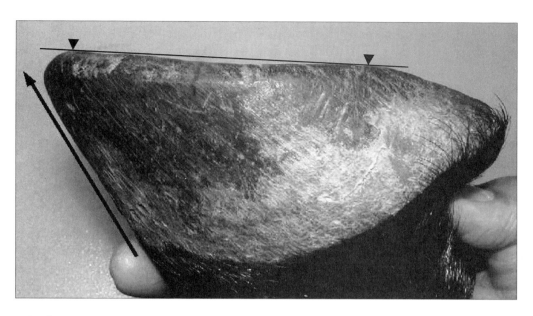

"Active" and "passive" wear

My study of wild horse hooves shows that there is considerable variation in the relative positions of active and passive wear along the bearing surface of the hoof wall.

(*Above, this page*) The "▼" arrows positioned on the image above correspond to two of those active wear pillars shown on the facing page (*above*). These indicate the hoof's "active" wear points, also called support pillars. These are the segments of the hoof wall that would support the hoof if the horse were standing on a flat, firm base of support (I used a flat board to pinpoint the support pillars). The passive wear areas lie in between these active points, and, on firm ground, we would expect that they bear less weight than the active points. The heel-buttresses without exception always formed the two rear pillars. But the location and size of the forward pillar, or pillars as the case may be, varied widely from hoof to hoof depending on the individual wild horse. I was struck, however, by the mirror image symmetry of the active-passive wear patterns for paired left and right hooves (not front to hind!) for each horse. In this particular hoof, the "toe pillar" (there is just one) exists right at the toe's center and is no more than a ¼ in. (1 cm) wide; if one looks closer still, the water line forms the most active salient of this pillar. The emergence of active and passive wear pillars can give the impression to those unfamiliar with true naturally shaped hooves, that the bottom of the hoof capsule is deformed or "unbalanced." This perception is due to the contours of the hoof wall, which can become extremely exaggerated — particularly among the most senior wild horses I examined.

For those readers now wondering how these active/passive "pillars" and "hollows" emerge during the trimming process, the answer is that they tend to form quite naturally on their own. NHC practitioners should recognize and facilitate them not only through trimming, but by encouraging horse owners to implement the other three "pillars of NHC": natural boarding, a reasonably natural diet, and natural horsemanship. Which is to say, the more natural the horse's lifestyle, the more pronounced will be the naturalness of his feet. I will be discussing all of these throughout the remainder of this Guide.

Overleaf continued
Wear patterns of the
naturally shaped hoof.

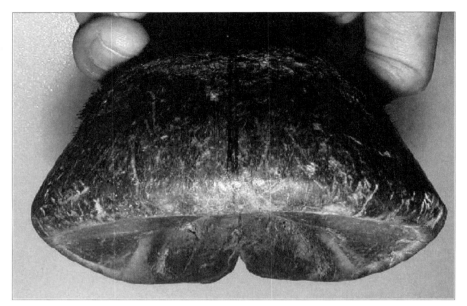

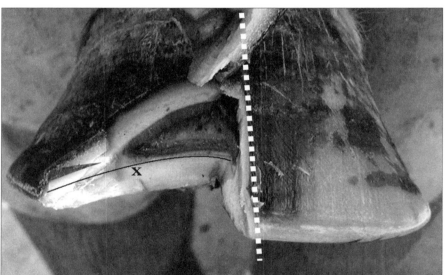

Sole Concavity

(*Above*) The bottom of the naturally shaped hoof, like this wild one, is somewhat concaved, like a bowl, neither flat nor bulging downward. The degree of concavity, however, will vary from horse to horse, some with very little and others considerably more. Much too much has been attributed to the importance of concavity; instead, it is the arched structure of the sole within the hoof that is significant.

(*Below*) In the cross-section of this domesticated hoof cadaver, the curved thin line (**x**) traces the convex upper ("proximal") surface of the arched sole. Where **x** interfaces with the sole dermis is the live sole plane (LSP). The surface that is ground bearing is called the hard sole plane (HSP). The thicker dashed line marks the center of the hoof wall viewed from the front. Arched structures are common throughout nature, and subsequently, architecture as they impart weight-bearing strength — precisely the case as the horse's weight presses down upon the hoof. I will discuss the implication of this in the naturally trimmed hoof in Chapter 7.

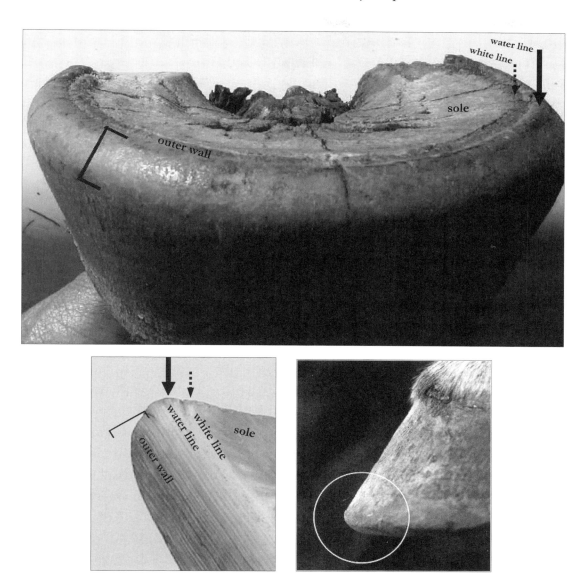

"Mustang Roll"

The mustang roll, which comprises the entire hoof wall, is a more complex wear pattern than first meets the eye.

(*Above* and *below*) The outermost part of the roll forms the *outer wall* (bracket). Just inside of and circumscribed by the outer wall, lies the *water line*. The water line forms a distinctly protruding ring of dry, extremely hard horn around the entire inner hoof wall; this conformation is something I observed in every wild hoof I sampled. For this reason, I think of it as "nature's horseshoe". Ironically, it receives its name due to its highly moist state further up inside the hoof where it lies in close proximity to the foot's blood supply. The water line plays a key role in the natural trim. The mustang roll terminates at the water line's juncture with the white line, which, ironically once more, is never white but somewhat tawny in color. The white line is a leaf-like structure that forms the hoof wall's attachment to the sole. During the debilitating foot disease known as laminitis, the white line characteristically distends and may turn shades of red as the sole-to-wall bonding mechanism inflames, perfuses with blood, and breaks down (discussed at length in Chapter 9).

(Continued from page 65)

Other Shape Characteristics of the Perfectly Natural Hoof

Many other visible features of the naturally shaped hoof are also of importance and worthy of our attention. I am discussing some of these here with the understanding that nature selects for variation and the degree to which these characteristics are more or less prominent in any given horse, including your own, is not to be misconstrued that one hoof is more natural, and therefore "better", than another. Notwithstanding management practices that are in conflict with NHC, all hooves are simply different from each other in the same way our own feet are different. In the following descriptions, I have focused on those characteristics which are probably of greater interest to horse owners. In some instances, my purpose is to dispel myths that have truly contrived to harm horses, in others to simply convey what is natural and nothing more. But in all instances, the shape characteristics discussed are based entirely on my observations of wild horse hooves in the horse's adaptative environment of the U.S. Great Basin.

Hoof Color

"Among the most egregious myths still circulating is that white-colored hooves are "inferior" to dark-colored hooves"

Much has been said about hoof color that, quite frankly, flies in the face of what is true and natural. Among the most egregious myths still circulating is that white-colored hooves are "inferior" to dark-colored hooves, resulting in some horses with white hooves being denigrated as inferior because of their purportedly problematic feet! In the few instances where I have pressed horse owners to explain this logic, I was astonished to hear such nonsense as, "Well, white hooves seem to be missing something that dark hooves obviously possess". What is that? "Well, you can see that the dark color is some kind of cement or something." Of course, what they are referring to is pigmentation, which is not "cement" and does not impart strength to the horse's hoof. Actually, white hooves are simply unpigmented. The fact is, no less than a third of wild horse hooves I sample in my studies were either completely white or were white-streaked with black pigment.[1] Further, my data has shown that white-colored hooves do not differ statistically from dark hooves in size, shape, or proportion. My observations were that they did not differ in terms of durability or functionality either. If my observations weren't enough, Dr. Doug Leach, a Canadian veterinary researcher who has studied hoof structure extensively, has corroborated my own findings. Writing in the *Journal* of the American Farriers Association, Leach stated:

> Hoof color has traditionally been implicated as an important factor in the durability and strength of horse hooves. However, it has been shown that black and white hooves do not differ in water content, chemical composition, hardness, or compressive strength.[1]

[1] *The Natural Horse*, p. 72, Fig. 4-4.
[2] Leach, Doug. "The Structure and Function of the Equine Hoof". *American Farriers Journal (5) (1) (1981) p. 179.*

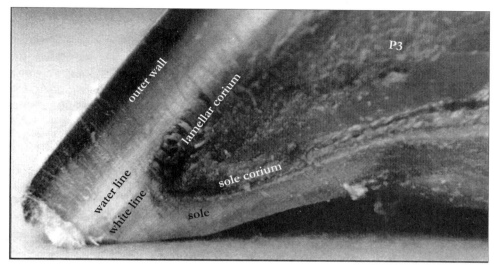

Observe in this interesting cross-section of a black wild horse hoof biospecimen that only the outer one-third of the hoof wall is pigmented. Another one third is partially pigmented. The inner one third, the water line, is unpigmented. This is in keeping with Dr. Leach's studies cited in the main text.

Leach also points out that only the outer two thirds of the hoof wall contains pigment, writing, "The inner third of the hoof wall is unpigmented." He also contends that if white hooves were inherently weaker, then a "vertical shear force" would erupt along the junctures between pigmented and unpigmented horn, causing breakdown in Paint Horses and Appaloosas that he studied. "Such breakdowns are not seen," he concluded.

Given the foregoing, I'd like to assume that the issue is over once and for all. But wherever I go, it seems, I continue to be lectured to the contrary by horse owners, farriers — even vets — and others who have nothing but the best of intentions and concerns for white-hoofed horses: "They must be shod because their hooves are white and weak." But such nonsense is actually acculturized into the mindsets of horse owners through their equestrian organizations and competitions. Perhaps the most glaring example is the "black washing" of hooves to hide the white ones within during horse shows!

White, like dark, colored hooves likely have to do with either camouflage or sexual selection — or both — in the wild. Both for sure harken back to the horse's adaptation 1.4 million years ago, and this is the way we should appreciate the manifestation of color. And before leaving the subject, I wish to point out that pigmentation is extruded by the same dermal structures that produce the hoof wall and sole.[1]

Front vs. Hind Hoof Shapes

I did not include a discussion of front and hind hoof size, proportion, and angle of growth, as I don't see these as wear characteristics; they simply define the shapes of the

(Continued on page 78)

Overleaf
"Watering behavior." In the wild, horses stand and bathe in the water from which they drink.
[Photo: *The Natural Horse: Lessons From the Wild*]

[1]According to Pollitt, "The cells which produce pigment are called melanocytes and are close to the germinal layer of the hoof epidermis at the coronet; they inject granules of pigment (melanin) into maturing epidermal cells and impart varuying shades of dark colour to the hoof wall." C. Pollitt, *The Horse's Foot*, p. 22, Fig. 71.

These exemplary front and hind hooves belonged to a wild mare. I found that on average front hooves are slightly wider than hind hooves across the toe and quarters, but nearly the same across the heels. On average, hind hooves grew down somewhat steeper at the toe (.e., toe angle) than front hooves.

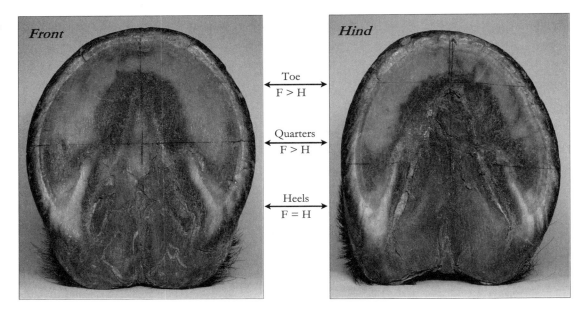

horse's feet as a consequence of natural selection (page 78, *above*). The matter is somewhat confused by the many misshapen hooves one sees commonly among domesticated horses — due to misguided trimming methods, shoeing, and neglect. An objective observer could readily conclude there is no such thing as natural front and hind shapes! This perception is reinforced by the many stock horseshoes that come in one shape, and are left to the shoer to "shape to the foot" or "shape the foot to the shoe" as the case may be. My observation has been that of the many shoes I have removed in my clinics and from client horses over the years, virtually none were given what I would consider to be a natural shape. As stated, the shape of the hoof is governed by the horse's adaptation as a result of natural selection. Thus, in every horse there are distinct front (left and right) and hind (left and right) hoof shapes shared by all members of his species, while every hoof is distinguished from the next by its size, angle of growth, and unique pillars of active and passive wear. Significantly, left and right hooves for any given horse are remarkably symmetrical, that is, are close mirror images of each other, right down to their individualized natural wear patterns. In Chapter 6, we will closer at both natural hoof shapes and wear characteristics as we begin to synthesize the elements of the natural trim.

"the shape of the hoof is governed by the horse's adaptation as a result of natural selection"

Lack of Relationship Between Toe Length, Heel Length, and Angle-of-Growth

I mention these measurable dimensions of the naturally shaped hoof, and their "mathematical" relationships to one another, because of their supreme importance during the natural trim. What their relationships in the wild show us is that the hoof's angle-of-growth ("toe angle") bears no relationship to the length of the toe, the length of the heel, or, for that matter, the length of the toe relative to the length of the heel. This is important because it relieves the NHC practitioner of the impossible task of lengthening or shortening the toe and heels with the objective of regulating toe angle. In *The Natural Horse*, I wrote:

> Also of interest was that toe angle did not appear to be a function of relative heel length. For example, two hooves with the same heel length and identical toe lengths could have entirely different toe angles (Figure 4-14a). Similarly, two hooves with different toe lengths but identical heel lengths could have identical toe angles (Figure 4-14b).[1]

In short, the hoof's growth coria will do this for us. I realize this contradicts everything most of us have been taught about "toe angle". But at issue here is the understanding that nature has selected for minimum toe *and* heel length, and simply accretes mass at a higher or lower angle-of-growth ("toe angle") as needed. Hence, by trimming the hoof (safely) to minimal toe and heel length — angle of growth (toe angle), then, quite independently takes care of itself. This is in stark contrast to the farrier and generic barefooter who are forever trying to "set angles" artificially through trimming, modified shoes, pads, and angle gauges, all of which invariably conflicts with what nature is trying to do — but can't under the circumstances. Again, the NHC practitioner simply lets "nature set the angle" for us!

Another related observation is worth discussing here too. This concerns the horse owner who wants hooves with "specific angles". One myth has arisen directly out of bogus farriery and veterinary science, and unnatural horsemanship ideology, that a higher angled hoof looks better, is sounder, and enables the horse to move better. Another myth holds that all front hooves should measure 45° at the toe. Nothing could be further from the truth in either case, and this type of thinking has led to more trouble for horses and their feet than I care to think about. Once more, nature sets the angle that is optimal for the horse, whether the angle be higher or lower from one horse to the next. My advice is this, if you want a horse with steeper toe angles, don't buy one with naturally lower angles! Better yet, just have the hooves trimmed according to NHC principles and don't worry about it. Your horse will move just fine no matter what his natural angles happen to be.

"if you want a horse with steeper toe angles, don't buy one with naturally lower angles!"

Sole Concavity vs. Sole Convexity

The characteristic of sole concavity was discussed in Chapter 3 (*Overleaf*, page 58). I'm laboring it a bit more here because of another persistent myth currently plaguing the horse world, particularly among "barefooters", and especially their horses when knives and Dremmels are deployed to "carve out the sole to get more concavity". The fact is, relative sole concavity varies as widely as angle-of-growth (toe angle): some hooves are more concaved than others. So, once again, if you want a horse with "lots of concavity", don't buy one that has naturally very little! The obsession with concavity, particularly among barefooters, is often taken to extremes — I have witnessed in astonishment distressed horse owners

"if you want a horse with "lots of concavity", don't buy one that has naturally very little!"

[1] *The Natural Horse*, p. 81-83

Throughout nature and in modern architectural masterpieces where structures are bearing extraordinary weight, we find the arch. The sole of the horse's foot is no different! Its naturally arched dome — the target of much too much carving — will *finally* be appreciated when the horse world's obsession with concavity is *finally* put to rest, and its convexity from above embraced.

whining, "Your horse has move concavity than mine." But all of this ravenous craving for concavity is simply misleading and overlooks what nature wants us to appreciate: that within the hoof, above the concavity, is a convex structure. Specifically, a sturdy dome selected by nature to resist and support descending weight-bearing forces.

Sole Thickness

Closely related to sole concavity is how thick the sole itself is — or should be. This would be a better obsession for the "gougers" out there as a 1 to 3 cm thick sole is not only natural, but necessary for any horse, particularly for those that are going to be ridden barefooted. It is ironic that the very persons obsessed with concavity are not at all averse to carving into the sole's natural thickness to "get that concavity", even at the risk of soring the horse and causing harm. NHC practitioners are trained in ways to determine sole thickness and to facilitate its natural thickness from trim to trim (Chapter 15). Trimmers who engage in the inhumane practice of sole gouging are no different than farriers who "trim to the bloodline" to make the hoof flat for the shoe, and then cauterize the foot through hot shoeing to mask the damage.

Hoof Balance

Hoof balance should be looked at in two ways. First, in terms of the hoof's active and passive wear pillars (*Overleaf*, pages 70-71), and second, by measuring the hoof along certain axes — for example, toe angle, hoof width, and hoof length — over time, and confirming that they have stabilized. Let's look a little closer at both of these signatures of the balanced,

"a 1 to 3 cm thick sole is not only natural, but necessary for any horse, particularly for those that are going to be ridden barefooted"

naturally shaped hoof.

The wild horse model shows us that size, shape, and proportion are static year round in wild horse populations of the U.S. Great Basin type environment (Figure 6-1, page 99). What this means is that their hooves did not grow into different shapes at different times of the year. Hence, the key elements of a naturally balanced hoof — size, shape, and proportion — also did not change during the year. The NHC practitioner understands this, and through the natural trim and related holistic practices, measures diligently to make sure data for the client horse isn't changing and that active and passive wear pillars are equally stable. In fact, when changes away from this stability occurs, the NHC practitioner will alert the horse owner that there are issues that need to be addressed.

When the key signatures of the naturally balanced hoof — size, shape, and proportion — remain the same following each trim session for one or more *hoof growth cycles*,[2] the hoof is said to be *biodynamically balanced*. Such a hoof exists in an equilibrium with its environment marked by optimal health and soundness. This may also mean that some part of, or even the entire hoof may require no trimming because new growth is offset by a commensurate amount of hoof worn away. I will use the term biodynamically balanced throughout the remainder of these natural trim guidelines with this implied understanding of stability, health, and soundness.

---

[1]See: "*hgc*: Hoof Growth Cycle" . J. Jackson, Bulletin #100 (4/28/2003), Natural Hoof Care Series, Star Ridge Publishing (www.star-ridge.com). One hgc = ~9 months at H°TL=8.25 cm at capsule growth rate 1 cm/mo.

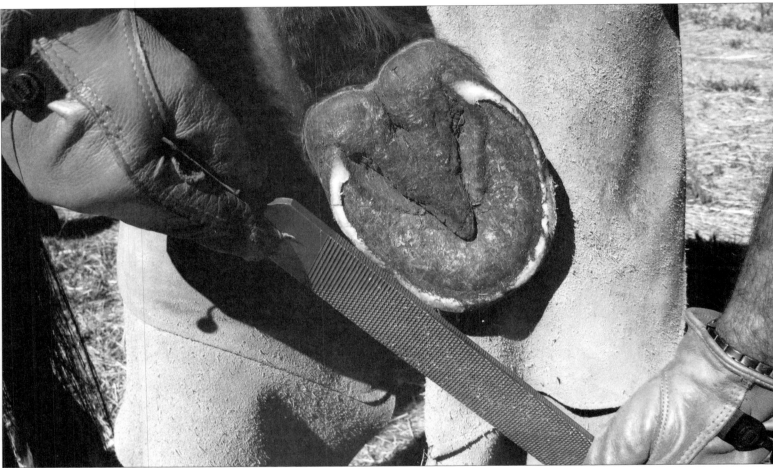

Jill Willis

I'm taking a swipe at one of the hooves that are worked hard in our Paddock Paradise (pp. 42-47). So efficient is the natural trim when done according to NHC guidelines, that I can trim our four horses to near perfection in less than an hour — with breaks along the way! I had to overcome the Farrier Principle to arrive at the door of NHC. Passing through that door was the greatest blessing of my professional career.

CHAPTER 5

What Is a Natural Trim?

*natural (nach/ er al) existing in nature; in accordance with the principles
of nature; as formed by nature without human intervention; wild condition.*

At the core of the natural trim is the very meaning of the word *natural*. There is some warranted confusion here — given the standard dictionary definition of the word quoted above — whether a trim method can be defined as natural when human "intervention" is involved at all in the process. Arguably, the term natural has been so wantonly savaged through commercial exploitation and gimmickry that the answer called for is an immediate and resounding "no". Such denigration aside, however, the horse's foot has proven to be more than tolerant of us in the matter of trimming — inviting actually — when we rise to the laws of nature and apply certain common sense *principles* based upon them in our work. When we do this, bogus and exploitative dimensions to the word *natural* quickly fall by the wayside, while genuine meaning stands firmly in their place. Such is the reality of the natural trim when anchored firmly to these principles, as is the whole of NHC.

In asking the horse world to move away from the conventions of shoeing, in order to "go natural", it is, to my way of thinking — as one who once shod horses — to be clear as to why shoeing is harmful and why going natural is the superior path to take and always in the best interest of the horse. And when this is then satisfactorily put behind us, we are next compelled to ask what are nature's principles that govern the natural trim? And, in the fullest meaning of the term, what precisely is a natural trim?

The Farrier Principle

In the introduction to this book, I laid out the historical premise for why people came to shoe their horses — and still do. The rationale for horseshoeing today is no different than it was at the industry's inception 800 years ago in Renaissance Europe. I call this the "Farrier Principle". Ask any farrier, and they will tell you: *the horse's foot needs protection and support.* This sounds reasonable, even humane, at face value. But today, in the Information Age, this rationale can only be described as specious and self-serving of everyone but the horse, who today, as always, truly suffers from the horseshoe's inherent pernicious effects. And the fact is, modern transportation has replaced any purported absolute "need" for horses as a means of conveyance in any civilized society.

Long before there was any discussion of NHC as there is today, I had to ask myself, what are the ramifications of telling horse owners to de-shoe their horses? Would it bring more harm to the horse's feet than the effects of the shoe I had come to know as a practicing farrier? This weighed heavily on me when I wrote *The Natural Horse* in the late 1980s. My farrier colleagues advised me against any such advocacy, or, at the very least, they argued, I should couch it within the safety net of competent farriers who would see horse owners through the transition. So I advised just that in the book. But following the book's release, horse owners — not farriers — took up the cause. Facing broad farrier resistance, many implored me to teach them the new "natural trim" method, to go around those too close-minded to help, and do it themselves. It was now clear to me that the Farrier Principle was standing in the way of farrier acceptance and crossover to NHC as I had envisioned. What to do? As I wrote in the introduction to this book, I opted to train horse owners, who, along with a small number of progressive-minded farriers, then joined me in spawning the barefoot movement we know today.

Not to turn my back entirely on my own former profession, I also wrote a series of articles for the American Farriers Journal and the European Farriers Journal on my research findings, the value of the wild horse hoof as a model, and how farriers can incorporate the natural trim into their professional practices.[1] A dialogue soon arose between the farrier community and the burgeoning numbers of barefooters. Though not always friendly, it was at least informative, giving me further insights into the rigid thinking that is so harnessed to the Farrier Principle, and why the addiction to shoeing is so unrelenting among its practitioners.

At first, I thought that the farriers I was hearing from directly, or from horse owners, were joking when they asserted that the horse's foot is incapable of going barefoot. That domestication in the broadest sense had at long last ruined the horse's foot. Their evidence lie under the shoe itself. In their minds, the damage that I perceived done to the hoof wasn't a direct consequence of shoeing, but the reality of the hoof itself with or without shoeing. To serve the civilized world, the horse had to be shod. The human race had rubbished the horse's foot, and there was nothing more to discuss. And in spite of an avalanche of evidence to the contrary, the Farrier Principle would be invoked by its adherents to the bitter end to defend their institution. Publicly, at least. Privately, I began to learn otherwise.

Behind the scenes, I have met with several of the world's most prominent farriers. The purpose of these meetings has been to find a way to integrate NHC into the world of the farrier. Without going into detail, our consensus is that education must lead the way and

---

[1]The following list of articles I wrote for the American Farriers Journal are archived online at www. americanfarriers.com: "What You Can Learn From The Naturally Shaped Hoof" (Sept/Oct, 1992); Forging "The Naturally Shaped Hoof" (Dec, 1992); "The Natural Healing Pathway" (Dec, 2004); "Spirit of the Natural Horse" (Jan/Feb, 1992); "Hoof Size vs. Proportion" (May/June, 1994); "Going Barefooted!" (Dec, 1997); "Farriery Implications For Natural Healing Of Laminitis" (Jan/Feb, 1995); "Logic Of The Frog, Pt. 1" (Sept/Oct, 2004); "Logic Of The Frog, Pt. 2" (Nov, 2004); "Challenging Hoof Balance Theories" (Sept/Oct, 1999); "Boot Up Your Shoeing Income" (Apr 2003).

that suitable educational models for teaching NHC must be created and implemented. To this end, I am collaborating with various parties to make this happen. And at the risk of being redundant, this has been my vision all along.

The antidote to the Farrier Principle, of course, is the artful science of NHC. I will let it speak for itself in the pages of this book and others I have written, and in the growing barefoot movement that follows the principles of NHC and not the reckless delusions of gurus and their unwitting worshippers or the armchair experts who know even less than the farrier has forgotten. This is not to say that the alpha and omega of NHC is completely worked out and that our house is completely in order. While the principles and practice of the natural trim are sufficiently worked out at this point in time to introduce it successfully to the world of the farrier for implementation in the field, tackling the immense landscape of the Four Pillars of NHC is very much a work in progress. The natural diet of the horse is still unknown (and too few want to follow the reasonably natural diet we know is healthier than many of the commercial feeds), too few horses are enjoying the benefits of natural boarding, the worlds of classical and natural horsemanship are yet un-fused, and the hoof boot of the future is yet to be designed. Of the latter, I have no doubt that it will be the farrier who brings it to us one day.

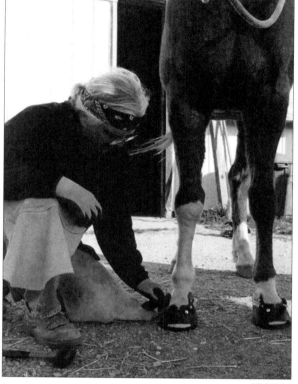

Jill Willis

Guiding Principles, Ethics, and the Natural Trim Defined

When we speak in terms of, or act upon, nature's principles for guiding the natural trim, it is implicit that the adaptation of *Equus ferus caballus* is a constant undercurrent either giving, or taking away, impetus to anything done to the hoof. This ancient force, the culmination of 55 million years of evolutionary natural selection, cannot be ignored; to the contrary, it must be understood, integrated, and cultured through the broad holistic spectrum of NHC practices. The natural trim, for certain, even with its own spectra of complex, interventional mechanics, cannot stand alone to bring the domesticated hoof into alignment and harmony with the underlying forces of nature. NHC practitioners understand that to successfully execute the trim in accordance with nature's guiding principles and within the holistic fold, there must be ethical adherence to two timeless tenets derived from the 5th century BCE Hippocratic Oath and observed by all responsible health care practitioners and humanitarians ever since:

>*Primum non nocere* — First, cause no harm

>*Vis medicatrix naturae* — Respect the healing powers of nature

These are truly inspiring words to abide by, and my opinion is that the horse world, and hoof care providers of all disciplines in particular, could do much to get in step with them! Nature's guiding principles for the trim flow readily from these two admonitions.

When I first wrote the guidelines, I included what I refer to as the "Four Guiding Principles of the Natural Trim". These are based entirely on the wild horse model, and, therefore, connect us directly to nature's principles and the powerful forces of adaptation that created the horse's foot through the evolutionary descent of *Equus ferus caballus* through natural selection. The first three principles cross-link to the first Hippocratic admonition to cause no harm; the fourth principle "indirectly" connects us to the second admonition to "respect the healing powers of nature". I would not think of trimming the horse's foot without these Guiding Principles in mind at every moment. They have brought me peace of mind as a NHC practitioner over the past 30 years, and certainty that my efforts are always in the best interest of the horse.

The Four Guiding Principles of the Natural Trim

1. Leave that which naturally should be there. Refers to the protection and preservation by the trimmer of the integrity of the basic anatomical parts of the hoof, such as the frog, bars, sole, and hoof wall. Principle #1 speaks to the "cause no harm" clause since these structures are routinely removed excessively — and not infrequently — altogether surgically by inappropriate farrier, veterinary, and barefoot trim methods (*facing page, top*). I view such excesses as inhumane, entirely unnecessary, and contraindicated by NHC principles and methodology.

2. Remove only that which is naturally worn away in the wild. This means that when the hoof (i.e., epidermis or capsule) is reduced by the trimmer, only that which would be worn away in the horse's wild state is taken. Principle #2 also implies that which is being removed should be trimmed away because it is excess growth. Similar to violations of Principle #1, the cause no harm clause is invoked when excessive (but not total) capsule is removed (*facing page, bottom*).

3. Allow to grow that which should be there naturally but isn't due to human meddling. Instructs the trimmer to use restraint when faced with hooves that have been over-trimmed in some part (such as a heel-buttress), and, particularly, to refrain from removing epidermis from the opposing structure (e.g., the opposite heel-buttress) so as to establish an ersatz "balance" that only worsens matters for the horse. This also applies to misguided efforts to force one hoof (e.g., the left front) to look like the other (the right front), for example, by over-thinning part of a hoof wall. Finally, Principle #3 admonishes the trimmer to not compensate the over-trimmed hoof by using horseshoes, wedging tech-

(*Continued on page 88*)

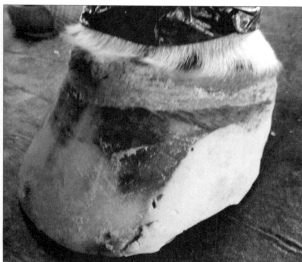

Double toe wall resection facilitates entry to the internal structures of the foot. Metallic straps are screwed to the wall to keep hoof and shoe together. This procedure and all the others shown here. evoke the NHC "cause no harm" clause and demonstrate a lack of understanding of the foot's ability to heal itself ("respect the healing powers of nature" clause).

The entire quarter and heel wall has been removed. This is not uncommon in the traditional and unnatural treatment of major wall splits ("quarter cracks") and foot infections. Such hooves typically only require NHC intervention to rebalance the capsule and facilitate healing.

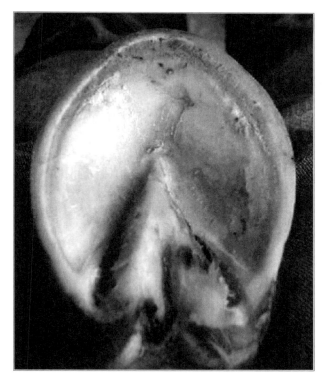

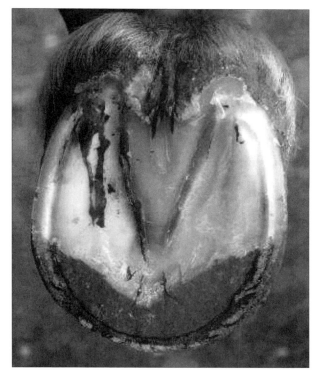

The entire solar dome has been sculpted paper thin to "counter hoof contraction"; of course, this is nonsense since the protective epidermal armor has been effectively removed and the hoof, in pain, will contract in response.

Other misguided "barefoot" trimmers also cut out the bars to the same end with the intent of "decontraction" for "increased hoof mechanism". All inhumane, all unnecessary, all based on a foundation of bogus science.

(Continued from page 86)

nology, and acrylics to "give it a better angle" (*facing page, top*). As always, the trimmer is to give the hoof time to heal, grow and renew its own structure.

4. *Ignore all pathology.* Warns the trimmer not to focus on pathology (if present) or violations of the three previous principles, but, instead, to look intuitively to 4th-dimensional changes (healing changes over time — "respect the healing powers of nature") and faithfully adhere to NHC principles and practices. Pathology invariably takes care of itself when we do healthful things. Experience has shown that beginning NHC students are very vulnerable to psychological trauma and panic when confronted with extremely deformed or inflamed hooves, such as horses afflicted with acute and chronic laminitis or severe neglect (*facing page, bottom*). Principle #4 also applies to the risks of "dirty window syndrome", that is, obsession with minutia, perfection, and pathology — a proven corridor to invasive, harmful trimming and violations of Principle #2. It is easier to see and understand nature's 4-D healing forces through the lens of health, than through disease, and one is then less like to fall victim to "fixing" problems rather than focusing on emerging health.

§

The Natural Trim Defined

Technically, the natural trim is concerned with and defined as the humane transposing or "mimicking" of natural *wear patterns* documented in wild horse feet onto the hooves of domesticated horses.[1] When these wear patterns are diligently and repeatedly applied to the hoof at roughly 4-5 week time intervals — and always as much as possible within the larger holistic fold of NHC — the natural trim (governed by the Four Guiding Principles) triggers a cascade of integrated biodynamic (i.e., living) forces that produce and reinforce naturally shaped hooves. This melding of forces is sometimes described as a reinforcing "cycle of

(Continued on page 90)

---

[1]Of course, here I am referring to the wear patterns described in the previous Overleaf (pp. 46-53). I recommend reviewing these again in the context of the current discussion of the natural trim.

> "the natural trim is concerned with and defined as the humane transposing or "mimicking" of natural *wear patterns* documented in wild horse feet onto the hooves of domesticated horses"

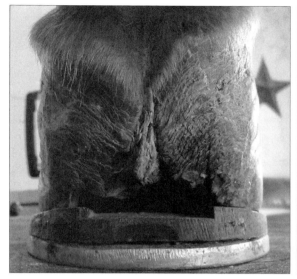

The farrier used a wedge pad to elevate the hoof's heels that are already too long; plus, an "egg bar" shoe (shoe that is continuous like an "0") to provide support that was already there in over abundance with the hoof's long under-run heels. The farrier was certainly industrious in creating this illogical support structure for what is a clearly laminitic hoof (Chapter 7): the toe has been rasped back into an unnatural bend (called a "bull nose"), stress rings abound, the egg-bar shoe providing support too far behind the heels where such support never exists in a naturally shaped hoof, and so forth. The absence of logic here in most every respect makes this hoof a remarkable candidate for NHC!

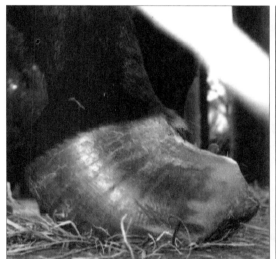

It is hard for many to perceive that the end of the hoof at left is, in fact, part of the bottom of the foot! Clearly the farrier or barefoot trimmer did not know what else to do, but cut off the end of this chronically laminitic hoof, thereby creating a "tube" of sorts of the hoof. The horse, in fact, is walking on the back of his heels! The practitioner then closed off the end of the hoof with a cemented mesh, probably to protect exposed internal structures and mitigate hypersensitivity. The hoof, if trimmed to the 4 Guiding Principles, would have transformed dramatically in the span of two to three trim sessions and the horse would have immediately been standing on the ends of his heel-buttreses as he should at the end of the first session!

form and function" (*facing page*). This cycle, in reality, defines the specific role and limits of the natural trim. And active within its penumbra are the collateral influences of the horse's temperamental character and physical conformation, the environment, and, never to be underestimated or ignored, the impact of human meddling. Briefly, let's follow the cyclical force field that follows from the natural trim:

1. Natural trim mimics natural wear patterns of wild horse feet

The cycle begins as the NHC practitioner trims the hoof by mimicking the *natural wear patterns* seen in the wild. This is done regardless of the damage done to the foot due to shoeing, unnatural trimming methods, and lifestyle complications. The Four Guiding Principles govern how this is achieved without causing harm while respecting and incorporating the individual horse's unique conformational and other attributes that will always influence future growth (size, shape and proportion). Other than possible booting, this ends the trimmer's role at the hoof; NHC holistic practices are then implemented.

2. Natural wear patterns stimulate natural growth patterns

Immediately following the trim, the foot's sensitive (innervated) and vascular dermal structures responsible for creating the capsule (the foot's epidermal armor) respond by producing growth patterns that correspond to the natural wear patterns. This characteristic growth response seems to be driven genetically by the powerful underlying adaptative force. New growth will reach ground level in approximately 9 months, that is, one hoof growth cycle (*hgc*) or the time it takes for the foot to completely reproduce itself.[1]

3. Natural growth patterns create natural hoof shapes

With each subsequent trim session, the generated growth patterns continue to position mass in the direction of the underlying adaptative form, in effect, posturing the capsule for optimal function (Chapter 7). To be clear, the foot is *not* adapting to the environment, but is overcoming the pernicious effects of misguided human meddling.[2] The result is a hoof that, under the influence of NHC holistic interventions, becomes increasingly more naturally shaped over time with each trim, called 4th dimensional (4D) changes in hoof mass. I view these efforts as a quest of sorts to tip the scales of "holistic" and antagonistic "antiholistic" forces in the favor of the naturally shaped hoof. This "tug of war" between the two forces is taken up in considerable detail in the training of NHC practitioners. A few

(Continued on page 92)

---

[1] For example, a biodynamically balanced hoof with a toe length measuring 3¼ in. (8.3 cm) will take less than 9 months at a growth rate of ¼ in. (1 cm) per month; the calculation is: $1 \ hgc = 3.25 \ in \times 2.54 \ cm/in \div 1 \ cm/mo = 8.3 \ mo$. SRP Bulletin #100 (4/28/2003)

[2] The adaptation took place 1.4 million years ago (Chapter 1, pp. 31-37).

Relationship of the natural trim to the biodynamic cycle of form and function

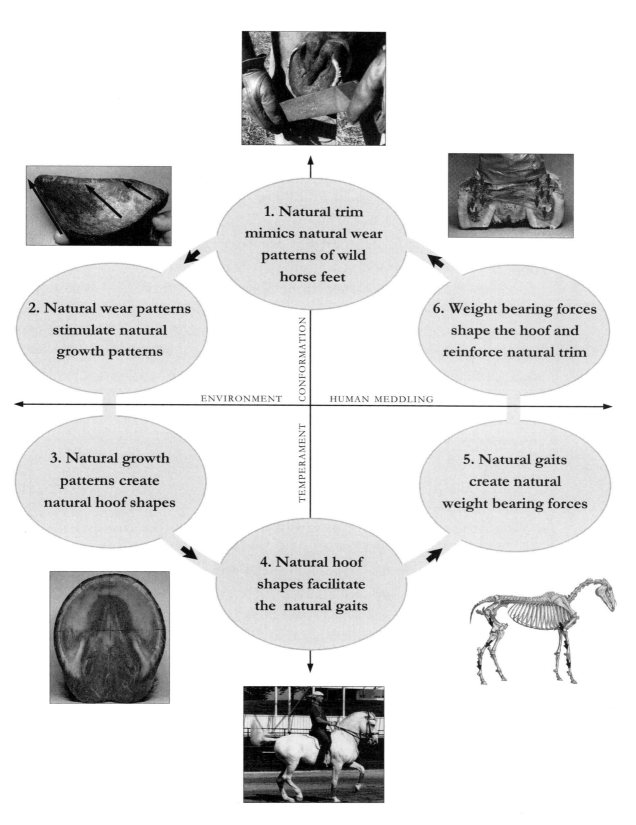

1. Natural trim mimics natural wear patterns of wild horse feet

2. Natural wear patterns stimulate natural growth patterns

3. Natural growth patterns create natural hoof shapes

4. Natural hoof shapes facilitate the natural gaits

5. Natural gaits create natural weight bearing forces

6. Weight bearing forces shape the hoof and reinforce natural trim

CONFORMATION

TEMPERAMENT

ENVIRONMENT

HUMAN MEDDLING

words about this, however, are worthy of the horse owner's attention since the general care of the horse is largely the focus.

We recall that NHC is founded upon the four pillars of natural horsemanship (riding/ training), natural boarding, a reasonably natural diet, and the natural trim. In the aforementioned tug of war, these are contraposed by unnatural horsemanship practices, unnatural boarding conditions, and harmful feeding regimens. I've depicted these opposing biodynamic forces in the illustration at right (*facing page, above*). The arrows represent their relative influences on the natural trim (NT), here the effects of the natural trim itself. Next, we see that bi-directional arrows ($\leftrightarrows$) lie between NT and A°. A° is the underlying angle-of-adaptation, which, in life, is measurable as N°, the natural angle of growth (which we measure at the toe) that the hoof would transform to if the horse were turned loose in the wild in his natural adaptative environment. In this scenario, strong holistic forces (black arrows) have canceled weak anti-holistic forces (ascending grey arrows) of NHC, and the effects of the natural trim (NT) are in a healthful equilibrium ($\leftrightarrows$) with nature (A°).

One can determine this stability, or instability as the case may be, by evaluating measurement data for the hoof over time and correlating that to management practices.[1] Indeed, there is very specific and telling "data" that correspond to these forces, and this information should be used to help horse owners make sound changes in their management practices. For example, in the "tug of war" seen in the illustration on the facing page (*bottom*), the effects of unnatural boarding practices on the hoof correspond to "shifts" in the hoof measurements over time. Another example would be the effects of an unnatural diet, which would generate similar shifts in the hoof's measurement data over time. I'll discuss some of these in very specific terms in later chapters.

4. Natural shapes facilitate the natural gaits

The initial growth pattern response to the trim, having reached ground level after 1 *hgc* (approximately 8 to 9 months for most naturally trimmed horses), now provides a more naturally shaped hoof (size, shape, and proportion) for the horse to move on. The horse can now move more naturally on his feet using his natural gaits. Obviously this is an area of intervention that horse owners can partake in by providing reasonably natural boarding conditions for their horses to live in, and engaging the horse as a natural rider.

5. Natural gaits create natural weight-bearing forces

The natural gaits now begin to organize and propel weight bearing forces as the horse moves more naturally on his feet. The feet must receive and resist these powerful forces

(*Continued on page 94*)

---

[1]The lay reader is encouraged not to fret about knowing how to do this — it is the job of the professional NHC practitioner!

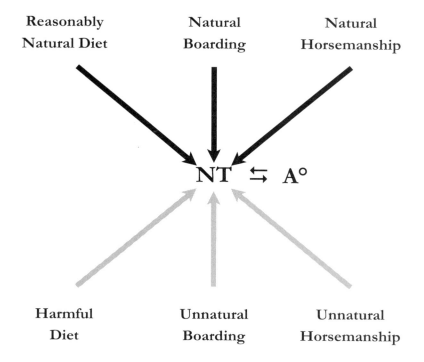

Reasonably
Natural Diet

Natural
Boarding

Natural
Horsemanship

NT ⇄ A°

Harmful
Diet

Unnatural
Boarding

Unnatural
Horsemanship

(Above) Tension between holistic and contraposing anti-holistic biodynamic forces on the natural trim (NT). The black arrows represent strong forces, the grey arrows weak forces, hence holistic forces are predominant and the equilibrium favors health and soundness.

(Below) At left, strong anti-holistic forces have overwhelmed NHC practices and destabilized the effects of the natural trim (NT). In this scenario, the horse, previously living under very natural conditions, was moved into a stall. Measurements collected by the NHC practitioner would show a shift away from A°. At center, the horse has been returned to a natural boarding facility, and trim effects begin at once to restore hoof measurements towards A°. At right, the effects of the trim have finally entered into a biodynamic equilibrium with the environment and stabilized the hoof measurements (note that the equilibrium here is identical to the one above). These "shifts" towards and away from A° correspond to measureable changes in hoof size, shape, and proportion; moreover, shifts are "data specific" and carry with them the individual "signatures" of diet, boarding conditions, and horsemanship. NHC provides the "Rosetta Stone" for interpreting these data shifts.

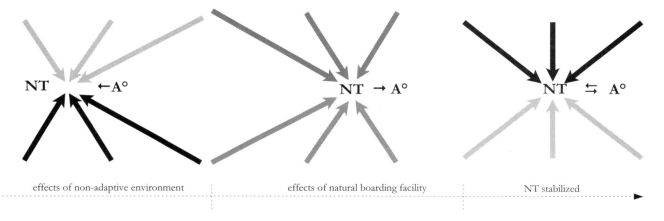

NT ←A°

NT → A°

NT ⇄ A°

effects of non-adaptive environment ⋮ effects of natural boarding facility ⋮ NT stabilized

delivered by the natural gaits, and as they do, the hooves are shaped. It is interesting to note that muscle groups, once organized around a less than natural — if not outright pathological — hoof conformation, also begin to transform. This is an interesting phenomenon to observe, particularly when natural riding is happening, wherein mass begins to dissipate over pathology, and accrete ("build in") where it should be. It is not uncommon to hear, "My horse looks like an entirely new animal".

Taking timely critical measurements of the hoof along specific growth axes is as important as the physician's patient chart. The NHC practitioner's "data chart" tells us how the hoof is doing over time.

The Healing Angle (H°) and
Other Critical Measurements

In the world of the farrier, measurements at the hoof are taken — if they are taken at all — for the express purpose of fitting the shoe to the foot. In some instances the farrier is directed to meet the arbitrary "toe angle—toe length—heel length" requirements of the many fickle equestrian disciplines. Given the actual complexities of the horse's foot and how the hoof grows according to the adaptive forces of nature, it is a sad state of affairs that any serious hoof care practitioner would subordinate their professional authority to persons who know less than them or who don't really know what they are talking about, except in the most self-serving of ways. Would the surgeon allow the patient to dictate what is happening in the operating room? This travesty is the result of neither party really understanding the relationship of "natural form" to "natural function", and, how certain capsule measurements, when taken accurately, are revealing of that vital relationship.

Genuine NHC requires that the practitioner not only take specific measurements, and at regular intervals, but also that they understand what these measurements mean in terms of capsule stability, soundness, and the horse's general well-being. In fact, recording hoof measurements, and interpreting their meaning at each trim session, is as important as the medical charts maintained and available for study or review by a physician. In these Guidelines, the student is taught what to measure, how to measure, at what point in time during the trim to take a given measurement, and what the measurements mean in terms of the Four Pillars of NHC.

Measurements should be recorded (tantamount to information put in the physician's medical chart), and kept by the practitioner (in hard copy or digital format) on each individual horse. Along with measurement data, the practitioner keeps a detailed record of the horse's history, including dietary information, veterinary care, boarding conditions, how the horse is ridden, and anything else that is revealing of the horse's treatment. All my client horses, for example, have their own "data booklets", which I can refer to at each trim session, or at any time an issue arises where they might be of help.

Acquiring accurate measurement data serves very specific objectives in the practice of NHC. These include the following:

- Evaluating hoof size, shape, symmetry, and proportion relative to the wild horse model.

- Evaluating natural hoof size and proportion relative to left-right, and front-hind, hoof shapes and symmetries for the individual horse.

- Ascertaining healthful and pathological growth changes in the capsule, such as club foot, laminitis, and run-under foot syndrome.

- Determining the effects of hoof contraction due to shoeing and invasive trimming methods.

- Custom-fitting of hoof boots.

There are seven critical measurements that enable the NHC practitioner to fulfill these objectives:

- H° (Healing Angle)
- H°TL (Healing Toe Length)
- B° (Basement Angle)
- B°TL (Basement Toe Length)
- HL (Hoof Length)
- HW (Hoof Width)
- CW (Coronary Width)

Each of the above is defined and their location pinpointed in the *Overleaf* (pp. 108-125). With the exception of "CW" (Coronary Width[1]) each of these measurements can be cross-linked to data ranges gathered from U.S. Great Basin wild, free-roaming horses (Figure 6-1). Generally speaking, when the hooves being measured collectively fall within these data ranges, and particularly when they do not change for the duration of one *hgc*[2], it is very likely that the hoof is naturally shaped. Hooves that fall outside these data ranges, or do not measure within them with stability (i.e., they are in a seemingly endless state of flux) for at least one *hgc*, are very likely unnaturally shaped and probably have serious problems that can be traced directly to violations of holistic NHC practices.

Of the aforementioned measurements, H° (Healing Angle) and H°TL (Healing Toe Length) deserve special attention. This is due to their strategic role in ascertaining the hoof's optimal angle of growth and toe wall length, and in aiding the NHC practitioner to establish safe cut-lines during trimming.

At this point, our discussion of critical measurements will become increasingly more complex as we delve deeper into the nuances of hoof size, shape, and proportion. This will become particularly apparent as we begin to assign values and points of reference to the more formidable landscapes of distressed domesticated hooves. But this groundwork is

---

[1]CW was not included in my wild horse hoof studies, as it was discovered years later during my study of the effects of shoeing on capsule stability.

[2]One *hgc* is approximately equivalent to 9 months of growth at H°TL = 3.25 in. (8.3 cm). See: *"hgc: Hoof Growth Cycle".* SRP Bulletin #100 (4/28/2003).

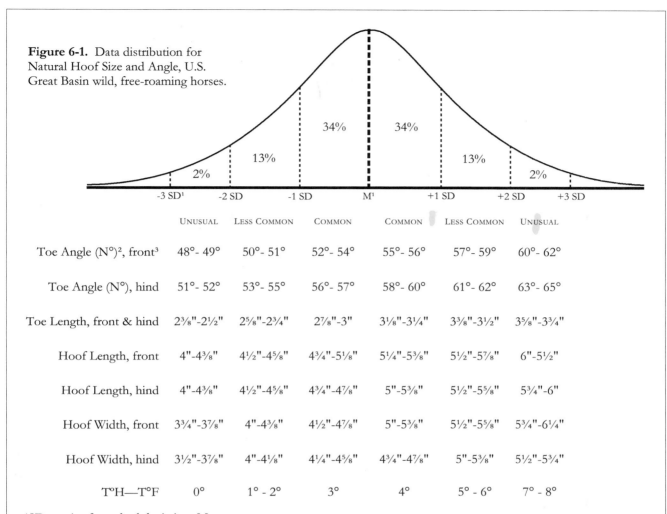

Figure 6-1. Data distribution for Natural Hoof Size and Angle, U.S. Great Basin wild, free-roaming horses.

	UNUSUAL	LESS COMMON	COMMON	COMMON	LESS COMMON	UNUSUAL
Toe Angle (N°)[2], front[3]	48°- 49°	50°- 51°	52°- 54°	55°- 56°	57°- 59°	60°- 62°
Toe Angle (N°), hind	51°- 52°	53°- 55°	56°- 57°	58°- 60°	61°- 62°	63°- 65°
Toe Length, front & hind	2⅜"-2½"	2⅝"-2¾"	2⅞"-3"	3⅛"-3¼"	3⅜"-3½"	3⅝"-3¾"
Hoof Length, front	4"-4⅜"	4½"-4⅝"	4¾"-5⅛"	5¼"-5⅜"	5½"-5⅞"	6"-5½"
Hoof Length, hind	4"-4⅜"	4½"-4⅝"	4¾"-4⅞"	5"-5⅜"	5½"-5⅝"	5¾"-6"
Hoof Width, front	3¾"-3⅞"	4"-4⅜"	4½"-4⅞"	5"-5⅜"	5½"-5⅝"	5¾"-6¼"
Hoof Width, hind	3½"-3⅞"	4"-4⅛"	4¼"-4⅝"	4¾"-4⅞"	5"-5⅜"	5½"-5¾"
T°H—T°F	0°	1° - 2°	3°	4°	5° - 6°	7° - 8°

[1] SD= unit of standard deviation; M = mean:average.

[2] N° is the "natural toe angle" measured over the MATW at limit line; N°, in these data ragnes, applies only to wild horses of the U.S. Great Basin studied by the author and cited in fn. 3 below.

[3] All measurements left or right hooves, ages 5+ (adults), *Equus ferus caballus*. Based on J. Jackson's Litchfield BLM Corrals data, Summer samples x 2 @ 125 horses each + Winter sample x 1 @ 125 horses = 1,500 F/H hooves measured (Bell curve modeled after Figure 6-2, *The Natural Horse: Lessons From The Wild*, p. 111, Northland Publishing, 1992).

foundational to the NHC practitioner's ability to navigate the horse's foot skillfully and confidently, and, therefore, it must be mastered. This will require much effort and study on behalf of the reader, with whom I am entirely sympathetic in what can only be described as the most daunting of tasks.

The Healing Angle (H°)

The horse's hoof is ever-demonstrating to us that it is either in a state of healthy equilibrium or in a constant battle to overcome our vices and ignorance as horse owners and professionals.[1] This is no more apparent than in its angle-of-growth, which is subject to change over time depending on the type of care given. When the hoof grows downward in close approximation to the wild horse model, we can say with near certainty that the horse is, at that moment in time, sound and healthy. When growth patterns diverge from that model, inevitably we will find the hoof, the foot, and the animal himself in duress. One important and useful indicator of the hoof's health and soundness relative to the wild horse model is its angle of growth at the toe wall, or "toe angle". When, as a result of the natural trim and related NHC practices, that angle measures with stability over time within the angle data ranges in Figure 6-1, the hoof will be found to be healthy and sound. Angle changes towards those data ranges as a result of NHC intervention are also viewed as healthful changes. Conversely, when angle changes move away from those data ranges, we will find the hoof (and the horse) to be in trouble and accompanied by unnatural care practices. NHC practitioners view the healthful changes in a hoof's angle of growth to be a product of the foot's biological capacity to heal itself ("healing powers of nature") and its inherent "will" or propensity to gravitate towards and align with A° — the hoof's angle of adaptation. For this reason, this angle of growth is defined as the "Healing Angle of Growth," or simply H°. H°, therefore, is an indispensable tool with which the NHC practitioner can gauge and evaluate how the hoof is doing over time.

In all of this, we recognize that H° actually only exists *in the moment*. Our misguided or holistic actions can tip the scales of healing to the detriment or benefit of the animal and his foot, and set that growth pattern in another direction entirely. This is to say that H° is not simply any growth along the toe wall, but *new growth emerging immediately from the coronary corium* (page 60). Ironically, then, we do not know what that new projection of mass is in absolute terms of growth, because we cannot see or measure it directly. But we can evaluate its history, and, when at last it becomes visible to the naked eye, measure it "indirectly" with our hoof gauges. These Guidelines provide criteria for locating and measuring H° in a standardized way that is vital to the NHC practitioner. Measurements are taken with the Hoof Meter Reader (HMR), a gauge that is calibrated to the wild horse data ranges in Figure 6-1.

H°, not surprisingly, is often confused with the term "toe angle" as used by farriers, vets, and horse owners. The two are not the same. Since this is the case, let me clarify the difference between the two.

Toe angle is the angle that the toe wall forms with the bottom of the hoof (*not the ground*), and can be measured accordingly with a farrier's angle gauge (*facing page*). The farrier is able

---

[1]"Of the 122 million equines found around the world, no more than 10 percent are clinically sound. Some 10 percent (12.2 million) are clinically, completely and unusably lame. The remaining 80 percent (97.6 million) of these equines are somewhat lame and could not pass a soundness evaluation or test." [American Farriers Journal, Nov./2000, v. 26, #6, p. 5.]

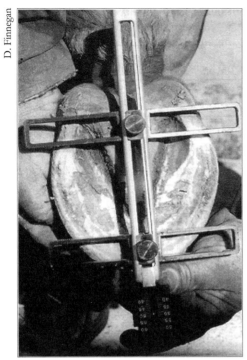

D. Finnegan

A more ingenious toe angle gauge used by farriers that measures toe angle in relation to the bottom of the hoof. The angle readout can be seen near the toe. Such a design, however, presumes a flat volar plane upon which to rest the arms of the gauge. As the bottom of a naturally shaped hoof is never flat along the hoof wall (due to active/passive wear), such a gauge is rendered useless.

to regulate toe angle by alternately lengthening or shortening the toe wall relative to the heels, and vice versa. Toe angle is also commonly associated with the concept of "break over", that is, the manner in which the hoof leaves the ground over the toe (hence, "break over"). It is widely believed that increasing toe angle by shortening the toe while increasing heel length through excessive growth or some artificial means (e.g., heel wedges), or "backing up the toe" by rasping the toe wall to less than its natural thickness, "speeds up" break over. Farriers may also "roll" or "square" the toes to further synergize the effects of elevating the hoof's toe angle and effecting breakover. These kinds of manipulations of the hoof are typically done to correct interference (caused by the presence of the shoe, excess toe length, and/or bad riding practices!) or enhance gait "action". H°, in contrast, has nothing to do with any of this, and NHC practitioners view such meddlings at the hoof as unwarranted, and in some instances blatantly inhumane.

Instead, H° — measured just below the coronary band over the toe wall, and always in relation to the ground (*not the bottom of the foot!*) — is closely associated with complex mass changes occuring anywhere in the hoof capsule from the coronary band down to the ground. These changes typically occur gradually over time, hence, they are referred to as 4th-dimensional ("4D") changes among NHC practitioners. As stated earlier, NHC practitioners track these 4D changes over time by keeping close tabs on H° as well as the other (six) codependent measurements.

In the naturally shaped hoof, the lateral profile (the hoof viewed from the side, page 109) of the toe wall is neither convex nor concave, but follows a straight line from just below the coronary band (called the "bull's-eye", page 116) down to the turn of the mustang roll (*facing page, above*; and page 66). H° is measured along this axis, as I said, below the coronary band. This often is not the case with many domesticated hooves, however, due to unnatural care. All unnaturally shaped hooves can be classified into two lateral profiles: those that bend forward of the natural profile (*facing page, middle*) and those that bend behind it (*facing page, below*). The two-prong goal of NHC is to stabilze H°, and to harmonize these "bends" in the hoof wall into "straight line" growth in alignment with H°. The natural trim, in conjunction with the other three pillars of NHC, facilitates these complex, 4-D healing changes.

Healing Toe Length (H°TL)

Once H° has been identified, the NHC practitioner sets their sights on H°TL (*facing page*). H°TL is a measurement of toe length in alignment with H° from just *below the coronary band, down to the ground*. Generally speaking, measurements that fall within the data ranges for toe length in Figure 6-1 indicate that the hoof is at its optimal toe length and requires no further shortening at the toe; measurements that fall outside these data ranges suggest that the hoof is excessively short (e.g., has been over trimmed) or too long (and needs to be trimmed). The NHC practitioner must consider other factors (e.g., presence or lack of obvious excess growth, previous data taken, and relative concavity) in reaching a final decision. H°TL, thus, plays a vital role in reducing capsule length to its optimal size — safely, accurately and quickly.

Trimming to H°

Once H° is stabilized, and only after H° is stabilized, it is then incumbent upon the NHC practitioner to sustain that angle of growth in the future following any given trim session. This is called "trimming to H°". Arbitrarily altering H° would be tantamount to saying that we know better than nature when we don't — practically an invitation to do battle! Would we change the natural angle of growth (N°) of a wild horse hoof? The exception would be that, for some reason, H° has changed of its own accord, in which case, we would then sustain that angle while investigating the cause.

Sustaining H° at the conclusion of any given trim session can be perplexing to beginners. This is largely due to the capsule's admittedly peculiar angle of growth (pages 66-67) from "toe to heel" and the illusions such growth presents to the untrained eye. At the heart of the problem is the common sense notion that to sustain H°, one must trim away the same amount of heel as toe. In fact, and due to the hoof's varying angles of growth from front to back, one always trims more heel away than toe to sustain H°! This may require some additional clarification, as follows.

(*Continued on page 104*)

Mass Changes in Angle of Growth Relative to H°.

H° is the capsule's projection of growth at inception. H°TL is the 4D history of that projection. In the illustrations, both H° and H°TL are constant.

(*Above*) The "straight line" descent of growth relative to H°, marked as H°TL, is representative of the wild hoof model and our goal as NHC practitioners.

(*Middle*) The descent of growth has departed from H°. Here, at the point designated as DTA (acronym for "diverging toe angle", or "divergent angle of growth"), the toe wall tracks forward of H°TL. This pathological change in capsule mass is typical of horses suffering from chronic laminitis and underslung ("run under") heels, due to which it is commonly called the "slipper toe" foot. The capsule is now too far forward under the horse, thereby impeding breakover and obstructing the natural gaits. Nature commonly responds in such hooves by elevating H°.

(*Below*) The lower hoof wall tracks behind H°TL. This is typical of what is called the "bull-nosed" foot, a pathological conformation caused by horseshoes set too far back on the hoof, and misguided trimming methods, both of which rasp away excessive amounts of hoof wall, called "backing up the toe". Ironically, this type of hoof work is done to "increase toe angle" so as to facilitate break over, but, in fact, has the opposite effect of unbalancing the foot and causing pain and tripping because the toe wall isn't where it is supposed to be. The capsule, having lost mass behind H° TL, is now too small and too far back under the horse, thereby obstructing the natural gaits. Nature commonly responds in such hooves by lowering H° and accreting extraordinary amounts of heel mass.

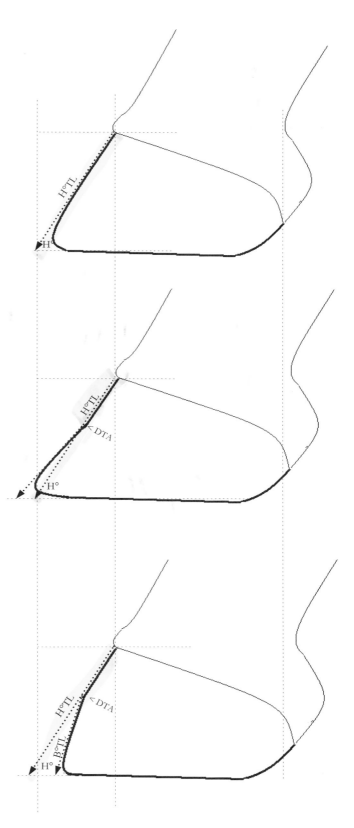

Consider the biodynamically balanced wild horse hoof on the facing page (*above*). I have marked the hoof's angles of growth at the toe, quarter, and heel. As can be seen, angle of growth is steepest at toe and progressively lower towards the heel, where it is the lowest. ▼¹ and ▼² locate the hoof's active wear pillars visible in this view. In the wild, the natural angle at the toe would remain the same year round due to natural wear in the horse's adaptative environment.

Next, I have drawn a similar hoof profile, with the same varying angles of growth as the wild hoof, to which I have added projected excess growth typical of what we see with domesticated hooves. I have marked the ▼¹ and ▼² support pillars in their pre- (excess growth) and post-trim positions. Now, let's analyze what and how much epidermis is being trimmed away to sustain H° at the conclusion of the trim. Let's assume, too, that H° had previously stabilized at 54° and that the hoof here with excess growth still measures at 54°.

First, note that as the capsule has grown longer, the distance between the ▼¹ and ▼² support pillars has become less and less. Note too that the length of new growth is shorter at ▼¹ (marked as x) than at ▼² (marked as y). In other words, $x < y$ (< = less than, hence, x is less than y). What this means is that 1) the support base of the capsule has shrunk proportionally with time, 2) the support base has advanced forward of its natural position, and 3), the heels have grown longer than the toe in the same amount of time and are too far forward under the horse (called "run under heels").

To sustain H° at post trim, a corresponding — but not equal — amount of wall must be removed at x and y. As you can see, more wall must be trimmed away at the heel than at the toe. The result will be the reverse of the above: 1) the support base will expand to its natural size, 2) the support base will move back under the horse to its natural position, and 3) the heels will be shorter and back under the horse where they belong.

It is interesting to note that horse owners always marvel at how so much heel can be trimmed away relative to the toe without lowering the hoof's toe angle. To the naked eye, it appears that the hoof's toe angle has actually increased. This is an illusion wrought by the visual clash between the hoof's pre-trim "run-under" profile and its post trim "natural" look. Part of what's happening too, is that as the hoof comes back under the horse, the bones of the digit (P1-P2-P3) realign and become less hyper-flexed, which also contributes to the "slung under" conformation.

Another area of confusion in trimming to H° concerns the reversal of the "long toe, run under heel" syndrome seen in hooves similar to the middle hoof on page 103. Such hooves are characterized by sweeping long toes, severely *run-under heels* (if you can imagine y totally out of control!), and low angle readings for H° completely off the data ranges for toe angle in Figure 6-1. Typically, the farrier — often under pressure from the horse's owner to shorten the toe and elevate the hoof's toe angle by "giving him more heel" — will attempt

(*Continued on page 106*)

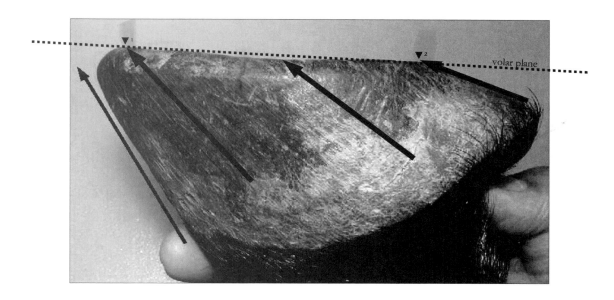

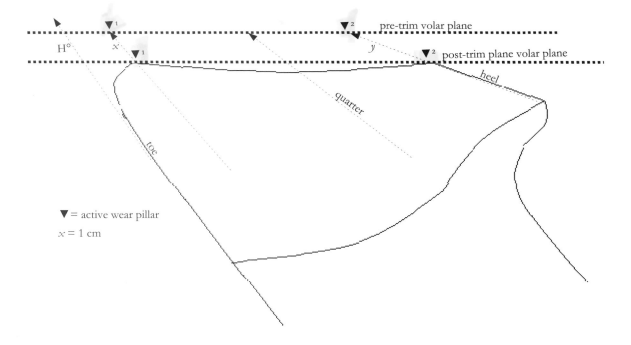

▼ = active wear pillar

x = 1 cm

(Continued from page 104)

(futilely so) to correct the problem by letting the heels grow longer and/or using heel lifts/wedges to raise the angle. But, as I've just illustrated above, the effect of this action is to migrate and shrink the support plane of the hoof forward of its natural position relative to H°. Hence, the problem is only compounded and the hoof continues on its "run away" forward migration. Faced with this specter, the farrier will then attempt to blockade this forward growth by setting the shoe back and aggressively rasping the toe wall back — only to find themselves now faced additionally with a "bull-nosed hoof" (page 103; Chapter 13) in the forward run away position! Many horses are euthanized at this point due to the concurrent and unrelenting pain many endure *(facing page)*. The way out of this conundrum, of course, is to bring the foot back under the horse by removing more heel — precisely counter intuitive! Of course, this has the effect of restoring (or setting in motion) the heels to their correct position back under the horse. H° will then modulate as nature sees fit to a steeper or lower angle of growth through redirected mass accretion, bringing the toe wall back into alignment with H° where it belongs. Natural trim protocols explained later in this text cannot only "correct" but also prevent these kinds of unnatural disasters from occurring.

§

For the remainder of this chapter (overleaf, pages 108-125), we will use the Hoof Meter Reader (HMR), Vernier caliper, and tape measure to take the critical measurements of H° (Healing Angle), H°TL (Healing Toe Length), B° (Basement Angle), B°TL (Basement Toe Length), HL (Hoof Length), HW (Hoof Width), and CW (Coronary Width). Additional terms such as DTA, MATW, and MAVP are also introduced, defined, explained, and subsequently used throughout the natural trim instructions in Part 2 of these Guidelines.

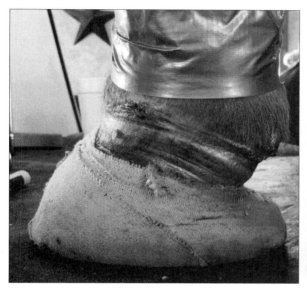

Pathological Mass Changes in Angle of Growth Due to Shoeing and Unnatural Trimming.

The laminitic hoof seen here has been further compromised by what can only be called outrageous shoeing and trimming practices. Yet, this has become fairly commonplace worldwide due to bogus veterinary science, complicit farriery, and ignorance of NHC by horse owners. These photos of cadavers were taken in one of my ISNHCP training camps. Ironically, while students looked on aghast as I removed the bandages and hardware, at the very same time a veterinarian was conducting the same misguided procedure on a horse just outside the clinic door in the main barn!

(*Above, left*) The ace bandage contributes nothing but a cloak to conceal the damage underneath to the horse's foot.

(*Above, right*) I've removed the bandage, revealing the blatant pretzel logic that went into creating this travesty of hoof care. The heels have overgrown to an extraordinary length, causing them to "run under". The toe, likewise, has also grown to great excessive length, which in conjunction with the long heels, caused the entire foot to be too far forward. To help counter this effect, the farrier nailed on an oversize "egg bar" shoe (*right*), to support the horse where the heels should be! To aid the foot's breakover, the farrier also backed up the toe, which bull-nosed the hoof. A wedge pad was also added to elevate the heels, thinking this would elevate toe angle and, therefore, also help breakover. Of course, none of these measures helped matters, but conspired along with other management problems (including diet) to kill the horse. The dashed line points to the approximate cut-line this hoof would have been trimmed to under natural trim guidelines. That and giving the horse a reasonably natural diet is all that was needed to bring this horse onto a healing pathway.

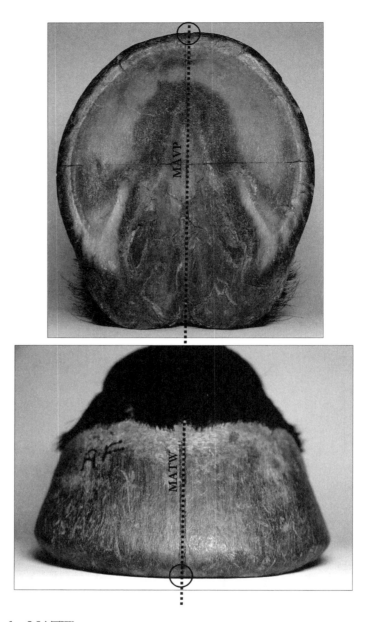

Measuring the MATW.

Two important lines are used to grid the bottom and front of the hoof: the MAVP and MATW. These gridlines form important reference points or positions, called *navigational landmarks*, for the NHC practitioner when measuring and establishing cut lines used in trimming. They also enable NHC practitioners to communicate clearly with each other when discussing trimming issues.

(*Above*) The MAVP (Median Axis of the Volar Profile), is a line drawn through the central sulcus of the frog, and which closely bisects the bottom of the hoof (called the "volar profile") as seen above.

(Below) The MAVP is then extended up the face of the toe wall, the line then being called the MATW (Median Axis of the Toe Wall). The intersection of the MAVP and MATW is marked with the circle.

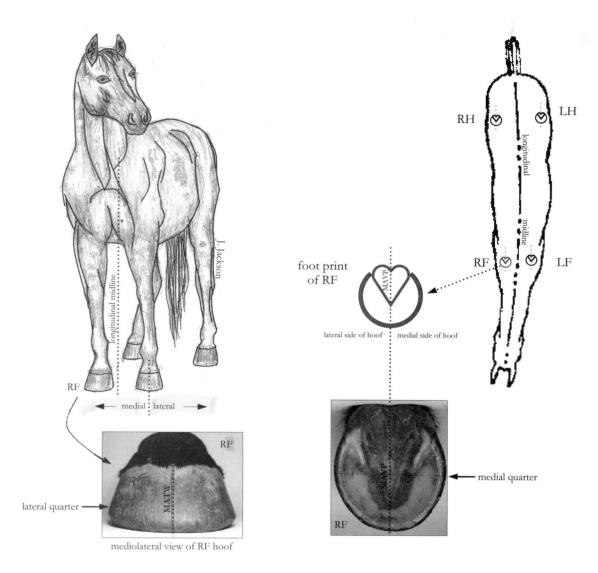

mediolateral view of RF hoof

Medial and Lateral Orientations.

Both the MATW and MAVP reference a "median" axis of the hoof. The term *median* (Latin: middle, or that which is in the middle) points us to another important navigational landmark: the *longitudinal midline* of the horse's torso.

(*Above, left and right*) This longitudinal midline divides the horse in half along his spine, from front to back. It serves as a necessary reference point when identifying one side of the hoof or the other. Specifically, that side of the hoof facing towards the longitudinal midline is the *medial* side of the hoof; conversely, the side facing away is the *lateral* (Latin: of the side) side. Hence, we can speak specifically of the medial or lateral bar, quarter, etc.

(*Below, left and right*) When these words are combined, *mediolateral*, the term becomes a navigational direction (rather than position) meaning from the medial side to the lateral side. I will use these terms throughout the trimming instructions.

Locating the Median Planes.

Two additional navigational landmarks are important to the NHC practitioner during trimming and measuring sequences. These are the Median Plane of the Toe Wall (MPTW), which passes through the MATW; and the Median Plane of the Volar Profile (MPVP), which passes through the MAVP. These two dimensional planes bisect the capsule along their respective axes.

(This page.)

(Above) Intersection of the MPTW and MPVP in relation to the MATW, MAVP, digital axis, and volar plane (representing the ground or other flat supporting surface of the hoof). These relationships are important and I will be referencing them through the trimming instructions, so it is time well-spent studying them closely

(Below) This wild horse cadaver hoof has been cleaved down the MPTW; the exposed sagittal section corresponds to the hoof outlined in the image above.

(Facing page.)

(Left side, 3A thru 3C) The MPTW passes through the MATW, bisecting the hoof's mediolateral profile (3A). The MPTW is also aligned with the MPVP, thereby bisecting the hoof's volar profile as well (3B). In 3C, the MPVP-MPTW axis is at right angle to the axis of the volar plane. This relationship will prove to be helpful later when balancing front feet during the trimming instructions.

(Right side, 4A thru 4C) In contrast to the front foot, the MPTW does not bisect the mediolateral profile of the naturally shaped hind hoof. This is due to the peculiar relationship between the hind hoof's MATW and MAVP, which do not align (4B). The planes of these two axes fail to align as well (4B,4C). This incongruity has given rise to an asymmetric relationship between the hoof's volar and mediolateral profiles, seen in each of these images. While no definitive research has yet taken place to explain this clash between front and hind hoof conformations, I suspect that it relates to differences in how the front and hind feet serve the horse's locomotive needs. The propulsory role of the hind limb, which also provides left and right thrust, would be favored by a the asymmetric conformation of the hind foot (Ref. *The Natural Horse*, "Hoof Asymmetry", p. 94).

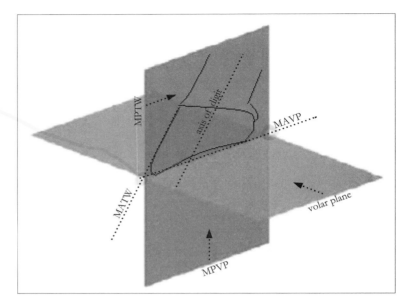

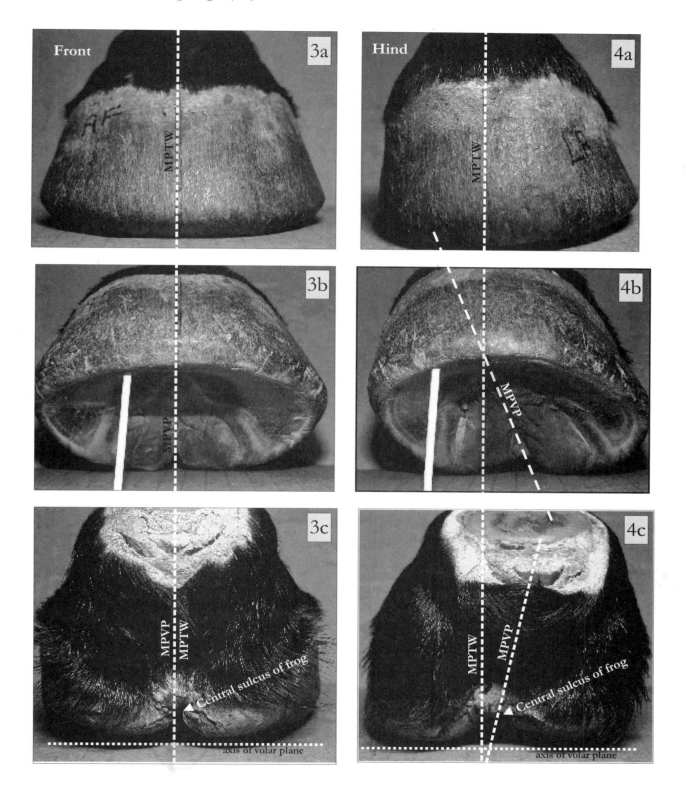

Measuring H°.

(This page)

(*Above*) H° (Healing Angle) is a measurement of the hoof's angle of growth along the MATW.

(*Below*) H° is gauged over the MATW with the HMR, whose calibrations are cross-linked to the wild horse hoof data ranges given in Figure 6-1. The edge of the gauge is positioned against or parallel to the hoof wall. This wild horse hoof measures ~57° (degrees) on the HMR scale (*right*), which indicates the measurement is natural and very common. (Compare with Figure 6-1, where 57° is located very central on the distribution bell curve.)

(Facing page).

Due to management problems, not all domesticated hooves grow straight along the MATW like the wild horse hoof. Using the hoof profiles discussed earlier on page 103, let's see how the HMR is adapted to measure such hooves.

(*Above*) This is the natural profile, similar to the wild horse hoof. To gauge H°, the angle readout dial of the HMR is set against or parallel to the toe wall, directly over and aligned with the MATW. H° measures 58°.

(*Middle*) There is a DTA midway down the MATW. Because H° is a measurement of new growth emanating from the coronary corium, it is gauged higher up along the MATW where it's growth history is most recent. Therefore, in profiles such as this one, H° is always gauged above the DTA, or above the uppermost DTA if there is more than one. Because the MATW is bent forward below the DTA, the lower toe wall interferes with normal placement of the HMR angle gauge. When this is the case, hold the HMR away from the lower toe wall, but parallel to the segment of MATW above the DTA as shown here.

(*Below*) Another DTA on the MATW, but the toe wall is bull-nosed and does not interfere with normal placement of the HMR. The angle gauge is positioned against the MATW like the upper hoof.

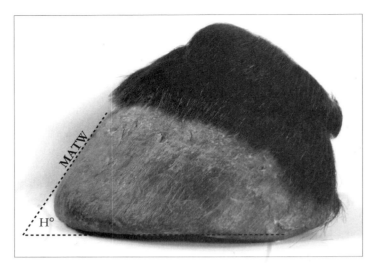

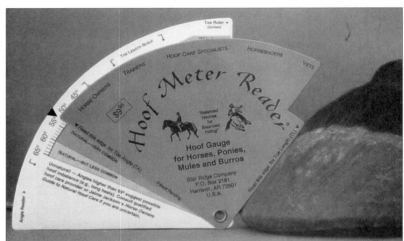

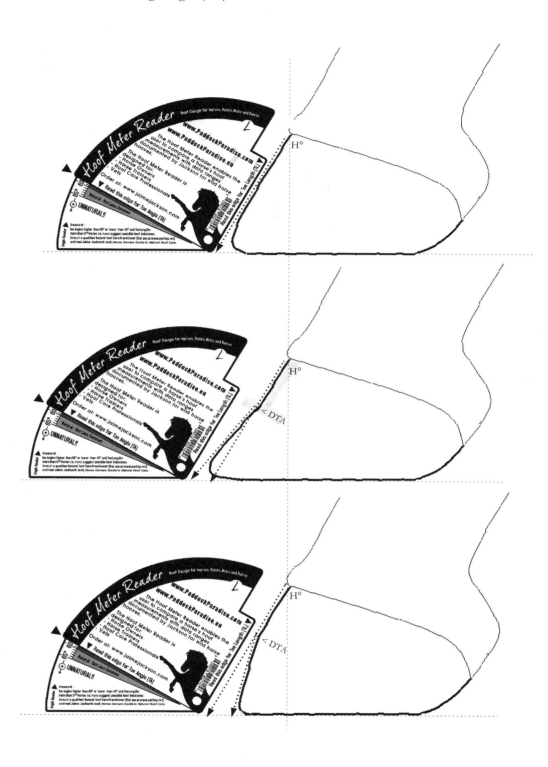

Measuring H°.

On this and the facing page are examples of hooves suffering extreme capsule deformity due to neglect, disease, and/or misguided hoof care methods. Because of their deformities, gauging H° along the MATW reliably is virtually impossible, at best guess work. In some instances, H° will simply measure off the HMR data spectrum altogether, either too high or too low.

(*Above and facing page*) H° is artificially elevated by presence of wedge pad in shod hoof #1. The MATW has been deformed into an arc of multiple DTAs in hooves #2, 4, and 6 thru 8, rendering H° completely unreadable. Hoof #3a is extremely run under, due to extreme sole-to-wall separation (#3b); one would have to position the HMR so far forward to clear the toe, you would need a telescope to read the gauge! Hoof #5 has deformed and rotated onto its side, upon which the horse walks (instead of the bottom of the hoof); hence H° cannot be read at all with the HMR as it has lost its mandatory ground-based reference. Hooves #7 and 8 are commonly known as "slipper toe" hooves.

In all these instances, the NHC practitioner will have to make important approximations of H° to guide them through the trimming. What is actually needed to get the trimming started is a reasonable estimation of H°TL, our focus in the following pages. But for now, please understand that attempts to measure H° in these kinds of hooves is futile, and not time well-spent. Natural trim protocols dictate that we now have no choice but to approximate H° and move to H°TL.

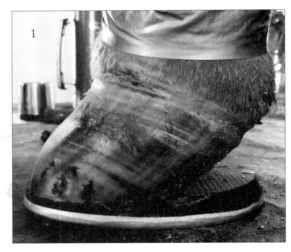

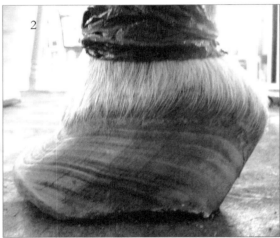

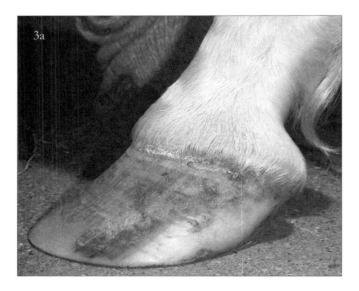

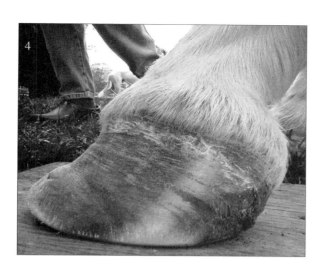

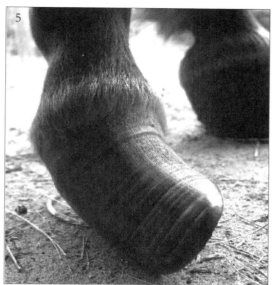

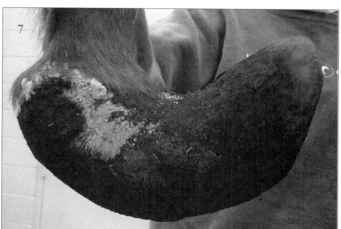

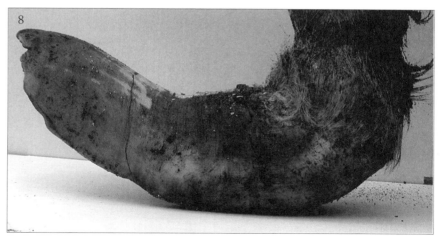

Measuring H°TL.

H°TL (Healing Toe Length) is a measure of the hoof's toe length along the MATW when aligned to H°. H°TL is a critical measurement that aids the NHC practitioner in shortening the hoof safely to its optimal length.

(This page.)

(Above) The MATW and H° are located on a wild horse hoof. The limit line (LL) must be located to determine the beginning of H°TL at the top of the hoof wall; the dashed arrow line (MATW) points to its terminus.

(Middle) The edge of the HMR angle gauge is positioned against or parallel to the hoof wall along the MATW. This wild horse hoof measures less than 2½ in (6.4 cm) on the HMR scale. Correspondingly, this measurement falls very much to the left on the bell curve (-2 to –3 STD) in Figure 6-1, meaning it is natural but unusually short in the spectrum of adult horses surveyed.

(Below) One of the peculiarities of the naturally shaped hoof is that the upper "neck" of the capsule (below the coronary band) tapers upwards to a narrower thickness than the hoof wall further below. Behind the tapered neck lies the epidermal coronary groove (p. 60) into which the coronary corium (p. 62) is situated. This tapering occurs over approximately ¼ to ¾ in. (1 to 2 cm) before the "true" natural thickness of the hoof wall begins.

(Facing page.)

(Above, right) Cross-section of wild horse hoof showing tapering neck (dashed line) of capsule that forms the coronary groove.

(Above, left) Same view of wild horse hoof, marking the MATW, coronary groove (CG), coronary corium (CC), crest (solid black line) of the hoof capsule above which lies the coronary band (CB), and limit line (LL) where the true natural thickness of the hoof wall begins. H°TL is measured from LL where the true wall begins, approximately ¼ - ¾ in (1-2 cm) below the top of the hoof capsule, down to the ground as shown here. "⊙" is called the "bulls-eye" and marks the intersection of LL and the MATW, and, therefore, the starting point of H°TL. To find ⊙, the coronary band is lightly palpated at the top of the toe wall along the MATW until the hard capsule is located. From here measure down ¼ to ¾ in (1 to 2 cm) along the MATW and mark ⊙.

(Below, left and *right)* Typical grid lines and navigational landmarks leading to ⊙ and H°TL. Students practice this on many hoof cadavers in my training clinics until they are confident and precise when measuring. I personally take these measurements with all my client horses.

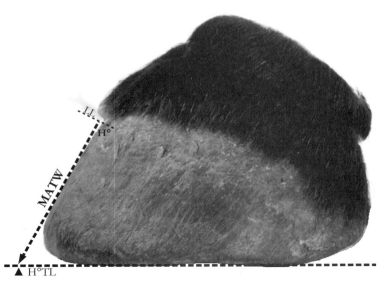

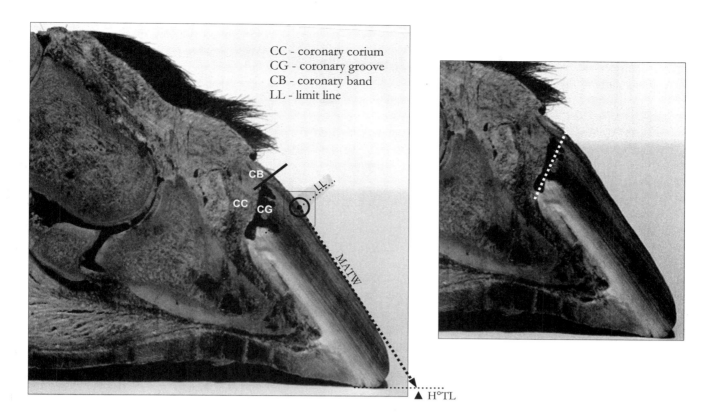

CC - coronary corium
CG - coronary groove
CB - coronary band
LL - limit line

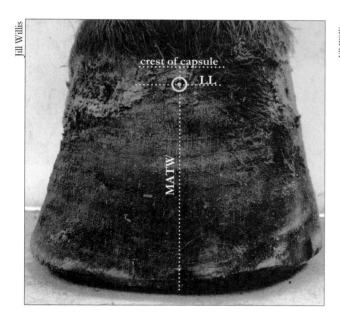

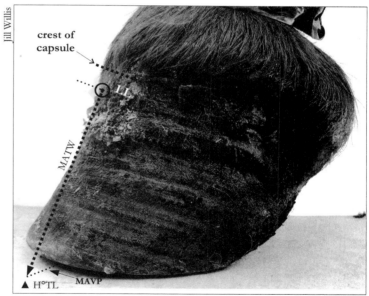

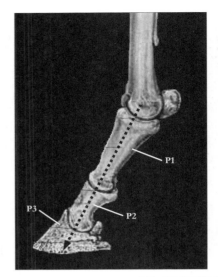

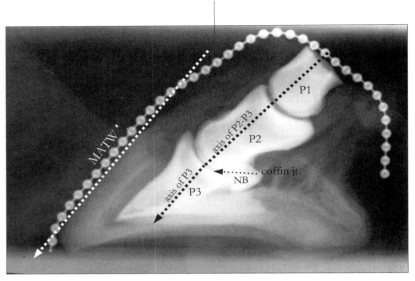

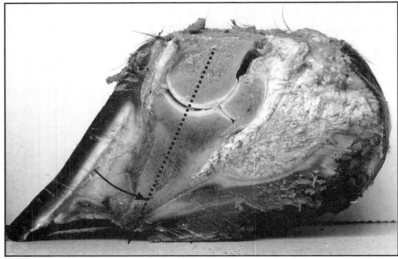

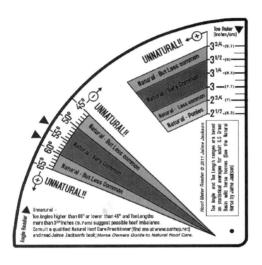

Measuring H°TL.

Measuring H°TL in deformed hooves is inherently problematic because H° itself is sometimes impossible to gauge (pp. 114-115). In the following discussion, I will lay out the rationale and protocol for estimating H° in deformed capsules, and then measuring H°TL as a consequence.

(*Above, left*) There is some suggestion that in naturally shaped hooves, the MATW closely parallels the face of the foot's distal phalanx (P3), and, by extrapolation, is parallel also to the remaining digital bones above P3. In this interpretation, the practitioner would attempt to gauge the slope of the pastern above the hoof to determine H°. This is problematic, however, due to the likely variable effects of normal interphalangeal ("between the bones") joint rotation, determined by the horse's stance. This is evident in the x-ray of the wild horse foot (*above, right*), where the digital axis (P1-P2-P3) is broken at the coffin joint (junction of P2 and P3). For this reason the MATW is not parallel to the digital axis. A similar problem exists in the chronically laminitic hoof (*below, left*) where the digit has moved down and away from the hoof wall (called *P3 rotation*) and the MATW. Moreover, without x-rays, it is virtually impossible to predict these relationships in deformed hooves.

(*Bottom, right*) Given the complexities of ascertaining where the digit lies in relation to the hoof capsule, and therefore, the unreliability of the slope of the pastern as a navigational aid for determining H°, the NHC practitioner instead sets the angle gauge to the *mean* front or hind values for H°, ~54° and ~58° respectively, and measures H°TL from there. Examples of this are given on following pages and in the trimming instructions in later chapters.

Estimating H°TL.

As stated on the previous page, measuring H°TL in deformed hooves may require making an *estimate* of H°. This is done when either H° cannot be evaluated due to toe wall deformity (e.g., multiple DTAs) or the toe wall angle at the bull's-eye is readable, but is either higher or lower than the angle ranges given on the HMR. Experience has shown that using the average/median values for front and hind H° values in Figure 6-1 work well for the purposes of estimating H°TL and facilitating favorable 4D changes in H°. This will required re-calibrating the HMR as follows:

(*Above*) First step is to mark the HMR angle gauge at 54° (front) and 58° (hind). This can be done with a Sharpie type pen.

(*Below*) The HMR has been set to 54°. The H°TL scale at right is now ready to use for deformed front hooves. Hind hooves will require setting the H°TL scale to 58°. Examples of setting the HMR thusly to deformed hooves are given on the following pages.

Note: H°TL here is a measurement axis, not a cut-line marker.

Measuring H°TL.

On this and the following three pages we will revisit some of the deformed hooves on pp. 114-115 with an objective of estimating H° and measuring H°TL. In this discussion, we will introduce a new measurement axis, B°TL (Basement Toe Length). It is defined as the length of the MATW when it is bent either forward of, or behind, H°TL due to the presence of DTAs. Its name is derived from its diverging angle of growth, B°, below H°.

(*Above, left/right*) The hind hoof at left, and its simulation on the right, are representative of (laminitic) capsules suffering from such severe stress that the MATW is bent into an arc terminating in B°TL. H° then cannot be read. When this is the case, the HMR is set to H° TL=58° (hind) and positioned next to the hoof one of two ways as follows:

(*Middle*) First, grid lines are marked and ⊙ located. With the HMR set to H°=58°, the H°TL dial is held to the near side of the hoof, and slid back until it intersects the bull's-eye on the MATW. That part of the capsule forward of H°TL will be obscured by the dial. The reading, however, is off the H°TL scale, indicating the toe wall can be shortened, the extent of which will be discussed later in the trimming instructions.

(*Below*) Alternatively, the angle dial is positioned forward of the hoof (i.e., B°TL), and read straight across in the direction of the arrow. In life, one would never place the HMR to the far side of the hoof, as this would put the practitioner at risk of being struck by the hoof if the horse lifted his leg forward.

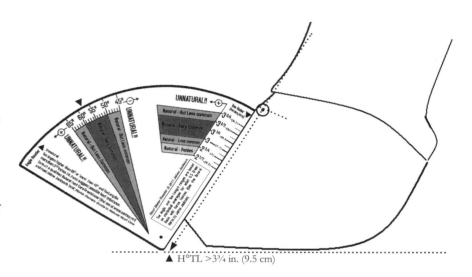

▲ H°TL >3¾ in. (9.5 cm)

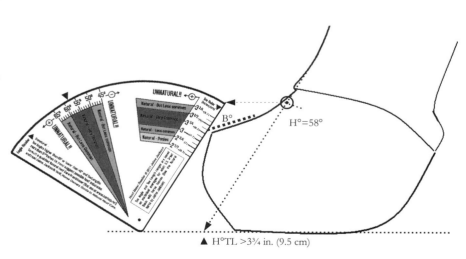

▲ H°TL >3¾ in. (9.5 cm)

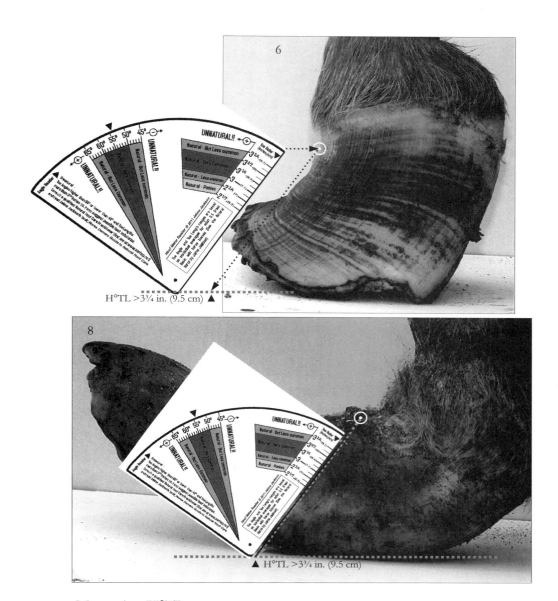

Measuring H°TL.

At first glance, one would think these hooves to be by far the most challenging hooves to measure. In fact, they are no more difficult to measure than the most naturally shaped hoof if the estimation method is used. These are both front hooves, so the H°TL angle gauge is set to 54°. In each case, I have set grid lines and located ⊙.

(*Above*) This is a clubfoot type conformation (chapter 11). I've elected to position the HMR forward of the hoof. Reading straight across, it is clear the hoof is in excess of the H°TL data range for natural and will require trimming.

(*Below*) Given the extraordinary length of this hoof's toe — over 12 inches (30 cm)! — it is necessary to slide the HMR along the near side of the hoof. Like the club foot above, this hoof exceeds the H°TL data range on the HMR and will require much capsule reduction.

Measuring H°TL.

This is a neglected "run away" hoof that has become "wry", meaning the capsule has grown down literally "lop sided". Conventionally, these are very perplexing hooves to measure, however, they yield to our grids and navigational landmarks as readily as the most naturally shaped hoof. With beginners, the principal challenge in measuring H°TL in the wry hoof lies in ignoring its pathology and simply measuring the capsule according to our natural trim protocols.

(This page)

(*Above* and *below*) The MATW is curved — the defining characteristic of the wry foot. The MATW may be skewed to the medial or lateral side, in this case, it is to the medial side.

(Facing page).

(*Above*) Not only wry to the medial side, the capsule is also bull-nosed by a single DTA (▼). I've set the bull's-eye at ¾ in. (2 cm) below the coronary band over the MATW.

(*Middle* and *below*) As with any severely run-under hoof, H°TL is measured at the bull's-eye with the HMR angle gauge set to 54°. The HMR is necessarily brought to the near side of the hoof and then aligned with ☉. Typical of overgrown hooves like this one, H°TL is off the data range for natural, indicating the toe wall will be shortened. This is such an interesting, albeit tragic, example of wryness, that I've included the entire trimming sequence in Chapter 12.

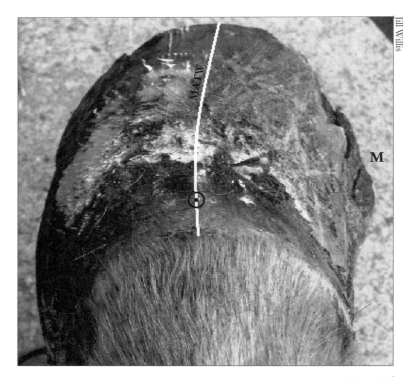

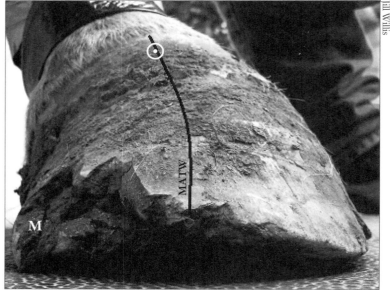

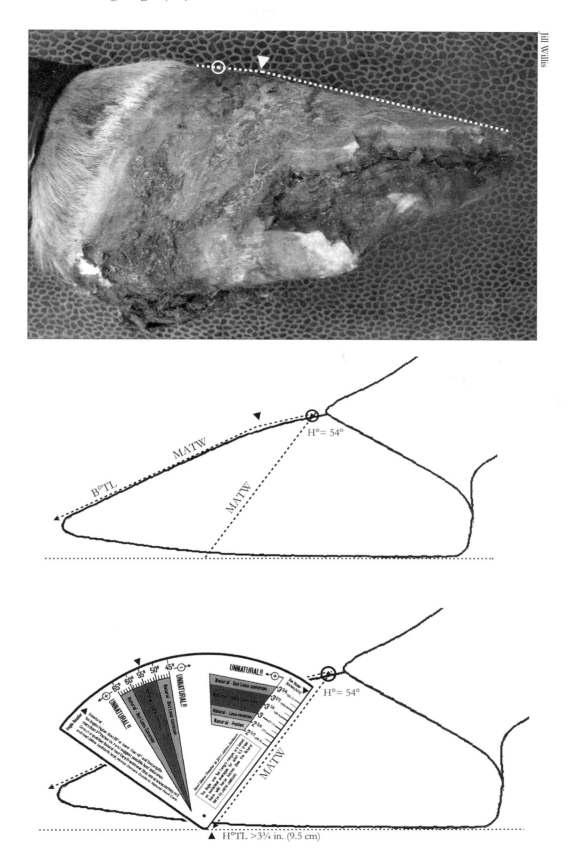

Measuring HW, HL and CW.

As a group of measurements, HL, HW, and CW provide clear indicators of changes in hoof mass. When these measurements are taken diligently at regular intervals, for example, they are revealing of how the hoof is changing following de-shoeing. Over time, as these numbers begin to settle and stabilize, and are correlated to H°, the NHC practitioner can deduce with reasonable certainty that healing from hoof contraction has concluded. Arguably, the only definitive way to evaluate hoof contraction and other changes is through what these measurement categories tell us very specifically over time. HL and HW are cross-linked to the wild horse hoof data ranges given in Figure 6-1.

(*Above*) HL (Hoof Length) is the length of the bottom of the hoof from the tip of the toe wall to the posterior most point of contact that the heels make with a level, unyielding surface (e.g., a flat board). It is measured along the MAVP with the vernier caliper.

(*Below*) HW (Hoof Width) is the widest width of the hoof, usually occuring across the quarters, and is measured at right angle (90°) to the MAVP.

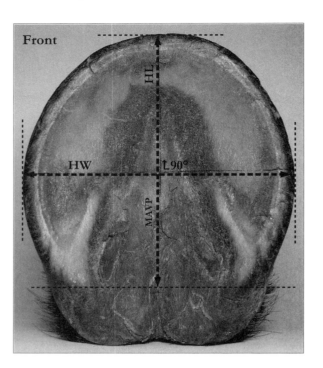

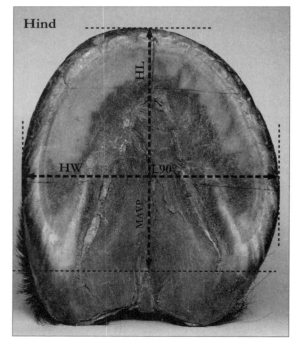

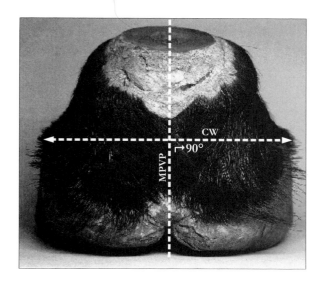

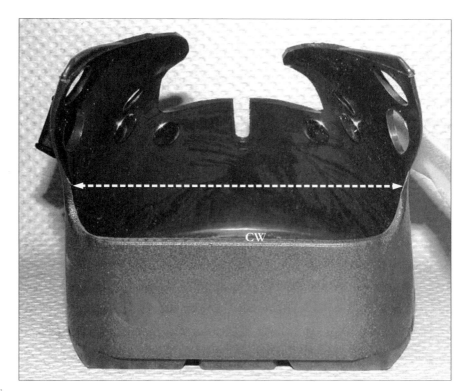

Measuring HW, HL and CW.

(*Above, left*) CW (Coronary Width) is a measurement of the hoof's widest width at its junction with the coronary band behind the pastern. Use the vernier caliper to take this measurement. CW is also measured at right angles (90°) to the MPVP.

(*Above, right*) CW is shown here with the hoof's contents removed and in relation to the MPVP.

(*Below*) CW is an important measurement when custom fitting hoof boots.

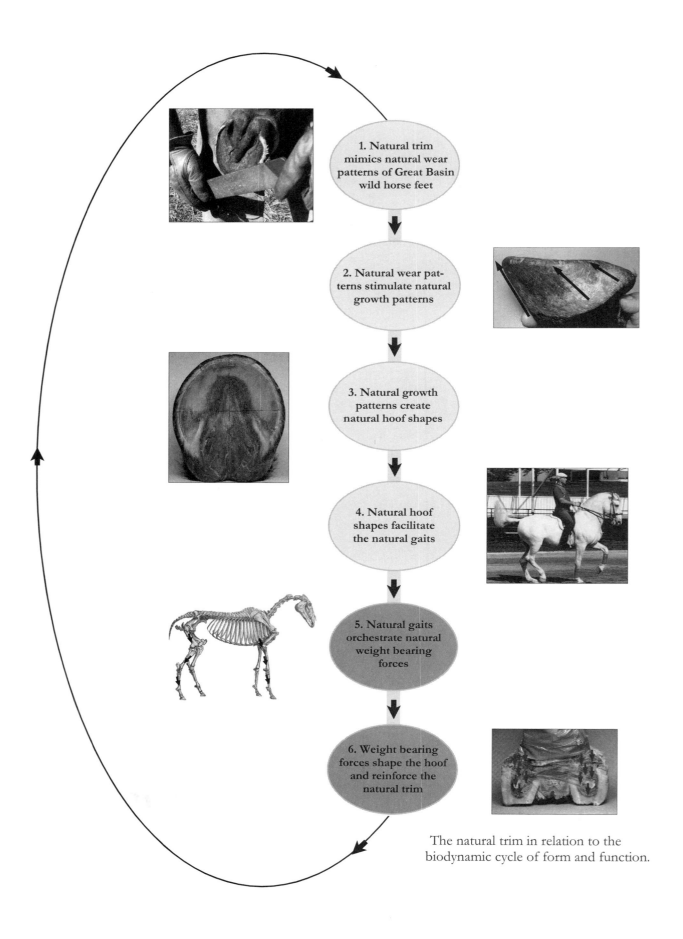

1. Natural trim mimics natural wear patterns of Great Basin wild horse feet

2. Natural wear patterns stimulate natural growth patterns

3. Natural growth patterns create natural hoof shapes

4. Natural hoof shapes facilitate the natural gaits

5. Natural gaits orchestrate natural weight bearing forces

6. Weight bearing forces shape the hoof and reinforce the natural trim

The natural trim in relation to the biodynamic cycle of form and function.

CHAPTER 7
Hoof Form and Function

We recall from Chapter 5 the limited, although significant, role of the natural trim in the biodynamic cycle of hoof form and function, delineated here again at left (*facing page*). For the NHC practitioner, the effect and consequences of the trim upon the hoof's biomechanics and the horse's ability to move naturally on his feet are of no less importance than the proper execution of the trim itself — if one can even imagine such a dichotomy. Indeed, as soon as the hoof hits the ground, the horse feels what we have done to him, and instinctively adjusts his manner of going — unconsciously partnering in our efforts. His contribution comes through the execution of his natural gaits: the walk, trot, canter and their myriad variations. By moving naturally, the horse delivers weight bearing forces that pass into the hoof, pressing it against the ground, shaping it. When the Four Pillars of NHC are integrated into this locomotory chain of events, the hoof is driven into a biodynamic equilibrium with its environment. Because the horse is living in domestication, many challenges contrapose this equilibrium and the outcomes are not always pretty. Several of the trimming examples in these Guidelines are representative of this. For the sake of discussion here, however, let us proceed as though our management practices are in good order, a qualified NHC practitioner has done their work well, the horse is moving naturally, and the hoof is biodynamically sound and naturally shaped.

So, in this best of all worlds, it is logical to ask, what happens to the hoof under the natural locomotive force that coincides with optimal form (i.e., natural shape) and function? The short answer, and the most important, is that the hoof is rendered sound and healthy (and with the implicit understanding that the holistic practices of NHC have been reasonably implemented too). The long answer, which helps us to understand why the hoof is biodynamically sound and naturally shaped, lies in understanding first, the natural gaits of the horse, and second — because it is a direct consequence of the first — what is known as the "hoof mechanism".

What Are the Natural Gaits?

Most horse owners and professionals serving them are quite adamant that they know what the horse's natural gaits are and how to get the horse to use them. Most will say, "The walk, trot, canter, and gallop". Others will point additionally to the "gaited" horse with his striking paces. From the standpoint of natural selection, some of these "gaits" aren't natural at all, but are "man made", spurred forward by an eclectic collection of riding disciplines, no riding discipline whatsoever, and outright circus. These compel horses to use their gaits for different purposes: racing, jumping, pulling carriages, dressage, carnival, cattle penning, and so forth. What else is there to know? My opinion is that this is a problematic and hasty backdoor approach to understanding the natural gaits and getting the horse to use them. The matter is far more complex, in my opinion, with many fairly serious consequences for the horse.[1] The horse isn't simply a car with gears to shift, he is a living animal designed to behave and move in accordance with his specie's evolution. Logically, then, let's tackle the subject from the perspective of our wild horse model and NHC.

The Natural Gait Complex (NGC)

I approach the natural gaits through what I call the "natural gait complex" (NGC). In keeping with our wild horse model, NGC is defined as *the natural manner in which wild, free-roaming horses of the U.S. Great Basin move as a result of herd behavior.* As one can imagine, this is going to get us much more involved than simply defining the "walk, trot, canter" or what gaited horses do! The key word here is "behavior". The reason is that in the horse's natural world his movements are determined by his instincts and the social behaviors that flow from them. This raises important questions, such as what those behaviors are and how the horse moves in relation to them. One could say, "I don't care, I just want him to walk, trot, canter, gallop, halt, side pass and just go and do whatever I tell him to do." There are two fundamental problems with this approach. First, it ignores equally the psychological, physiological and biomechanical limits imposed upon the horse (and his feet!) by natural selection. And second, it consigns the horse to whatever mental burden and physical exploits his rider deems appropriate, regardless if they clash with his biology. Obviously, commanding the horse to move in ways that his species is not anatomically or psychologically equipped to, and/or, working him beyond his limits, natural or not, isn't exactly in his best interest, even if it suits the fancy of his owner. While this may have been the case broadly before automobiles replaced horses for transportation, it certainly doesn't seem reasonable or appropriate today.

NHC advocates approach NGC from the standpoint of the laws of nature, including the horse's DNA, since these are what shape his innate behavior complex, manner of movement, and ultimately, his hooves. The following are certainly less common ways of looking at NGC, but, from the standpoint of NHC, they are certainly important and relevant. I view them as fundamental "truths" and they are presented here in no particular order of importance:

Truth #1: Horses are animals of prey, and think and react accordingly.

This is a hard point to fathom in our modern age — one so detached from nature —

[1]Ibid., FN, p. 100, *American Farriers Journal*, Nov./2000, v. 26, #6, p. 5.

Jaime Jackson

Life in a stall is no life for any horse. This jail cell, replete with bars, prevents a horse from being a horse. When I took this photo, it was a sweltering 110+ degrees (F). Three doors down, one horse appeared to spend his entire day with his teeth clamped to the steel rimmed door out of sheer boredom. In inner alleys of the barn, many horses lived without the light of day for 23/7 or longer, assuming someone gave them any turnout. At night, the artificial lights go on, and loud music is turned on to "keep them company". My client's horse was one of those back in there, living in darkness much of the day, his stall so dim he could barely be discerned except his faint outline. One day, I looked in and found him standing with his head lowered towards one of the pitch black corners. His state of depression overwhelmed me — I then lobbied hard to get him out of there. I succeeded briefly, but the inconvenience to the owner, coupled to an out of the blue diagnosis of "hind end" nerve damage rendering him a "poor candidate for the rigors of outdoor living", brought it all to an end. I then resigned my services, rather than be complicit with circumstances I believe are completely and inexcusably inhumane.

Jaime Jackson

There's quite the story behind this photo, which I took in the mountains 100 miles east of Carson City, NV, c. 1983. Arrows point to the dominant (alpha-1) bay stallion, and his "next in command" sub-dominant alpha-2 buckskin stallion. Each alpha stallion has his own family band. The alpha-1 stallion's alpha mare is just out of view behind him. The buckskin's alpha mare stands nearby him. Each mare had a youngster at her side. I learned to "speak" their language (one of gesture, posture, and deep intuition) after so much time among them, and I "asked" this "herd" to let me travel with them in formation in close proximity. The whole process took 5 minutes, with much preliminary "discussion" between the two alpha stallions. Their dialogues included trotting slowly in place ("piaffe") head to tail, while at the same time vocalizing sounds at just above a whispering pitch. Once they worked it out, they then turned to their respective alpha mares, and carried out the same communication head-to-tail. Finally, the bay stallion turned to me with a brief but very penetrating stare: I took it as his "green light" to get in formation. The buckskin in the photo is actually "holding" his family in place; in another minute the bay stallion will move his bunch to the front (i.e., to the right in the photo), the buckskin taking the rear guard in the forthcoming procession. Far out of view on the left was a bachelor band of six younger stallions — all of whom I would describe as behaving with much apprehension. Notice the incredibly rugged terrain, volcanic rock everywhere, and not a blade of what I would call grass anywhere! Yet every member was fit, sound, and the pinnacles of health. The kind of hoof each wore will be taken up in the next chapter.

BLM

Wild horses "on track" in the U.S. Great Basin. The third band member on the left is a mule, a rare occurrence, but it does happen when wild horse herds interface with wild bands of burros.

where horses are commonly understood in terms of our anthropomorphistic sentiments and/or commodity exploitations. But the horse simply puts up with us — and what choice does he have? Animals of prey invariably move in familial or bachelor bands, their survival instincts dictating this propensity (*facing page* and *above*). But back in civilization, horses are typically isolated from each other by their owners for reasons that can only bewilder and torture their species. Here's some of the reasons I've personally heard:

- I'm afraid my horse will fall and hurt himself if I turn him out with other horses.
- I don't want bite marks on his coat.
- Shaggy winter coats are such a turn off – he looks so much better indoors wearing his blanket.
- It takes too long to catch him; he won't come to me.
- She colics if she gets wet.
- My horse loves his stall.
- My animal communicator told me that my horse wants me to know that he doesn't like other horses, and prefers being alone in his stall.
- Pasture turnout is for persons of lower socio-economic status.
- He's just too out of control when I give him turnout.
- It's the barn rule, and I have to abide by it.

Clearly, such attitudes violate the horse's biology, and give rise to stall vices and other aberrant behaviors derived from close confinement, abnormal stress, isolation, large "set meals" followed by long periods with nothing to eat causing dietary distress,[1] and the inability to move freely. These are all prescriptions for distressed animals, lameness, colic, and laminitis, and the horse world has done a superb job of ordering them up!

Truth #2: Horses instinctively use flight when feeling threatened.

This is distressing for many horse owners to accept, who often misconstrue it to mean the horse is "just being difficult" or "psycho". Col. Hans Handler, Director of the Spanish Riding School half a century ago, wrote, "People think that a horse is stupid when it shies from a flying sheet of paper only to leap into the path of a moving car, but one must remember that fear, developing at times into outright panic, is a fundamental characteristic of the horse."[2] Unfortunately, acting on his instincts often results in punishment, which instills yet more fear, and only fuels the flight instinct. Attempts to restrain the flight instinct, particularly when it is being instigated or created by the handler, leads to resistance and a breakdown of the NGC. This is when the "fighting" begins and people get hurt, and horses become distrusting, resentful, and, if psychologically traumatized, dangerous — if they haven't been injured themselves.

Truth #3: All horses naturally live in family or (all male) bachelor bands, never alone.

The message here, and it is a powerful one to be heeded, is that horses *need* to be physically with other horses, not partitioned-off "stall mates". This is part of their biology — and not a "personal preference" or an abstract concept horses ponder over!

Truth #4: All band members (family and bachelor) live in social hierarchies governed instinctively by pecking order or "relative dominance" (RD).

Few horse owners aren't aware of "pecking order" dominance among equines. But because horses are often segregated from each other (e.g., life in a stall), the process of how horses work things out among themselves is often misunderstood. At the heart of the pecking order process is the reality that no two horses are ever "equal" — one will always be either "above" (alpha or dominant) or "below" (beta, subordinate or subdominant) the other. Threats of aggression (e.g., ears pinned back) and outright aggression (e.g., kicking and biting) are all fair game. This is their way to work things out, and the pecking order more or less continues on throughout their lives together. But the reality of dominance is also "relative" and makes for interesting observations. Consider one such interplay among band

---

[1]The horse appears to secrete hydrochloric acid 24/7 for digestion, hence the biological need for constant foraging, granzing, and browsing.
[2]Hans Handler, *The Spanish Riding School*, (New York: McGraw-Hill, 1972), p. 139. This is a book worth reading from cover to cover if copies can be found. It was already long out of print when I referenced it in my first book, *The Natural Horse*, in 1992.

mates:

- Horse A (dominant) drives horse B (subordinate to A) off of his hay pile.
- Horse B then drives horse C (subordinate to B) off his hay pile.
- Horse C, in turn, drives horse D (subordinate to C) away from his hay pile.
- Horse D then drives horse E (subordinate to D) off of his hay pile.
- And, finally, horse E drives horse A off of his pile!

In other words: A>B>C>D>E>A. To make matters even more complicated, if horse B & horse E are buddies and decide to eat together peacefully, horse A may have to go elsewhere to make trouble, and the hierarchy of relative dominance will shift accordingly. Add yet another horse (or two) to the group, and further rather complex changes will unfold. In all of this, and this is my point in bring the foregoing up, is that much movement is driven naturally daily, hourly, and by the minute, as a result of relative dominance. Horses standing around in isolation are deprived of this important dimension of their biology . . . and the natural movement it unleashes.

> "movement is driven naturally daily, hourly, and by the minute, as a result of relative dominance"

Truth #5: Bands occupy well-defined "home ranges", within which all movement follows from structured inter-band and band to band socialization + the demands of survival.

The home range is simply the land occupied by family and bachelor bands. Wild horses appear not to be necessarily territorial, but do naturally prefer to stay within familiar grounds, providing that their survival needs (e.g., forage and water) can be met there. The U.S. Great Basin supports thousands of wild horse home ranges, many of which overlap each other. Where they intersect, bands interact and may exchange band members (e.g., daughters leave to form their own families with nearby alpha stallions seeking mates), while rival stallions typically battle to defend or take over harem mares during the breeding season.

Truth #6: Bands travel along well worn paths from one activity to the next in "pecking order".

As I wrote earlier, bands tend to move along well-worn "tracks" (or "paths"), often single file — but always by pecking order. For example, much of their time is spent foraging as they move along their tracks. This flexes and strengthens neck and back muscles while shifting their center of gravity forward, an effect that presses much body weight down upon the front hooves, shaping them. This happens much of the day and night — nothing to ignore! It also — due to natural selection — favors their digestive systems, nibbling as they go, never too much, or all, in one place at one time.

Summary: Natural Gait Complex (NGC)

There is a tendency among horse owners to view the natural gaits strictly through movement — walk, trot, canter, etc. — rather than through behaviors that define how, when, where, and to what extent they use them. These are such significant contributors to the natural cycle of hoof "form and function", that to ignore them, is to dismiss their many benefits not only for hoof care, but as models for riding/training, understanding their species, diet, and boarding (i.e., the four pillars of NHC). Indeed, we cannot expect our horses to possess exemplary hooves if they are to lead lives sheltered from the rigors of the natural gait complex (NGC).

The Natural Gaits

The natural gaits distill right out of the natural gait complex (NGC). Once more in keeping with our wild horse model, the natural gaits are defined as *the physical manner in which horses of the U.S. Great Basin naturally move in accordance with their natural gait complex (NGC)*. This makes sense since the natural gaits arise out of behavioral motivations. However, their biomechanical complexities, locomotive variations, and relationships to NGC seem to befuddle countless horse owners, if there's any thought given to it whatsoever. Many streams of opinion concerning what is natural movement for the horse fly in the face of the wild horse model. And here, precisely, in my opinion, lies the foundation for most motion-based lameness in horses.

The *walk* (4 beats), *trot* (2 beat) and *canter/gallop* (3 or 4 beats) are the foundational movements of the natural gaits.[1] Variations of these natural gaits include their lateral movements, in-place movements, and movements above the ground. I still hold, as I wrote in my book, *The Natural Horse*,[2] that horses rarely move backwards except for the briefest passage to turn around or in preparation to rear. There is no logic in horses moving backwards for any other reason, as there would be no survival value — the final determinant in the horse's natural world. Don't misunderstand me, it's not that they can't move backwards, it's just that they don't. I wouldn't even make an issue of this if it weren't for the fact that some riding disciplines use backing to "strengthen the hindquarters" and others "for fun". But with hock injuries rampant in these disciplines, and the psychological stress of 25 yard backing "sprints" being no laughing matter, it is worth considering that nature did not select for

---

[1] I have witnessed these foundational gaits among our wild horses of the Great Basin. I have not witnessed such extraordinary gaits as the pace, Fox Trot, running walk, etc., and these appear to be manmade either through riding or selective breeding practices. Nevertheless, no definitive scientific study of the natural gaits of the horse have been conducted in the Great Basin to the best of my knowledge; therefore, I am not prepared to rule out the possibility that the "man made" gaits may be natural. One way to find out would be to turn these "gaited" horses into the Great Basin wilds and see what happens to their gaits over successive generations. If they are natural, surely nature will select for them.

[2] Table 3-2, p. 37.

backing in these ways. Hence, they are violations of the natural gaits and, therefore, can, and do, predispose the animal to injury.

It isn't really my intent here to delve into the tenets of natural horsemanship based on the wild horse model — an enormous undertaking deserving of its own book!. But the equestrian who strives to train and ride in harmony with the natural gaits, will absolutely aid in the natural shaping of the feet because the natural gaits of the horse are the main driving (locomotive) force of naturally shaped feet. Delivered into the hoof, these forces, individualized by conformation and temperament, act to shape it by pressing and grinding it against the ground. When the horse is kept and ridden barefoot (boots if necessary or desired), fed a reasonably natural diet, boarded in a Paddock Paradise type environment, and given the natural trim, naturally shaped feet are the result. Examples of this are the hooves of Jill's and my horses in their Paddock Paradise, discussed in Chapter 2 (page 42) and again in Chapter 8.

As an NHC practitioner dealing with domesticated hooves for nearly forty years, I have learned first hand that the locomotive force can also be channeled or obstructed to the detriment of the hoof's form and function. Shoeing and unnatural trimming methods are obvious causes. It can also be sent astray through unnatural riding practices and diet — the former delivering the force as nature never intended, the other metabolically breaking down the structure of the hoof at its germinal cell matrix. And if boarding conditions are unnatural, shaping forces also become aberrant. As depressing as this sounds, it is the plight of most domesticated horses, in my opinion. *Unnatural horse care practices break down the hoof and obstruct natural movement.* Happily, the holistic practices of NHC provide an effective and proven way to generate optimal hoof form and function.

The Hoof Mechanism

The "hoof mechanism" (or simply "mechanism") is a little known subject of hoof science among horse owners, hoof care professionals, and vets — at least in the United States. As a topic of discussion, it seems much more prevalent in Europe, where it apparently originated. This is no doubt due to the farrier and veterinary sciences that have a professional hoof care tradition dating back a thousand years. The mechanism is a model for understanding how the hoof behaves when subjected to the weight-bearing force. The prevailing model of the mechanism that I was introduced to in the early 1970s as a young farrier — but now reject as invalid — is still the accepted one today: the hoof lands, spreads apart a little under the weight of the horse, then springs back together again when the hoof leaves the ground. This inherent flexibility of the hoof, to widen and spring back into place, is attributed to the presence of the frog, aided by the concaved sole which is thought to give somewhat like a trampoline under the horse's weight. This expanding and contracting action of the hoof is also believed to play an important role in the circulation of blood to and from the hoof — aided, many argue — by the pumping action of the frog as it presses upwards by the force of the ground against the vascular system within the foot. Finally, the consummate action of the mechanism is thought to be responsible for absorbance and dissipation of *concussional forces*, shock waves caused by the hoof's collision with the ground.

This model was introduced widely in the U.S. to the barefoot hoof care movement during the early 2000s, and is currently bandied about and debated among its many factions. Farriers, field vets and veterinary researchers in the U.S. continue to have little or nothing to say on the matter, but when pressed, more or less point to the conventional model, which, as it turns out, is muddled by the presence of the horseshoe.

The problem I always had with this model, is that, on closer scrutiny — particularly when held to the light of the wild horse model — it doesn't really add up. The central argument for the model centers largely around highly questionable "evidence", all of which, to my way of thinking, can be explained away by NHC principles and practices based on the wild horse model. I think it is important to tackle this subject in these Guidelines because many blatantly harmful veterinary, shoeing and trimming methods are rationalized by this conventional model. For this reason, I think it is important to delineate its mechanics, explain what its consequences are when applied in hoof care, and, later in this chapter, counter it with a different model that truly makes sense and is completely consistent with our wild horse model, and NHC principles and practices.

Hoof Mechanism: Conventional Model

According to convention, the hoof in flight, lacking any weight-bearing force upon it, is in its most contracted form (*facing page, top*). When the hoof next enters support (weight-bearing), the ground-bearing surface of the hoof wall is said to spread outward (*facing page, center*), evidenced by the grooves pressed into the heel branches of the horseshoe by the hoof wall (*below*). Following the diagrams on the facing page, we can see that as a reciprocal consequence of the outward expanding of the lower hoof wall, the upper neck of the hoof wall contracts and the coronary band (necessarily) descends slightly, more so at the back of the hoof where the relatively flexible frog is situated (*facing page, bottom*). Further, the concaved sole also gives under the descending weight, and, accordingly, takes a somewhat lower position during support.

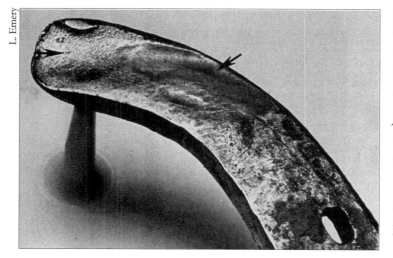

L. Emery

In addition to the "flattening" of the concaved sole, is the belief that the frog then becomes a key player in the mechanism. This is said to happen as

Conventional Model for the Hoof Mechanism

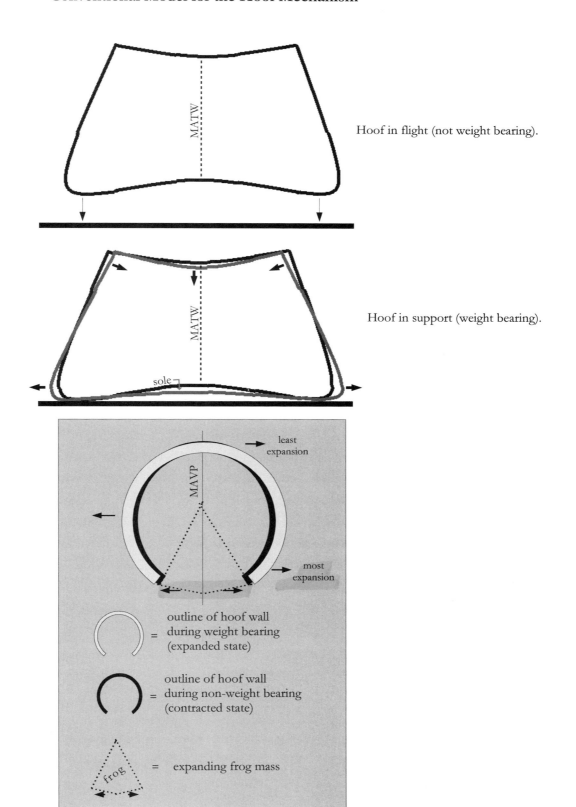

Hoof in flight (not weight bearing).

Hoof in support (weight bearing).

least expansion

most expansion

= outline of hoof wall during weight bearing (expanded state)

= outline of hoof wall during non-weight bearing (contracted state)

= expanding frog mass

a result of pressure exerted upon it from below by the environment: first, by aiding the sole in bracing the digital cushion above it against the descending weight bearing force; second, by squeezing the foot's vascular tract above it, in effect, serving as an important "pump" to return blood to the heart; and third, by dissipating concussional shock from the environment through its relatively moist body to the digital cushion, and elsewhere within the foot. The logic of all of these effects are truly inviting and seem to address what appears to be going on during the hoof's support phase. But after conducting my research with the Great Basin horses, I have long since stopped thinking along these lines.

In summary, the above is the main gist of the conventional hoof mechanism model as I understand what is being said by its adherents, and as I more or less accepted myself without much thought early in my career. I personally might not have given it any further thought in relation to my work as an NHC practitioner were it not for its implications in the field. My counter opinion is that it is incomplete as a model for the natural biomechanics of the hoof, and that many parts of it are incompatible with what we now know to be true in relation to equine natural state. No surprise then that many hoof care procedures done to the horse, based upon this model, result in harm. Some of the most egregious are worth discussing here as the NHC practitioner is sure to run into them sooner or later.

Conventional Mechanism and Laminitis

Laminitis is an inflammation of the dermal tissues responsible for producing, maintaining, and connecting the hoof to the horse. It is widely known that when this painful inflammation is severe enough, the hoof's fibrous attachments to the horse (discussed shortly) can completely fail. At its extreme, the hoof quite literally falls off the foot, called *hoof slough*. In many acute cases, the lowermost bone of the digit, P3 (coffin bone), is thought to tear away painfully from its attachments to the inner hoof wall, to which it is normally firmly attached during loading. And having lost its mooring, its sharp distal edge is then free to slice through the sole under descending body weight pressing upon it. These pathological changes are referred to as *P3 rotation* and *P3 penetration*, and are well known among horse owners today because laminitis is so epidemic and widely talked about.

From the standpoint of the conventional mechanistic model, the capsule's normal flexions must be arrested somehow so as not to further stress the inflamed and "tearing" hoof to horse attachments. Admittedly, there is a certain logic to stabilizing the capsule under the circumstances. By way of comparison, when we break a bone in our leg — the doctor stabilizes the break with a cast to prevent movement, and we use crutches to preclude weightbearing. Where I disagree with convention is that the fibrous attachments binding the hoof to the horse are not, in my opinion, weight-bearing (they don't support the weight of the horse), and that the natural flexions of the capsule during support don't really contribute to the wear or weakening of the attachments either. Therefore, in my opinion, there is no jus-

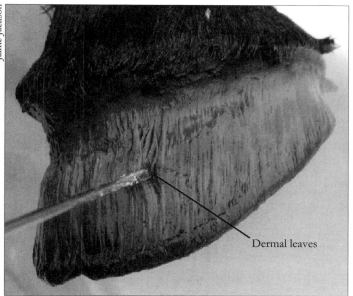

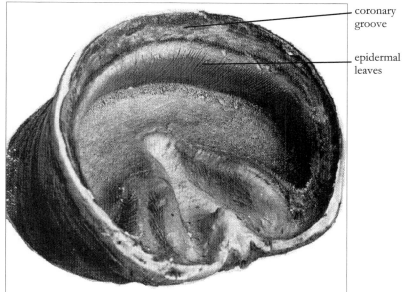

coronary
groove

epidermal
leaves

Dermal leaves

Leslie Emery

Dermal and Epidermal Leaves of the Horse's foot.
Approximately 600 dermal and epidermal leaf-like structures intermesh to form a bond between the hoof and the horse. This attachment mechanism inflames and fails during laminitis, defined as the "separation of the hoof from the horse".

tification for mechanically stabilizing the capsule by whatever means; moreover, doing so only exacerbates matters. Yet, this is precisely what vets and farriers do — based on the logic of the conventional mechanism — and why I'm taking issue with this model here.

When I first became aware of laminitis many years ago (as a farrier), I would ask, "What caused this?" In fact, little more was thought about its cause than one might discuss what caused a bone to break. The mentality was, "Just fix it". After all, when the horse is standing (or laying) there in agonizing pain, people want something done about it, and investigating the cause does not alleviate his pain or bring comfort to his stressed owner. In life, this often meant, then as now, procedures such as casting the hoof in therapeutic shoes (e.g., the heart bar shoe), adding flat or wedge pads under the shoe to mitigate internal locomotive stresses, cutting tendons that cause the coffin bone to move, and/or drugs. Causality or prevention are frequently on the back burner. Because NHC is focused on prevention, we're not going to do that. Instead, let's look closer at the reasoning behind shutting down the hoof mechanism during laminitis as convention would have us do.

It is well known that P3 (coffin bone) is attached to the inner hoof wall by means of a complex network of some 600-plus vertically oriented pairs of dermal and epidermal leaves (called lamina). These reach from the lower shoulder of the coronary groove down to the sole (*above*). The dermal leaves are *interdigitated* with the epidermal leaves, meaning the dermal leaves are situated in between and bonded to the epidermal leaves along their entire lengths on either side. The fibrous body of the dermal leaves, called the *lamellar corium*, is firmly attached to the entire face of P3. Hence, according to convention, a horse is said to be literally suspended by this lamellar, or "leaf like", bridge, attached on one side to P3 and on the other to the inner epidermal hoof wall. According to Dr. Christopher Pollit of the Australian Laminitis Research Unit (Queensland University), "In life, the hoof's distal phalangeal attachment apparatus is impressively strong; during peak loading the hoof wall and the distal phalanx move in concert and separate only when laminitis interferes with lamellar anatomy."[1]

Looking a little closer at this "attachment apparatus", there are actually two different networks of interdigitated epidermal leaves involved (*facing page, top*). The *primary epidermal leaves* (PELs) are part of the inner hoof wall and, therefore, grow down with it after they are produced by the Supercorium (page 60) at the lower shoulder of the coronary groove. Each PEL is separated from its interdigitated dermal leaf by a *secondary epidermal lamina* (SEL), which proliferates through the *basement membrane* (BM) that coats the entire outer dermal leaf (DL). Together, the SEL, BM, and DL form a contiguous body that is firmly attached to the face of P3. In life, as the hoof wall grows down, the PEL move past the SEL-BM-DL matrix and P3 (*facing page, bottom*). This complex leaf-based connection between the coffin bone and the hoof wall is called the *lamellar attachment mechanism* (LAM). It is also the supposed "bridge" which must withstand loading during support, according to Pollitt (and just about everyone else!). In contrast to the durable, rigid, and ever-descending epidermal hoof wall (including the PEL), the stationary LAM is, notwithstanding its SELs, very much "alive" and flexible given its highly vascular, innervated, somewhat fibrous, and flaccid constitution. Hence, it is this "side" of the lamellar bridge that is subject to inflammation and is the instigator of failure during laminitis.[2]

In my training clinics, students dissect this part of the inner hoof to understand its structural integrity as a purported weight loading structure. All agree, myself foremost, that such a moist, almost flaccid structure is physically incapable of sustaining the thousands of pounds of weight bearing forces they are said to endure during loading — no matter what their orientation and quantity. Moreover, the sharp, distal peripheral edge of P3 would clearly lacerate the soft dermal tissues surrounding it if subjected to those forces, regardless

(Continued on page 142)

---

[1]"Update On the Anatomy of the Inner Hoof Wall.". Dr Chris Pollitt. BVSc, PhD. Reader in Equine Medicine, School of Veterinary Science, Faculty of Natural Resources, Agriculture and Veterinary Science, The University of Queensland, AUSTRALIA 4072

[2]According to Pollit, the LAM failure is due to the proteolytic actions of a unique class of enzymes that digest the bonds between the PEL and the SEL-BM-DL matrix. Other mechanisms in the keratinizing process subsequently restore the bonds to newly arrived PEL. Calling it a "normal process gone wrong", Pollit has shown that during laminitis, there is a massive proliferation of these enzymes, which then overwhelm and destroy the LAM, causing the hoof wall to separate from the horse.

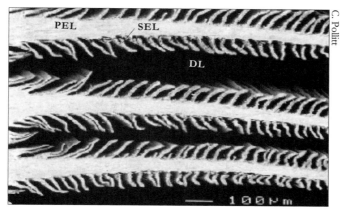

C. Pollitt

Interdigitation of the lamellar attachment mechanism (LAM). PEL = primary epidermal lamina; SEL = secondary epidermal lamina; DL = dermal lamina.

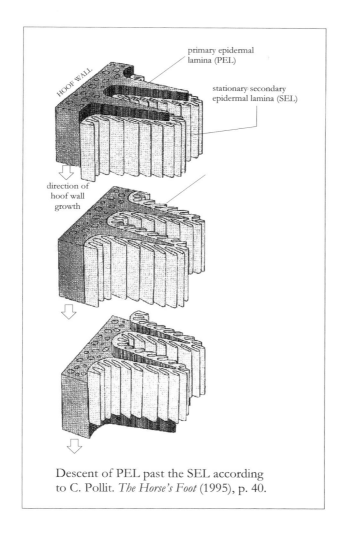

Descent of PEL past the SEL according to C. Pollit. *The Horse's Foot* (1995), p. 40.

Photographs of wild horse hoof imprints in central Nevada.

In these images, wild horse footprints reflect the hoof's volar profile during loading (weight bearing) on hardpan and loose soil. In both instances, mechanistic forces act in concert with the principle of relative concavity.

(*Left*) As the foot enters fully into support, only the hoof wall has pressed visibly into the ground, suggesting relatively firm substrate. In keeping with the hoof's natural relative concavity, no impression is made in such firm ground by the passive bars, solar dome and frog.

(*Right*) Here the horse is moving upon less firm ground. Once more, the hoof wall has pressed deeply into the earth reflecting weight-bearing forces mounting there (i.e., peripheral loading). Because the substrate is not dense and compacted (i.e., hardpan), soil is trapped in the dome, and under pressure from loose soil below, also renders an impression of the bars, solar dome, and frog. In accordance with the principle of relative concavity, weight loads principally over the hoof wall, passively elsewhere.

Photo credits: Luca Gandini.

(*Continued from page 140*)

of LAM failure. Nevertheless, convention says this is so, and that P3 must be supported and normal mechanistic forces halted when the LAM fails, or the digit, spearheaded by P3 under the weight of the horse, will slice through the bottom of the foot.

With such an ominous threat of disaster, and symptoms to support it, there is little for a conventional believer to do but truss up the foot with shoes augmented with side clips to prevent wall expansion during support, heart bar shoes to oppose the descent of P3, a tenotomy to mitigate the tug of the deep digital flexor tendon upon P3, pads to lift or lower the axis of the hoof to make it work less during support and manipulating breakover, performing a surgical resection or grooving of the hoof wall to relieve any pressure building up within the capsule, and providing drugs (which often trigger laminitis!) to kill pain and sensation. It's a long list of possible interventions, and pressure to act on as many as one can more often than not gets down to the depths of the owner's pocketbook, fears, and gullibility. Are any of these procedures really necessary? If one subscribes to the conventional model for the hoof mechanism, then one's answer has to be "yes".

Conventional Hoof Mechanism and Peripheral vs. Solar Loading

While most proponents of the conventional mechanism model are in general agreement concerning the LAM's suspensory role during support, two opposing camps of thought have emerged in recent years as to what happens next. Disagreement arises over how weight bearing forces are borne by the capsule itself. One camp contends that primary weight bearing duties are assumed by the hoof wall, called "peripheral loading", with the sole providing passive support. This follows logically from the hoof's natural concavity which puts the hoof wall closest to the ground, and the sole further away — not unlike the arch of the human foot being passive to the heel and ball (fore-foot) during support. The opposing camp holds that the sole assumes active support duties, while the hoof wall provides passive support. Images of hoof prints on the ground — including those of wild horses! — are used by both sides as evidence of their claims (*facing page*). While I personally believe that weight-bearing forces are always channeled to the most distal (active wear) structures during support, which is the hoof wall, I don't agree with the explanation of how this happens according to proponents of peripheral loading, who cause great harm to the foot as a result of their specious logic. So far as "solar loading" is concerned, I think this camp has completely missed the mark, which becomes abundantly clear when we consider the harmful things they do to the hoof based upon their equally bogus logic. It is interesting to note that vets, farriers and many barefooters fall into the peripheral loading camp when the hoof isn't laminitic, but many shift to the solar loading camp when the hoof is laminitic! The latter camp, however, seems determined to "solar load" the hoof at all times, regardless of laminitis. A few more words about their reasoning and what they do are in order, since, to my dismay, it has become more and more commonplace even as it causes horses to suffer.

Proponents of solar loading believe that the sole and frog are the primary support structures, while the hoof wall is passive — the opposite of what nature has shown us to be true. Consequently their practice is to trim the hoof wall away so that the horse is standing quite literally on his sole and, when possible, the frog. When laminitis strikes, proponents really

Hoof trimmed to "white line strategy". I've included trimming instructions for rehabilitating this hoof in Chapter 10.

Jill Willis

move into high gear to trim the hoof wall away from the sole, since, according to their logic, the separating hoof wall is literally tearing the LAM and causing excruciating pain to the horse. What we see practitioners of this camp — mainly barefooters — doing is cutting through the hoof wall, and into the sole-white line junction, called the "white line strategy" (*above*). And many barefooters, faced with additional pain caused by their invasive trimming, use boots (instead of horseshoes) with sole/frog pads to step up active pressure on the frog and solar dome. Doing this, they claim, facilitates maximum sole and frog support, thereby eliminating any possibility of peripheral loading, and, hence, further failure of the LAM. Again, farriers are not above doing this either, although their strategy is to resect the toe wall altogether, then nail, glue or screw on a heart bar shoe with a sole/frog pad to relieve the stressed LAM. I have now seen the long term deleterious effects of all these "methods", and, in my opinion, there is nothing remotely natural or healing about any of it, and, accordingly, I strongly advise against it.

Conventional Mechanism and Hoof Contraction

During the late 1990s, what can only be described as "mass hysteria" broke out among throngs — possibly tens of thousands — of unwitting U.S. horse owners who were led to believe by fanatical "anti-shoeing" barefooters from Europe that their horses were at grave risk of a deadly hoof diseases purportedly caused by shoeing. For awhile, I was even taken in until I found out what they were up to in early 2000. Without naming the perpetrators, who are still active in the barefoot community today, it is worth discussing the ramifications of their "method" and its rationale, which, as it turns, out, is also rooted deeply in the conventional hoof mechanism model.

First, unparalleled specious logic and outrageous bogus science that flies in the face of reputable research and common sense, let alone the wild horse model, served as the foundation and launch pad for this group of misguided barefoot trimmers. Ironically, using "nature" in a purely opportunistic and exploitative manner — natural this, and natural that, but with no genuine foundation in the horse's natural world — their proponents managed to seduce countless horse owners into thinking that hoof contraction (caused by shoeing) was at the root of all evil. Hoof contraction, they held over people's heads who could not possibly know better, caused Navicular Syndrome, an alleged "hoof based" disease — tantamount to a death sentence to horses who would get it — already familiar to and feared by most horse owners. Stop the shoeing and follow their method to the letter, or face the deadly consequences of "navicular". Not surprisingly, the farrier industry, and the metal shoe in particular, became prime targets in their cause, alienating in the process, that entire industry from embracing the principles and practice of authentic natural hoof care. NHC was pirated in name, but not in practice, and then swept along willy-nilly in what may be the greatest hoof care scam in the history of modern civilization. What mushroomed instead was a bizarre *esprit de corps* and angry clarion call across the barefoot movement to de-shoe everything in sight in the name of fear and intimidation. A decade before this all happened, I had already been a barefoot advocate, and much of what I was saying, doing, and teaching got grouped in with this bunch. But those who knew me and my work well — farriers, barefooters, and horse owners — understood none of this craze was ever my calling. Ironically, to this day, many misguided horse owners still place me under the same barefoot banner — often with praise!

It is true that the horseshoe causes what is commonly known as hoof contraction, but the link to NS just isn't there. Most well-trained farriers understand that shoeing contracts the foot, of course, and many have used my natural trim guidelines first published in *The Natural Horse* (1992) in an attempt to help matters. Earlier, Emery's *Horseshoeing Theory and Hoof Care* (1978), an important work that greatly influenced my thinking and practices at an earlier time had also tried to address the problem. And before Emery and I, countless farrier texts in more than one language had addressed the issue of contraction down through the centuries. One of the earliest papers was by the early barefoot advocate and British veterinarian I quoted in the introduction, Bracey Clark. Clark even attempted to invent a horseshoe hinged at the toe in an effort to get the shoe to "expand and contract" in harmony with — yes, once again — the same hoof mechanism I'm addressing here. So, hoof contraction has been no stranger to the shoer, and no shoer of any reputable standing would intentionally try to make a foot contract. In this respect, the narrow-minded assail upon their industry was, in some measure, unfair and without merit.

What is actually happening during hoof contraction is that the foot, under pressure

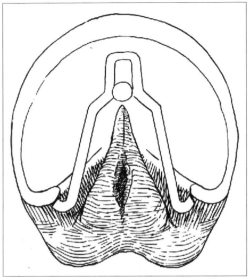

(*Left*) Scoring (aka grooving) the outer wall to facilitate de-contraction of capsule. (*Right*) Chadwick Spring. (J. A.W. Dollar. *A Handbook of Horseshoeing.* 1898)

from the shoe's metallic crunch, and unable to work directly against the ground, begins to weaken and atrophy. Epidermal mass is lost. But what every farrier and NHC practitioner should know is that mass lost to shoeing is re-accreted by the foot's dermal structures once the shoe is removed and healing time is allowed. Most hooves completely restore their mass within one to two *hgc*. This is something I observed in the mid-1980s as I begin my research with the natural trim following my Great Basin wild horse hoof studies. Later, I begin to appreciate the three-dimensional character of hoof contraction when attempting to keep hoof boots fitted during the first year or so after the horse's shoes were removed. Not only would boots no longer fit across the foot's volar profile just six months after they were initially fitted, they wouldn't fit around the neck of the capsule either in some hooves. Mass was building in along every axis of growth. I considered this an important finding and later formalized a study to evidence it before the burgeoning NHC community.[1]

Traditionally, farriers have tried many ways to reverse contraction by encouraging — sometimes outright forcing — the hoof apart. One regrettable method still practiced today (by shoers, vets, and barefooters) includes "scoring" the outer wall into or near the dermis, the idea being to weaken it sufficiently that it will then begin to spread apart. During the 19th century, the notorious Chadwick Spring was deployed to "spread the heels" by putting outwardly directed mechanical pressure on the bars. Certainly this could not have felt good to the horse! However, as crude and barbaric as these practices are, none rivaled, in my opinion, what the early barefooters would bring to the torture table. Before going into that, my point here is that down through the ages, solutions to hoof contraction were premised

[1] J. Jackson, "Does Horseshoeing Cause Hoof Contraction?" SRP Bulletin #111 (5/1/2003), p.3.

on the necessity of forcing the hoof to somehow get wider. Other than Clark, the idea of letting the horse go barefoot and letting the hoof enlarge again through new growth seems to have escaped the experts.

The purported causal relationship between hoof contraction and Navicular Syndrome (NS) was a critical bullying point to these new barefoot provocateurs. A scare tactic. But the line drawn between these two pathologies, in my opinion, was simply based on a fallacious indictment of hoof contraction since their explanation for how it causes NS is completely negated by the biomechanics of natural hoof form and function. Typically, in NS, one of the front feet becomes noticeably steeper down the toe wall and smaller in size — what I define as a "clubfoot". Its paired front foot is comparatively wider and lower angled. The horse will typically begin to "give" (limp) noticeably at the trot over the clubfoot while in a turn. Alarmed, the horse owner invariably calls the farrier and vet. The vet, familiar with the symptoms, tells the owner the horse likely has NS. Specialized shoes are sometimes recommended, along with pain medications, and stall rest; if one's pocketbook is deep enough, surgery may be conducted. But, if NS is the problem, none of these measures work, and so the horse can't be ridden. Most are then either put down or turned out to pasture if land is available and the owner can afford it and has a kind heart.

Enter those new barefooters. I soon discovered that their trim method was invasive (penetrating the dermis), left horses sore and bleeding, and solved nothing. I was also stunned to learn that they rejected the wild horse foot as a model because — and this is what I was told to my face — "wild horses have contracted feet and are in pain." How they came to that conclusion is beyond me, except, perhaps, that the sound, healthy wild horse foot truly doesn't resemble what they aspire to carve out of the hoof.

The premise for their trim is that the bars of the hoof, if allowed to grow excessively long, will pressure the navicular bone, the bone's protective bursa, and the deep digital flexor tendon. Conventional veterinary medicine had already targeted this zone of the inner hoof as the matrix of the problem, but did not necessarily implicate shoeing. Contraction was simply a symptom of NS. Some vets and farriers (like Emery) had postulated that NS was caused by the trim and how the shoe is applied to that trimmed hoof. Most authorities, while convinced that the cause of NS resided somewhere in the vicinity of the navicular bone, could simply offer nothing specific or a sure remedy. Emery pretty well summed up the situation:

> Many theories have been advanced about the causes of this lameness. However, most theories have been incomplete, or substantiated only by popular opinion rather than by research and careful observation. These theories often have been in conflict with each other and even with the material used to explain them. This lameness has not received more attention because its early signs and symptoms often are obscure, its causes are uncertain, and its treatment is considered hopeless.[1]

[1]Ibid., *Horseshoeing Theory and Hoof Care. p. 8.*

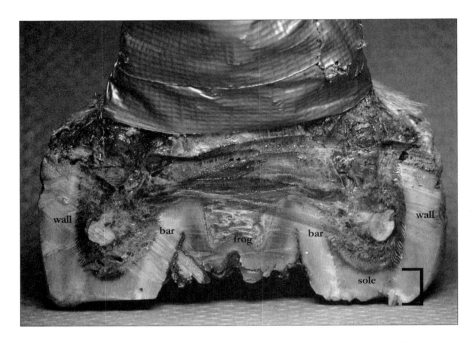

For the new barefooters, this uncertainty provided a perfect vacuum to fill and then use to whip up hysteria among horse owners and then march in their new cure-all, the "physiologically correct trim" method. The solution? Cut out the bars and seats of corn of the front feet until blood is drawn, and then set the front hoof toe angles precisely at 45 degrees. This, they claimed, prevented the bars from jamming the navicular matrix, weakened the back of the hoof so that its structures can move apart ("de-contract"), aligned the coffin bone (P3) to its physiologically correct position, and (to quote them) "to increase mechanism". These measures, we are told, would restore hoof health. All I can say is that the whole lot of it is unadulterated, sheer nonsense. But this is what they would have us all believe. Fortunately, nature tells us otherwise.

You can imagine the state of shock when I rolled out the wild horse hoof cadaver seen above for the creator of this physiologically correct trim method and her assistant.. The bars are not only dangerously long by their standards, they are aimed right at the navicular bone and deep digital flexor tendon (DDFT)! Of course, no such collision ever takes place because the internal biomechanics of the capsule relative to its contents work otherwise, and efficiently so, as nature intended. So, the "science" behind their "operative hoof mechanism" is faulty, to the say the least. But I offer up this important photograph for another reason as well.

If you look closely, you will see that the frog and the bars actually converge at the top of the bars. This is where their respective growth coria meet and differentiate, one producing frog epidermis, the other bar. Notice also the sole and how it unites each bar with the hoof wall. In fact, the bars are extensions of the hoof wall, wrapping around their respective seats of corn, and forming the heel-buttresses. Not surprising, these barefooters discovered through their cadaver dissections that by thinning the sole to nothing, or at most, paper-thin thickness, and cutting out the bars, the heel-buttresses are effectively dismantled. In the most grisly way, the bloodied back of the hoof is repeatedly flayed open, rendering the animal lame. Indeed, the hoof is mechanically unhinged and widened (de-contracted!) — but at what cost? Certainly not hoof health. Like scar tissue, frog mass typically is hyper-accreted by its growth corium to fill the gap, while the heel-buttresses reestablish them-selves further apart. Understandably, many hooves trimmed this way over a long period of time develop extremely wide frogs. Sometimes the pain and resulting infections and endless abscesses are more than the horse can take. In 2006, the British government brought ani-mal cruelty charges against one of these trimmers and the horse owner she was serving, successfully prosecuting both.

I would never recommend such a trim method to anyone for any reason. Once again, my point is that this inhumane method, like others discussed previously, follows directly from the logic of the conventional hoof mechanism.

Conventional Hoof Mechanism and Sole Concavity

. "Your horse has more concavity than my horse!" I'm not exactly sure when and where this obsession first arose in the barefoot horse community, but it is widespread and has cre-ated another aberration in hoof care that is also attributed to the conventional hoof mecha-nism model. Ironically, the rationale here is the opposite of the solar loading faction, even though it is derived from the same mechanistic model!

Instead of the sole leading the way in weight bearing responsibilities, the sole will be ex-cavated to extremes and the hoof wall put back in charge. What it says is that a "compacted" sole, meaning one that is relatively flat with little concavity, cannot "flex" as it should. In the words of its adherents, "There is insufficient mechanism." Of course, this is license to dig. But, in contrast to the de-barring faction that is going to take matters straight into the dermis, this group simply wants as much concavity as can be dug out up to but not actually reaching blood.

The justification for such sole thinning appears to lie in the alleged descent of the sole during support as the hoof wall moves outward under the weight of the horse. In their minds, a compacted sole is too rigid to accommodate this, whereas lots of concavity is really going to get the sole moving up and down like a trampoline. Moreover, the sole must give if P3 is going to descend somewhat to escape the neck of the capsule closing in on it. At all costs, the sole must be free to bend down and get out of the way, if the entire system is going to work right. Otherwise, adherents insist, the hoof will become contracted. That again.

I could go on with other convoluted examples of how the hoof can be assaulted to give it "enough mechanism", "more mechanism", or none at all if need be. A book could be written. Arguably, it is all testimony to human ingenuity, but unfortunately, does not really bode well for the horse. What we need, and need desperately, is a mechanistic model based on the sound, healthy foot of the wild horse. One that will work for our horses.

Hoof mechanism: NHC model

The NHC model for the hoof mechanism departs significantly from the conventional model described above. Any viable model that attempts to explain the biomechanical functioning of the hoof must be consistent with the hoof's natural state as we understand it among wild horses of the U.S. Great Basin, and should never advise or encourage any application that brings harm to the horse. The principles and practices of NHC, and specifically those that apply directly to the natural trim, has consistently shown that the wild horse model applies to all domesticated equines, regardless of breed or the animal's utility. Therefore, any mechanistic model of the hoof advanced by the principles of NHC must not only be consistent with the wild horse model, but be applicable in practice with all domesticated horses.

As I began to formulate and apply the NHC foundational principles for the natural trim in the early 1980s, it wasn't long before I realized that the conventional model for the hoof mechanism that I learned in the 1970s simply did not hold up to the test of reality within the new NHC paradigm. In short, I had but two choices: abandon the foundational principles derived from the wild horse model and revert back to the conventional model with all its problems and inconsistencies, or, accept a new model that nature seemed to be presenting that stood-up to NHC practices in the field based on the wild horse model.

Before going into detail, I want to say out front that the NHC model is a surprisingly simple, logical, and useful way to understand how the horse's foot works. I've tested it on thousands of horses over three decades with consistent success. Moreover, it does not open the door to the types of harmful procedures we've seen with farriers, generic barefoot trimmers, and equine vets rooted in the conventional model. Since it is entirely integrated with holistic NHC practices, it is something that horse owners can and should understand to help safeguard their horses from practitioners still entrenched in the old model.

At the core of the NHC model is the rejection of the conventional model's claim that the LAM (lamellar attachment mechanism — the PEL, SEL, MB, and P3) is a suspensory apparatus for loading the horse's weight at any given moment during the hoof's support phase. Also rejected is the premise that the hoof, under this weight-bearing force, expands outward or that the sole and frog yield like a flexible trampoline. Not rejected from the conventional model is that the foot's vascular system plays a key role in the hoof mechanism, and, in conjunction with the capsule's soft tissue structures, in absorbing and dissipating *concussional* forces, although these are viewed as minor compared to the *compres-*

sional force.

The NHC model, in contrast, holds that, during support, the weight-bearing force does not build upon the LAM, but instead, everywhere else around it within the capsule. As the force presses downward within the foot, pressure builds within the hoof capsule. In this interpretation, weight bearing is supported, contained, and countered by intra-capsular soft tissue mass, the foot's vascular system, and the entire capsule itself from the hairline to the ground.

The internal base of the capsule, we recall, is convex — an arched dome — hence, it is a strategically important structure in providing strength and stability to the capsule, aiding the soft tissue mass and vascular system to counter the massive compressional force building inside the capsule due to the horse's weight. Pressure (from the horse's body weight) upon this arched dome "locks" the hoof in position and stabilizes it, not unlike the dome of an Eskimo igloo bearing the weight of snow, or any arched structure in nature (p. 80).

Within the capsule, the vascular system contributes an intense resistance in the form of semi-closed system hydraulics. According to Pollit — and this seems to be consistent with the NHC mechanism — the venous tracks evacuating the hoof's vascular system are partially closed by pressure exerted upon them by the hoof's medial and lateral cartilages and surrounding soft tissue mass (e.g., skin). In this way, pressurized blood is trapped within the capsule, at the same time it is "pumped" at a reduced pressure to the heart. Pollit also identified the presence of *arteriovenousanastamoses* (AVAs) — shunts connecting sub-branches of the arteries and veins in advance of the foot's capillary beds feeding the LAM and growth coria. In this way, nature has created a foot that is able to equalize fluid pressure forces within and without the capsule by channeling blood to where, and when, it is needed. The vascular system within the hoof is tantamount to a water bed upon which the horse is suspended. As a matter of record, in 1908, forward thinking veterinarians of the British War Department released a publication to this effect:

> The blood supply is so bountiful that in addition to giving nourishment to the foot, it acts like a water bed, helping to equalize the tremendous pressures to which the whole structure is constantly subjected, and keeping the bones and sensitive parts contained in the hoof buoyantly supported, lie a big ship in a little dock.[1]

During all of this, the question begging an answer is what is happening to the LAM — one of the key players in the conventional mechanism model?

P3, the lowermost bone of the digit is busy responding to the opposing tensions upon it by the major extensor tendon and the DDFT. During flight and support these two major tendon networks, aided by other tendons/ligaments acting upon the entire limb, reciprocate to advance the foot through flight, support, and breakover. During support the shoul-

---

[1] *Animal Management, Prepared in Veterinary Department of the War Office.* London: His Majesty's Stationery Office, 1908. p. 221.

der joint is opening to the max (something one can feel if they put their hand upon it while walking alongside the horse), which has the effect of lifting or thrusting the horse off of his "water bed" as the muscles pull the lower leg upward in order to propel the horse forward. At this point, hydraulic pressure is greatest within the capsule and P3 and the LAM are completely non-weight bearing. P3 movement is limited to normal interphalangeal joint rotation. As muscle to tendon reciprocities continue the limb towards flight, the entire hoof is lifted from the ground. In this interpretation, it is not P3 that is making things move, but the nerves, tendons and muscles acting upon the entire limb and foot. This is also true of the horse's entire musculoskeletature. The skeleton serves as an apparatus upon which nerve to muscle to tendon activity sequences can take place in an organized way. Without this activity, the skeleton — simply along for the ride in the NHC model — will simply collapse to the ground. Without the skeleton, if we can even imagine such a thing, there would be just a mish-mash of disorganized living mass on the ground. Not a pleasant thought. Obviously, each needs the other. But my point here is that in the NHC model, bones carry no weight at all. They are acted upon, and carried along, entirely by the nerve-muscle-tendon activity sequences. Go ahead and flex one of your arms. Now ask yourself, what is doing all the work to make this happen? That's right, the arm bones are moved by the tendons, which are set into motion by the muscles, which are activated by the nerves — and ultimately your brain and mental desire to make it happen.

The LAM is itself in the same boat as P3 during support: essentially stationary, weightless (except its own mass), and "docked" (with p3) in the capsule's waterbed. But recall that the orientation of the dermal and epidermal (primary and secondary) lamina are all vertical. This makes sense, since pressure building within the capsule would be moving along their axis of orientation, instead of against it — sort of like the current of a stream moving in the direction of the banks. I will note here that when the hoof dermis is infected (e.g., if pricked by the shoer's nail and untreated), pressure due to abscessing pushes bacterial wastes up the same vertical dermal lamellar tracks, where they are evacuated through the soft perioplic epidermis covering the coronary band. Nature thinks of everything!

When the horse finally completes the propulsory force, the hoof is able to leave the ground (breakover), carrying the LAM with it. *Breakover*, in the language of the NHC model, is defined simply as the "cessation of the weight-bearing force".

I know I said earlier that this model is simple and easy to understand and that my long description may contradict this assertion. Actually, it is extremely complex (as are all systems in nature), but can be simplified enough so that we can understand and apply it to our work with horses. To this end, let me clarify what the hoof is doing with some simple line drawings and contrast these, side by side, with the conventional model (*overleaf*, pages 154-155).

Applications of the NHC Mechanism Model

How the NHC mechanism model is applied in our work surfaces again and again. Foremost, it means that we don't have to obstruct the mechanism and harm the hoof with all those mechanical devices and invasive techniques discussed earlier. Instead, we facilitate the mechanism by simply conducting the natural trim according to our guidelines, and by providing genuine NHC holistic care.

If ever there was a "daring" application of our mechanism model, it would be in relation to the hoof suffering from acute laminitis — P3 rotation, P3 penetration, and hoof slough. While I instruct students that these are medical emergencies requiring veterinary intervention, at the same I also encourage them to advocate for allied NHC intervention. I tell them that the NHC model is really the only rational, front line defense against the terror that otherwise is likely to happen to the laminitic hoof. Given the veterinary industry's entrenchment in the conventional hoof mechanism model, such an undertaking is problematic from the word go. The mere threat of P3 rotation and sole-to-wall separation is enough to make the average owner willing to cling to any pitch for the heart bar, pads, surgery, etc. The suggestion that we make no effort to provide support to P3 borders on heresy for some. To offer, further, that there is no need to because there is no weight bearing force on P3 (and the LAM) is grounds for losing all credibility in that moment! The decision for treatment rests entirely upon an understandably confused horse owner. For this reason, I have always taught students that education represents the very front lines of the NHC revolution. Things have to be sorted out, explained, and where possible, demonstrated without excuses over the final outcome.

Against this backdrop, but armed with the foundations for the NHC hoof mechanism — for the first time in the 1980s — I made the decision to remove the shoes from a horse stricken with acute laminitis. As is usually the case, the owner allowed this only because the horse lay at death's door in complete agony. The vet had sad nothing more could be done to help, and the owner did not want to give up on the animal if there was a sliver of hope. This was my first test of the NHC mechanism model, and it was proven then, and time and time again since, to my satisfaction beyond all doubt. The details of what happened are now a common story in the current mainstream of NHC protocol: NSAIDS are given by the vet. Inflammation abates. The cause is removed. The horse is fed a reasonably natural diet. And healing time is allowed. As I think of it, "Nature and the hoof mechanism working hand in hand." For the NHC practitioner, education and advocating unrelentingly for NHC holistic prevention is the main work front. The natural trim is but a 20 minute intervention.

Overleaf
Hoof mechanism
models contrasted.

Contrasting the conventional and NHC models for the hoof mechanism.

On the facing page is a diagram of a hoof that is going to go down two "mechanism" paths: on the left, the NHC version, on the right the conventional. These are greatly simplified schematics, with only a few structures identified so that the essential differences standout. There are no dimensions attached to the drawings and they are not to scale. As a pragmatist, I don't think I need to complicate in order to do our work, and do it well according to this understanding, and to rest assured that we are acting in the best interest of the horse. I would encourage research scientists to delve into the deeper nuances if they like and recommend any studies on nature's model. In life, those of us who do this work in the field and face the consequences of our actions, need to be perfectly clear about what we're doing and that we are not causing harm. The NHC model leads us away from the serious issues inherent in the conventional model and into a place that harmonizes with common sense, reality, humane care, and the wild horse model.

(1) The hoof is mediolaterally cross-sectioned, and in flight. All the key players are identified and have been defined and discussed in previous chapters. The things we want to keep our eye on are the before/after positions of the bull's-eye (limit line), mediolateral angle of the hoof wall (73°), the distal edge of P3, and the arch of the sole where it intersects the MPTW. These targets are the main watersheds between the NHC and conventional models.

(2a) The NHC model has entered support. There are no visible changes occurring in this view. The arch of the sole has locked everything in place (evidence for this has now been captured on film in slow motion, and can be seen on the Internet at:
http://www.youtube.com/watch?v=sPipjsRep9U).
Not visible are the hydraulic forces concentrated in the dermal space between P3 and the capsule. Not within view also, are changes across the back of the hoof, where it gives outwardly in very small measure across the heel bulbs. The effect of this minor "give" is to facilitate shock absorption as the foot enters support — not flatten the arched sole which would weaken the capsule's structural integrity that must support thousands of pounds of pressure. Nevertheless, as we have already seen, the weight bearing force over the heels is still sufficiently great to press grooves into the branches of a steel horseshoe!

(2b) Many significant changes have occurred in the conventional model, according to its authorities, and are depicted here. The neck of the hoof wall is pressing inward as the lower wall deflects outward (3 degrees of change). Of course, for this to happen, P3 must descend further into the capsule to avoid being crushed by the descending hoof wall. In turn, the sole must flex downward like a trampoline to provide room for P3's descent. Contrast these changes in the side-by-side illustrations.

(*Bottom, left/right*) Looking at the rim of the hoof wall relative to the MAVP, we see very minor expansion in the back of the hoof with the NHC model, and, as expected, much more with the conventional model.

Summary

In the horse's natural world the hoof behaves during support as nature intended it to. Fifty-five million years of natural selection defines what this is. I believe the NHC model brings us closer to the truth. I can understand, however, why advocates of the conventional model believe as they do. When the foot is trussed and choked in steel like a straightjacket, surgically modified where vital parts are altogether missing, repeatedly abused by nipper and knife, drugged, and prevented by whatever justification from moving freely, naturally and *without pain*, one can believe just about anything.

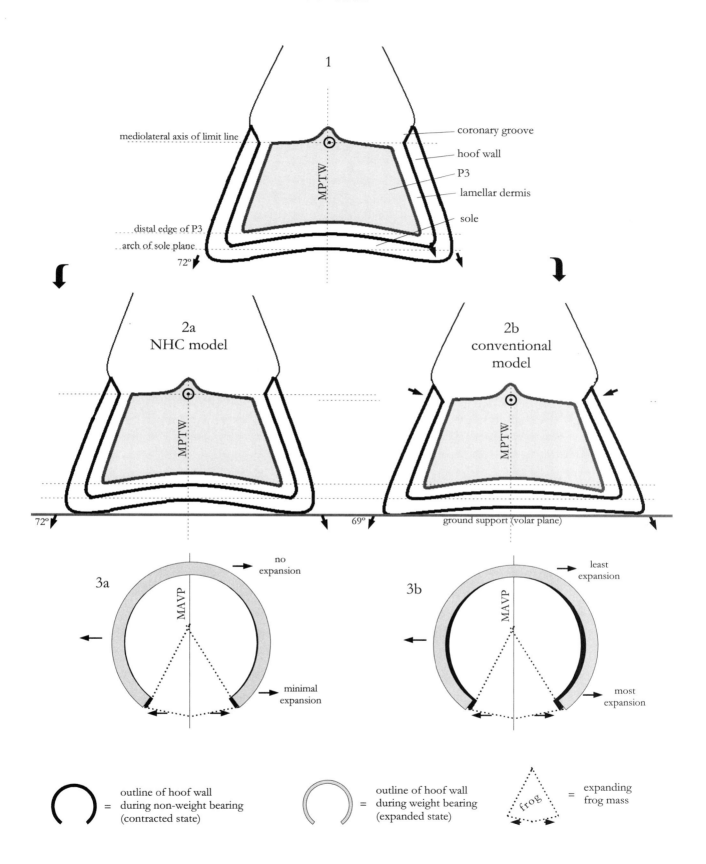

Part II: Practices
The Natural Trim in Action

I saw the angel in the marble and carved until I set him free. — Michelangelo

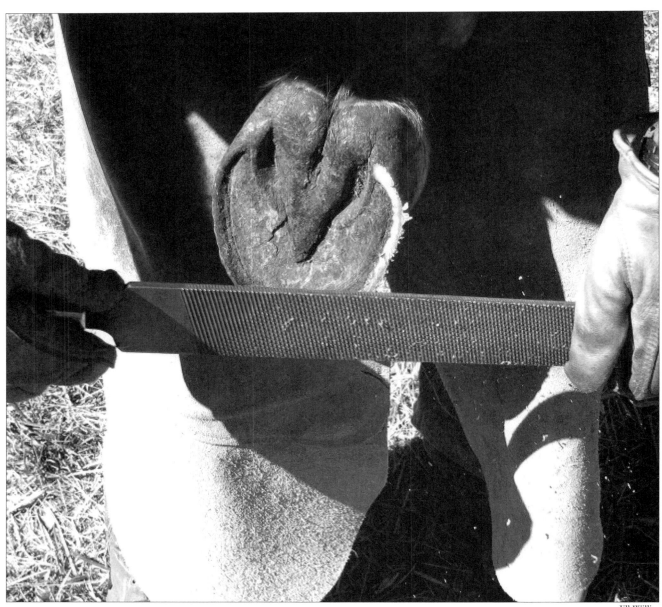

Jill Willis

158

Readying Ourselves to Trim

Armed with the Four Guiding Principles, restrained by the ethical admonitions of Hippocrates, knowing how to measure with precision, and harboring no harmful delusions regarding the hoof mechanism, the NHC practitioner has little more to do than carry out the explicit directive of mimicking the natural wear patterns of the Great Basin wild horse hoof. Typically, the trim is conducted in 20 to 30 minutes, plus time for several brief rest breaks for the trimmer and horse, interspersed with timely "treats" and praise to reward the horse for his cooperation. Neglected hooves, depending on the amount of excess growth, will take whatever time is necessary. As will foals being introduced to trimming, starting at four weeks of age. Dangerous, unruly horses won't be trimmed at all until readied. Generally speaking, such horses will require preliminary ground training and hoof handling by the horse's owner or an expert. Unless agreed to in advance, this task falls outside the responsibility of the NHC practitioner, whose role it is to conduct the trim.

To explain the nuances of the trim, I've selected four highly contrasting hoof types that are representative of what NHC practitioners face in the horse world today: the laminitic hoof, the club foot, the wry foot, and the biodynamically balanced hoof. Each type, of course, has its variations, and, not uncommonly, there are overlaps between the types, such as the laminitic hoof that is also wry. But the student of NHC should take comfort in knowing that, to master one type, is to master all its variations.

To the most seasoned and accomplished NHC practitioner, the biodynamically balanced hoof offers the greatest challenge of all, even though it requires the least physical energy to exert, and only a fraction of the time of any of the others to complete. This is because such hooves have arrived at the door of "wildness" in most respects, and nature requires exponentially greater mental attention to detail and professional restraint when taking the very least of excessive growth. The hoof must be attended to patiently and astutely, studied like a documentary with an important message, because more time will be spent contemplating the action to be taken, than the time wielding the tool itself. Rushing to trim what little is there is an invitation to regret one's action, because the eye and hand are no longer working together and mistakes are inevitable. Speed, I teach my students, arrives through efficiency and foresight, not the hand moving quicker than the eye — the objective of a magician's slight-of-hand. Four horses in my care have reached the threshold of biodynamic balance in the past year, and each can be trimmed (with a half time break) in 8 minutes. Even so, by a long shot, they are the most complex hooves I have faced in my near 40 years in the field, surpassing in terms of professional intimidation even the most notoriously twisted slipper-toe that pathology has to offer.

We will start the trimming with one of these biodynamically balanced hooves, the right front foot of a 25 year old Arabian gelding named "Apollo". This alpha male is a friendly, intelligent, and remarkable athlete. The contrast between Apollo's hoof and the cadaver specimens that will follow, will be glaringly obvious to the reader; less so, however, will be the steps to the final destination, even though they are identical. Only to repeat myself, to the NHC practitioner, the difference lies only in the amount of work to be done. Always, always — the less there is to remove, the more biodynamically balanced is the hoof, the more challenging is the practitioner's path to completion! This is the irony and burden our profession shoulders because nature imbues such hooves with the delicate nuances of "form and function" that must be understood and cultivated. Sooner or later, every hoof strikes back in revolt when we roam astray from that path: nature will not tolerate incompetence. Apollo and his pasture mates' hooves speak to this truth.

Finally, I wish to echo my words recalled from the foreword of this book, the instructions that follow will serve the student best if used in conjunction with formal training under the guiding hands of qualified NHC practitioners. So what follows is simply what I do, and an opportunity for the reader to look over my shoulder for a brief look at the natural trim in action.

Managing the Horse through Relative Dominance (RD)

Of the many things I learned from the wild horse in his homeland, and value as much or more than anything else, is the socialization structure through which they communicate with each other. At the foundation of that structure is what biologists call "peck ordering" behavior. In their world, it is understood among every member of their species that all social life is governed by hierarchy. I gave examples of this earlier, where one member is either alpha (dominant) or beta (subordinate) to the next. There is no such thing as "democracy" or "equality" in their world — these are the philosophical constructs and legal precepts of human institutions. Forget them when dealing with horses, because they are abstractions that mean nothing to their species. The NHC practitioner, accordingly, has one singular objective before trimming any horse, and this is to assert their position of relative dominance (RD) above the horse in the pecking order. Because if this doesn't happen, the horse is obliged by his DNA to assert his dominance over the practitioner. It's just the way things are. Once "dominance" is established, horse and human can partner as a team.

An entire book could be written about this, and I have been implored by others to do just that. Obviously, that isn't going to happen here, but I would like to discuss some of the main principles of RD, and refer the reader to a related monograph that I wrote for

ISNHCP students to develop their horse handling skills as part of their training. This is the *AANHCP Field Guide to Sequencing*.[1] RD is a big part of that document.

At the heart of RD in the horse's natural world is the implicit understanding that once one family member subordinates their authority to another member, that member assumes protective responsibilities towards the subordinate. I approach every horse I trim with this in mind. And until this is achieved, I run the risk of that horse becoming difficult and even violent with me.

I wrote about the alpha "monarch" stallion in my book *The Natural Horse*. This is the exact role I must assume with each horse. Once this position is attained, trimming is essentially problem free — nothwithstanding physical debilitations the horse may be suffering requiring my special attendance.

In the wild, alpha or beta propensities are established in the individual's DNA. As I explain to students, at the moment the newly arrived foal hits the ground, gets on his feet, and begins to explore his surroundings, every member of his family knows the alpha has (or hasn't) arrived. And that it's just a matter of time before he asserts himself. Obviously, though, the little one cannot establish his authority through size and force, because he is still a baby. So he asserts it through other behaviors — pinning his ears and other threatening gestures. As he grows older, his play time transposes into fight time. That's his way. Among male horses, this can get pretty brutal, always exciting for humans to watch. Among females, the tone is different, but the kicks and bites are just as painful. Whatever it takes to assert and remind others of one's alpha position is the order of every day.

When I approach a horse the first time, I introduce myself. Not as a friendly "nice guy" asking for cooperation. As I teach students, this is the worst thing one can do to assert one's dominance. That is "beta behavior" and has no place in NHC practitioning unless one welcomes getting kicked, bit, pushed around, and dismissed by the horse from the proceedings! That this doesn't happen more in the horse world is because most horses are naturally "band betas" in their DNA. People just get by, although not without many unpleasant consequences.[2]

So what I do before trimming is assume an alpha demeanor when approaching the horse. I let him know by my upright and confident carriage, "the alpha has arrived!". Only abused, severely dissociated horses, will not respond through ear radar, alertness, and attention to me as I walk around them reading their signs. These are the dangerous horses among us, and, with few exceptions, I will decline to trim them until matters are dealt with appropriately by the owner. If you want to get kicked, bit, and run over . . . here is your

---

[1] *AANHCP Field Guide to Sequencing*. See in appendix.
[2] Several years ago, the America Holistic Veterinary Medical Association published some findings on U.S. horse owner injuries, specifically those severe enough to require emergency room treatment and more. I did the calculation, and it was about one case every 10 minutes!

opportunity at last!

In the horse's family circle, being an alpha means commanding, not being commanded. The alpha *asks* for nothing, the alpha *requires* and *exacts* cooperation. Asking, or worse, begging the horse to cooperate is annoucing your beta status. Expect trouble, possibly cooperation if you're lucky to have a beta who is more beta than you! Exacting compliance is how one asserts one's higher position in the horse's natural social hierarchy. How this is accomplished will depend on two things: first, the alpha or beta demeanor of the horse; and second, the alpha or beta demeanor of the NHC practitioner. Putting an alpha horse with a beta person is asking for trouble. It can be done, but the person must entertain no delusions about the meaning, methods, and responsibilities of the alpha in the horse's natural world. I hate to say it, but that eliminates most horse owners I know.

Because I am a confirmed alpha type, 99% of horses I approach understand and respect this within seconds of my arrival. All ear radar focuses upon me as I approach and walk around them. They know, "the alpha has arrived!". I don't have to say a word. Because the concept of RD is often poorly misunderstood in the horse world, and because it plays a central and ongoing role during trimming, I normally dismiss the horse's owner from helping manage the horse. Unless I have schooled them on what to do, I will either manage the horse myself (called "free reining"[1]), or, as is the case in my practice today, I am assisted by another NHC practitioner who is schooled in RD.

In the moment, literally, that the horse has accepted his beta position to my satisifaction, I instantly praise and reward him (usually sliced carrots or apple pieces). This is done with the utmost humility and restrained composure with the rare alpha persona horses (male and female "monarch" types), who, by their mental stature and sense of authority, require respect and appreciation for their acquiessence to higher authority. With the much more common beta persona types, I am usually more vocal and treating of them. They welcome this. But in either case, at the moment of subordination, I have then and there assumed the most important responsibility in their minds: it is my job now to protect them from threat or harm, real or imagined. To ignore this facet of RD is to lose their trust, and, rightfully so, their compliance. This is the way it is in their natural world, and they expect this from us.

So, if you were to observe me closely in my work, you will see that at all times I am in close communication with the horse and handler. It is a very busy affair, and I am given to fits if the handler strays to talk with others while I am at work, and ignores the process. As the alpha "in charge" (which every trimmer should be), I expect all immediate participants — trimmer, handler, and the horse — to keep their fingers on the pulse of what's happening. This is an animal of prey, given to fear and flight, and the handler and I are wise to be vigilant.

[1]See "Step 12. Trimming without handler", *AANHCP Guide to Sequencing*, p. 23.

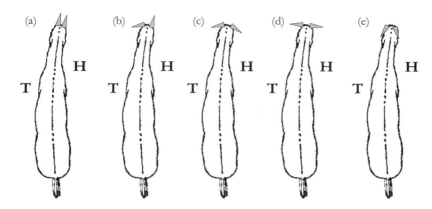

Ear Radar

- Direction of the horse's ears communicates his attentiveness and attitude towards the NHC process; T = trimmer; H = handler:

  (a) Attention is elsewhere (handler should investigate).

  (b) Attention is divided between trimmer and elsewhere (trimmer should sense this, handler should investigate).

  (c) Horse is attentive to trimmer and handler.

  (d) Horse is not fully attentive, possibly dozing (handler should get horse's attention).

  (e) Horse is disturbed or angry, and there may be tail swishing trimmer should exit from under horse, resolve issue).

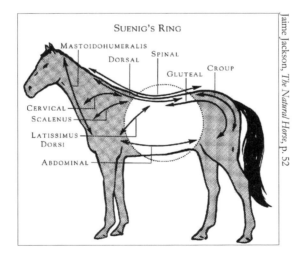

SUENIG'S RING

MASTOIDOHUMERALIS
DORSAL
SPINAL
GLUTEAL
CROUP
CERVICAL
SCALENUS
LATISSIMUS
DORSI
ABDOMINAL

Jaime Jackson, *The Natural Horse*, p. 52

The handler's job is to observe the horse's surroundings for potential threats or disturbances so perceived by the horse, and report them to the trimmer. The position of the ears are revealing (*above*). At my end, down under the horse, other information is received from the horse. Through his "muscle ring" (*above*) described by Suenig in his classic erudite work, *Horsemanship*, the horse conveys subtle and vital communications to me; this is completely undiscernable to all others with the possible exception of the most asture handler who possesses the lightest hands deployed forward on the ring:

The regular engagement of the hindquarters is produced by muscular pulsations that are elicited by the controls via the central nervous system, and in turn they produce pulsation of the extensor and flexor muscles that extend along the spinal column through the neck, returning along the belly to the pelvis. These wavelike movements will be shorter or longer depending upon the framework, that is, the degree of collection.[1]

Through the muscle ring, the horse lets me know many things: if he is tiring, unbalanced, afraid of something, annoyed by the handler, in pain, getting sleepy, resentful or angry because he was not treated during break time, a foot is being trimmed out of sequence, not sufficiently collected over his support diagnonals (*facing page, above* and *below*), standing on something uncomfortable, and so forth.[2] Over the years, I learned — conditioned myself — to heed and respond, not ignore, these communications from the horse. Countless times I have heard, "Jaime makes it look so easy!" The truth is, it is easy, or at least more fluid, when you and the horse are in "dialogue" and operating as a team.

Why Treat?

In return for subordination, an alpha will let the beta eat with them, as Jill's 25-year-old Apollo does with his young six year old male pasture mate, Chance — and out of the same hay bag. It is a reward, or perhaps an expression of tolerance is a better way to put it, in a world of relative dominance (RD), but always, always, at the discretion of the alpha. Rewards, from our human perspective, and that is all we can truly be, position us a humanitarian step beyond tolerance as we deal with this other species. This can mean many things to the horse as I always say. Treating, as I do with carrot slices, for example, is but one instrument of kindness that I deploy, and always in the appropriate *moment*. This is vastly superior to the bleak alternative of subjugation through fear and violence, a path I will not take. If, in the wake of an act of RD, I do not receive the beckoning facial expression of invitation from the horse, something I see in his eyes, I know I have not earned this animal's trust and cooperation -- yet. To suggest that a horse's trust and cooperation cannot or should not be incurred through any act of kindness, such as treating, grooming, even hugging, is a step back to the other dark side of intolerance. Fortunately -- and why otherwise? -- horses are not stupid and all welcome kindness from humans (especially food!), although acts of

(Continued on page 166)

[1] Waldemar Seunig, *Horsemanship* (New York: Doubleday, 1956), p. 127. I quoted from this important foundational cornerstone of natural horsemanship in *The Natural Horse*, p. 52.
[2] All of these concerns are discussed in the *AANHCP Guide to Sequencing*.

Horse's left and right support diagonals

- The horse is able to support himself during trimming while standing on either his left or right diagonal

- The horse instinctively moves his free leg (the one not supported by the trimmer) into a tripod position with his support diagonal. Example: if trimmer is working with LF hoof, horse will form a tripod with his right support diagonal (RF & LH hooves) and RH hoof.

A horse that is standing "square" or whose hooves forming his support diagonal are not directly under his body, is *not* balanced for trimming.

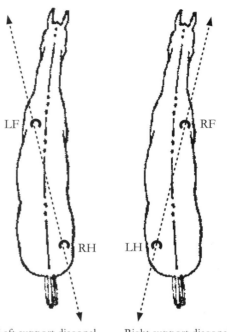

Left support diagonal   Right support diagonal

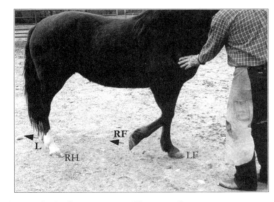

Setting the horse's left support diagonal.

(*Above*) Horse is standing on his *left support diagonal* (RH & LF), so I am pressuring his right chest muscles so that (*right*) he will step back half a stride onto his right diagonal (RH & RF). So positioned, the horse is free to form a support tripod with his RH foot and his LF hoof is available for trimming. Alternatively, the RH hoof may be taken, and the LF hoof forms the tripod. This technique is also effective for lifting any hoof to be trimmed, as it also sets the existing support diagonal. For example, in the instance at right, the trimmer would grasp the RF hoof in flight, before the left diagonal (RH & LF) has left the ground to move rearwards; the horse would instinctively move the LH hoof to form a tripod with his left diagonal. Setting the diagonal is the most effective technique available to the practitioner for balancing the horse using the horse's natural gait complex. Ironically, compelling a horse to "stand square" to be trimmed without attention to his diagonal supports is an invitation to resistance, rather than cooperation.

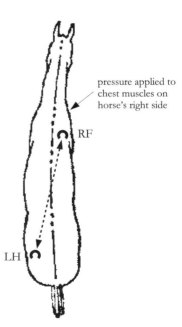

pressure applied to chest muscles on horse's right side

Right support diagonal

(Continued from page 164)

kindness do not in and of themselves incur submission in the pecking order.

Horses know we are not horses and can see, hear, and smell that we do not live our lives as they do, in the same way that they know the mountain lion who feeds upon his young lives his life differently. This is why they are always anxious to depart from us for their own, when treats and halters are withdrawn at the gate. They, as prey animals, just need to know that we will not cause them harm, and in return, most will tolerate us. But to submit to the human's will as a subordinate cooperator, that is something else entirely. One either forges the alpha position, as I do with every horse I trim before work commences, or one "isn't in" the pecking order at all and the horse will simply tolerate us, if we are lucky. That, to my way of thinking, is dangerous for an animal given to flight, especially when one must work as I do under the animal and always within kicking and biting range. Down there, there is no place for allegory and anthropomorphism, only the raw realities of pecking order and where one is positioned in it. As an alpha, I do what is necessary to attain and sustain this unique position. And with it, once more, comes the responsibility to protect he who subordinates his position in the pecking order. Ignore that responsibility or violate that responsibility with injustice and one is instantly demoted in their world.

Done within the context of RD, treating is more than an act of kindness, it is an entirely appropriate and important tool to *reinforce* subordination without fear. Treating reinforces this in the most pleasant of ways, the threat of violence in the least pleasant of ways. But both, let the race of humans know, are part of RD in the horse's natural world. And in the one where I must dwell in close contact with him in my work; down here, at his hoof, the instruments of RD are everything. A fool's paradise for he who thinks otherwise! It is surprisingly simple, though, and from what I have seen, it speaks as much to our own character as that of the horse. To feel the tension of RD, is to feel the wildness within the horse without fear. A connection and rewarding journey I wish all could experience.

Positioning Yourself Under the Horse

With a clear and operative understanding of RD, you are ready to get under the horse to trim. When beginning, there are two objectives: one, learning efficient body positioning; and, two, teaching the horse the complementary positions he must take so that both partners are equally comfortable, balanced, and mentally prepared for the tasks ahead.

Natural trim protocol calls for an ordering of trimming steps. This ordering is called "sequencing". Things are done in sequence because work steps are then orderly, efficient and understood by both partners. This is particularly important to the horse, who will act upon his great memory to cooperate and help. For example, sequencing requires that the feet are attended to in strict order with rest breaks taken between each foot. Height adjustments in the hoof stand are made during half-time breaks (when we shift from front to hind hooves). Breaks are important because they facilitate rest and mitigate fatigue — keys to efficiency. I conducted a study of AANHCP practitioners that contrasted those who sequence with those who did not. On average, those who sequenced spent consistently less time trimming than those who didn't! Horses were demonstratively more cooperative as well. Breaks are also times to reward and praise the horse, as I discussed earlier.

Sequencing, as I teach in the ISNHCP training camps, includes the following ordering of hooves: LF (midway break) - RF — half-time break — LH (midway break) - RH (praise/reward horse). In the following pages showing AANHCP certified practitioners and ISNHCP students, I've laid out the sequencing positions of trimmer and horse according to this ordering of hooves (*overleaf*). The supporting positions of the handler are included in some of the images. Study these images and my comments closely, and then practice. In my training clinics, I teach sequencing independent of trimming until it is confirmed. At the same time, they are instructed in cadaver trimming without the complications of sequencing. After two weeks, students are then taught to integrate both of these facets of the natural trim.[1]

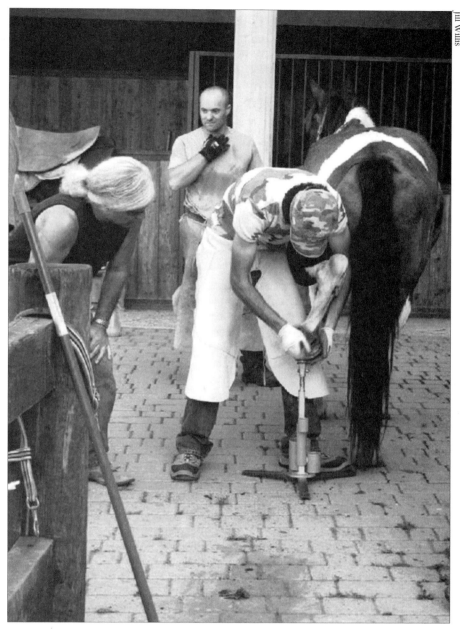

Teaching sequencing to a young student in Italy. In the *Overleaf*, we'll go step by step.

§

With the above all borne in mind, let's proceed on to the natural trim mechanics for the four hoof types. I recommend that the reader refer back, as many times as necessary, to

[1]For an example of six of my NHC colleagues sequencing while trimming side by side during a public demonstration in Denmark, go to: http://www.youtube.com/watch?v=KoZKkvZzzKw

(*Overleaf*)
Sequencing:
step-by-step.
[All photos by Jill Willis]

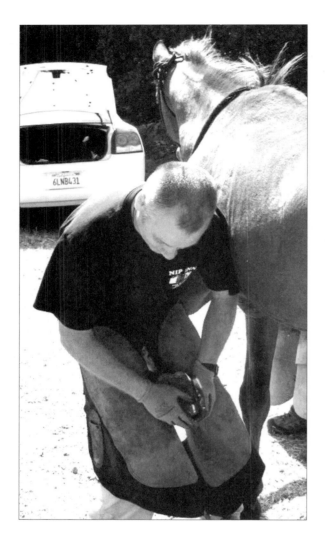

Sequencing: Left Front Hoof.

For a complete description of sequencing to go along with these images, refer to the *NHC Field Guide to Sequencing.*

(*Above, left*) This is the "classic" trimmer's position used by barefooters and farriers alike. Toes are pointed inward, which locks the hoof between and just above the knees. Legs are bent and ready to move up and down, and left to right, if movement is needed. The back is kept relaxed and bends with the legs. Resisting straightening legs while bending back, a prescription for back pain. As a general rule, the trimmer's heels should be positioned at shoulder-width to stabilize one's center of gravity.

(*Above, right*) This is the forward position for front feet. The hoof is taken from the classic position, then, turning towards the horse, the hoof is placed on the knee and brought forward. Once the hoof is stabilized on the knee and the horse is balanced in the forward position, the hoof stand is brought to the hoof. There is a tendency among beginners to do the opposite, that is, position the hoof stand, and then move the hoof to it. This is problematic because the horse should be balanced first in position. If he isn't, then the trimmer is stuck moving stand and hoof together to a better location for balance, or starting over. Tiring and inefficient!

Sequencing: Left Front Hoof (cont'd).

(*Above, left* and *below sidebar*) Next, the hoof is positioned on the grip head of the hoof stand. The hoof is set between the point-of-frog and the toe wall on the hard sole plane (HSP), over the MAVP. The grip head is aligned with the MATW.

(*Above, right*) Try to keep at least one foot on a leg of the hoof stand at all times for stability. The right knee is held against the back of the hoof for stability; the horse senses and appreciates this. Both hands are now free to work. If stability is compromised through bad technique, the trimmer is left to "one handed" work — inefficient and the signature of professional incompetence. To finish, the hoof is taken back to the trimmer's knee, the hoof stand moved to the side, and then released. Gently push the hoof off the knee rather than carry and release it. If the horse suddenly snaps his foot, you can be injured if you are holding firmly to the hoof.

§

I recommend using tripod stands like the one here for added stability. Round bases are inclined to slide on some flat surfaces, whereas the tripod "digs in". Tripods are more stable also on uneven ground. Many of the popular round base hoof stands are so large that they render it virtually impossible for the horse to be on his diagonal, and for the trimmer to maneuver through some of the key body positions necessary in sequencing.

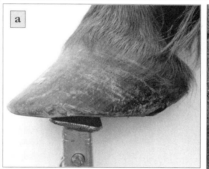

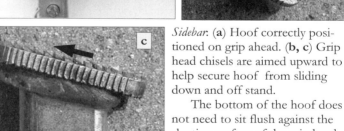

Sidebar: (**a**) Hoof correctly positioned on grip ahead. (**b, c**) Grip head chisels are aimed upward to help secure hoof from sliding down and off stand.

The bottom of the hoof does not need to sit flush against the slanting surface of the grip head. Rather, aim to position upper edge of grip head on the hard sole plane between the toe wall and point-of-frog over the MATW; this will avoid weight-bearing pressure on the frog, and possible discomfort to the horse.

Sequencing: Right Front Hoof.

Following a short midway break, during which the horse is praised and treated, and the trimmer takes fluids, the hoof stand is brought around to the horse's right side.

(*Above, left*) Classic front hoof position once again. When correctly executed, the horse will be balanced and cooperative. The trimmer should be equally balanced with both hands free and independent to work.

(*Above, right*) As with the LF hoof, the RF is taken first to the trimmer's knee, then set on the grip head. Here, the hoof could be positioned a little higher on the thigh so that the hoof can then be lowered onto the grip head instead of lifting it up to it. This is more critical for "stiff" and "heavy handed" horses. The handler takes position on the opposite side, her hand lightly/passively at the halter. If you look close here, and in other photos in this series, you will see the halter tied around the horse's neck, forming two "reins". This is called "free reining", and it enables the handler or trimmer to use the direct and indirect rein to help position the horse. What does the horse's ear radar tell you? Of course, that his attention at the moment is not with the sequencing. The trimmer will feel this inattentiveness through a change of muscle tension in Suenig's Ring (p. 163), and ask the handler to investigate for potential trouble.

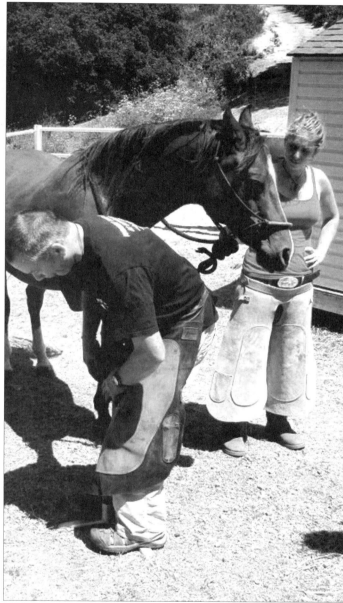

Sequencing: Right Front Hoof.

(*Above, left*) The hoof has been taken to the grip head. The trimmer is standing to the outside of the hoof (i.e., away from the horse's midline), securing the tripod with both feet. This facilitates working the medial side of the hoof. The horse's radar is attentive to both trimmer and handler.

(*Above, right*) The trimmer has moved to the opposite side, and is now able to see and work the lateral side of the hoof with both hands. Moving to and from the medial and lateral sides of the hoof is called "walking the hoof stand". With practice, movement is very fluid and horse's tend to find it interesting to watch. As with all hoof stand work, the horse's weight is taken entirely by the hoof stand, relieving the trimmer of much body stress, particularly the back and knees.

This concludes the "front end" work of the natural trim. A half time break is now taken. I will stop for at least 2 minutes to take fluids, reward the horse, and prepare the hoof stand for the final trim run.

Sequencing: Left Hind Hoof.

(*Above, left*) This is the classic stance for working with either hind hoof sans the hoof stand. Toe's point inward, legs bent, and back relaxed. Do leg bend (deep squat) exercises to condition yourself for the classic position. I do these and weightlifting 3 days a week to sustain upper and lower body strength. Note the handler, who maintains constant communication with horse while on the same side as the trimmer. There are two reasons for this positioning: one, if the horse spooks, he will be more likely to move away from the trimmer; second, the horse can more easily keep his eyes on both of us. To aid in this, the handler turns the horse's head slightly to the working side.

(*Above, right*) The hoof stand is brought forward on the trimmer's knee (as done with the front hoof), and placed on the grip head. Careful attention is required to place and sustain the toe wall on the grip head over the MATW. What must be avoided is putting the coronary band on the grip head, as this is soft tissue subject to abrasion. Notice that the horse's lower leg is vertically oriented (white arrow) and bent at the fetlock joint. This is an extremely comfortable position for the horse, and renders the leg light and easily movable up and down. I call this nature's "hind leg elevator", and teach students to set the elevator on the vertical before positioning the grip head.

Sequencing: Left Hind Hoof.

(*Left, above* and *below*) This is a body position that I innovated for NHC practitioners. The hoof is brought to the outside and placed on the trimmer's thigh. The trimmer's back presses lightly against the horse's side (abdomen). A bit intimidating to beginner's, most are surprised at just how comfortable it is to assume, and how readily horses adapt to it. In this position, the trimmer works two-handed, and has full access to the lateral side of the outer wall.

(*Above, right*) Next, the hoof is brought forward (on the trimmer's knee) and set on the grip head. In this position, the trimmer has ready two-handed access to the medial wall. As in all instances, the hoof is returned to the trimmer's knee, the hoof stand moved aside, and then released.

Sequencing: Right Hind Hoof.

Following a midway break, we are ready for the final run down the right side.

(*Above, left*) The hoof has been brought to the classic position, hoof stand to the side. Handler in the correct supporting position.

(*Above, right*) Trimmer is double checking the "elevator". Toe wall is positioned on grip head, over the MATW. Both feet secure tripod. Right knee/thing supports the hoof. Knees are bent and back relaxed. During training, and for the purposes of confirming sequencing, I will — as I've done in all these photos — have students "tag team" with each other and instructors — sometimes while the hoof is on the grip head. This builds confidence and fluidity. Horses find it interesting and always cooperate to be a part of the action — and for the praise and treats!

Sequencing: Right Hind Hoof.

(*Above, left*) Everything is in good order, and the trimmer has deployed the nippers. Right ear radar is directed at trimmer.

(*Above, right*) The hoof is brought forward to the grip head and secured with the knee. Most students will move straight to this position and bypass the "outside" position until they gain confidence and fluidity working with horses they know and trust. Eventually, it is adopted in most cases without second thought.

Okay, we are done! As I said at the outset, sequencing requires practice to master. In time, it will become second nature to you and the horse.

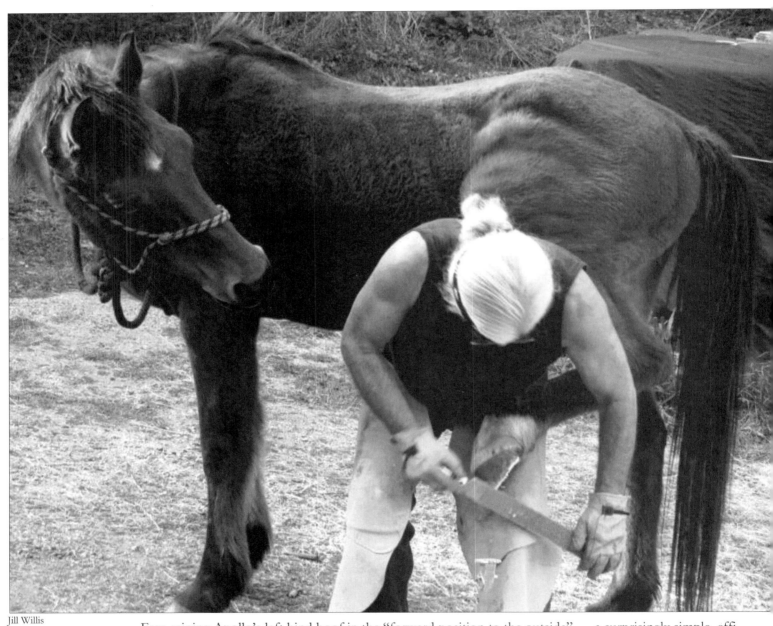

Jill Willis

Free-reining Apollo's left hind hoof in the "forward position to the outside" — a surprisingly simple, efficient, and effective way to balance and trim the lateral wall without the hoof stand. Apollo is balanced and comfortable on his left diagonal. Trained to "sequencing", Apollo is attentive and cooperative.

CHAPTER 8

Trimming the Biodynamically
Balanced Hoof

I wrote in an earlier chapter that when the natural trim is carried out as an integral part of the four pillars of NHC, the hoof enters into a biodynamic equilibrium with its environment. Since this represents the pinnacle of NHC, I want the reader to be clear about what this means exactly. Indeed, what is a "biodynamically balanced hoof"?

First, as I define it, the term biodynamic refers to the hoof's "living relationship" with the environment. This is no different than the horse's living relationship with his environment. The word has no other meaning beyond this until we talk about the specifics of his environment. In the wild, we have seen what this means regarding the shape and function of the foot, which, like the animal himself, exists in harmony with the environment. In domestication, we realize that the biodynamic relationship may not be so harmonious! But when we say, a "biodynamically balanced" domesticated hoof, we are talking about something that is akin or parallel to the wild hoof, yet is domesticated because it is managed by humans. With this specifically in mind, let's now add depth and meaning to the term as I shall use it in this chapter and throughout the remainder of this book. A biodynamically balanced hoof is a naturally trimmed hoof that is distinguished by . . .

- hoof health
- hoof soundness
- natural wear patterns
- natural growth patterns
- natural shape/size/proportion
- distinct areas of active/passive wear that do not change from trim to trim

. . . as documented in the hooves of U.S. Great Basin wild, free-roaming horses.

Since we now know what this means in terms of the wild horse model, and in relation to the four pillars of NHC, our work is straightforward. And our expectations of the biodynamically balanced hoof should come as no surprise.

Our subject for this photo essay are the hooves of our 25 year old Arabian gelding, Apollo, whom I introduced along with our three other horses in their Paddock Paradise in Chapter 2. My approach to trimming Apollo's hooves is the same as all other hooves discussed in this book. Paddock Paradise has immensely helped Apollo wear his feet naturally. I am able to trim all his hooves in just eight minutes, as there is little excess growth to trim

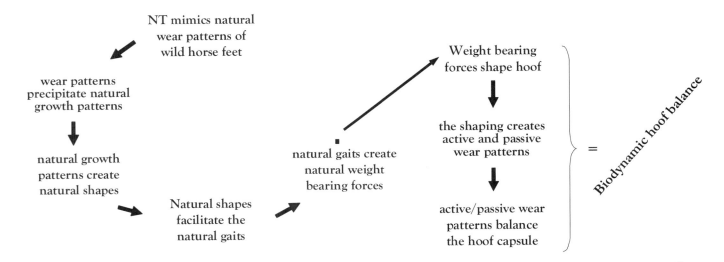

away. My attentions will focus principally on sustaining his well-established *active* and *passive* wear patterns — a key signature of biodynamically balanced hooves. Active and passive wear, we recall, emerges out of the reinforcing cycle of "form and function" discussed in Chapter 4. Recalling the illustration depicting that cycle (*above, left*), we can expand it to include the formation of highly callused active and passive wear (*above, right*). We see here that the weight bearing force shapes the hoof, and, in the process, forges areas of active and passive wear. These are highly individualized wear patterns that are unique to each horse — no two horses being identical. As they emerge, the horse is balanced upon them. As I said, we will be looking for these in Apollo's hooves.

It is worth mentioning that active wear tends to develop more over the medial side of the hoof wall and (to a lesser extent, the) sole in the biodynamically balanced foot. Unless worn away through sufficient movement, it is common that we see more horn "build up" to trim away along that side of the hoof. I attribute this to how the horse moves to the left or right, with the inside of the hoof (front and hind, but more so with hinds) pushing against the ground more than on the lateral side. This propulsory force signals the foot's dermis to produce more growth because there is more active wear there. I see this in all of the hooves of our horses living 24/7 in their Paddock Paradise.

Before describing the trimming sequences, I want to add that within 24 hours of trimming our horses' hooves, their volar profiles go through some rather extraordinary changes. The water line becomes more distinct and the hoof wall from the white line to the outer wall becomes more rounded and prominent — the mustang roll, in other words, takes on more definition. The areas where I trimmed harden off and, for lack of a better word, "bulge" to the extent that the water line segment of the mustang roll rises an eighth of an inch (3 to 4 mm) above the white line — exactly as we see in the wild horse hoof.

All the photos in this series were taken by Jill Willis.

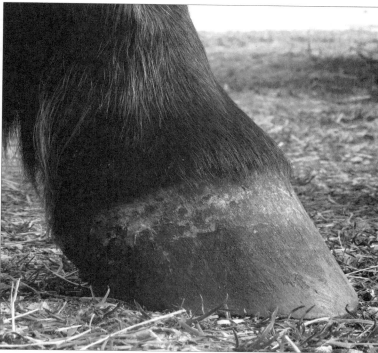

(*Left*) 25 year old bright-eyed Apollo and his three band mates live on the ridge of a coastal mountain, pocketed with deep oak forested canyons, cool ocean winds and fog, with soil that is a mixture of plain dirt, dry grasses, and gravelly rocks as seen in the photos above. Consequently, their feet show a similar kind of rugged wear and tear I saw in our U.S. Great Basin wild, free-roaming horses As hooves approach such "wildness" in shape, size, and proportion, our work as NHC practitioners becomes exponentially more complex.

(Above) This is Apollo's left front hoof (LF), which we will follow through one entire trim sequence. Along the way, I will contrast it with his other hooves when they better illustrate some nuance of the trim or tool usage. To start, his LF measures under 3 in. (7.5 cm) at the bull's-eye over the MATW, so there will be relatively little work to do. But what we do will be exceedingly important to sustaining his biodynamically balanced hoof. As stated in this chapter's introduction we will go right after his active/passive wear points, which will harbor the main areas of excessive growth. Apollo is trained to sequencing and works closely with me during the trim. The approximate "real time" for trimming all four hooves is 10-12 minutes, and typically each front hoof will take 3 minutes to each hind at 2 minutes per hoof. Let's go!

Apollo: Pre-trim Evaluation.

(Above This is Apollo's left front hoof (LF), which we will follow through to the end result. Black arrows point to the three areas of active wear. Their relative positions must be sustained above (i.e., remain distal to) the passive wear areas between them as I lower the entire hoof wall to the hard sole plane. "M" marks the medial side of the hoof (towards Apollo's body); MHB and LHB to the heel buttresses. In the biodynamically balanced foot, these areas of the volar profile endure greater active wear and produce more growth.

White arrows point to hardened flaps of frog horn. These flaps are not symptoms of thrush, and are sometimes seen in wild horse feet during winter months when tissues hydrate and separate. The test for thrush lies in evaluating the epidermal integrity and odor of the central cleft of the frog. This is done carefully with a probe — the job of a competent NHC practitioner — which I do not recommend horse owners attempt on their own without instruction.

(Below) This is an important view. The markers correspond to those in the image above. The bracket frames an exemplary "mustang roll" — all naturally worn; the nearby arrow points to the hard rim of "water line" that continues around the entire periphery of the hoof wall. The "white line" lies just inside the water line, but is indiscernible in this view.

§

Both views on this page tell us that little work will be necessary to finish the job, in contrast to the prodigious tasks involved to accomplish the same thing with the cadaver specimens in the forthcoming photo essays in following chapters!

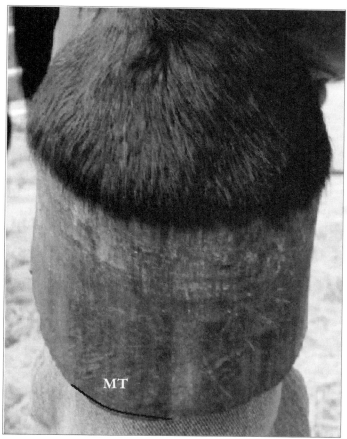

Apollo: Pre-trim Evaluation.

Two bird's eye views of the same (active wear) toe wall pillar. Left unchecked by insufficient wear, active wear pillars can continue to "over build" and cause hoof imbalance.

(Left) We are looking straight on from the front as the hoof rests on my knee. I've marked the medial toe wall (MT), and drawn a line around that segment of the toe, beyond which is excessive growth (*"flare"*) due to active wear.

(Below) In this view we are looking straight down from above. This is the ideal position to sight excess growth (*flare*), and to evaluate hoof shape and symmetry (front feet) and asymmetry (hind feet). With few exceptions (due to sufficient natural wear, such as we see in the wild), all hooves will require rasping the outer wall in this position on the hoof stand to remove flare and complete the mustang roll. As a farrier, I once did this work with the hoof on my knee, but learned later as an NHC practitioner, that to do the job properly and completely (and more easily!), a hoof stand is necessary.

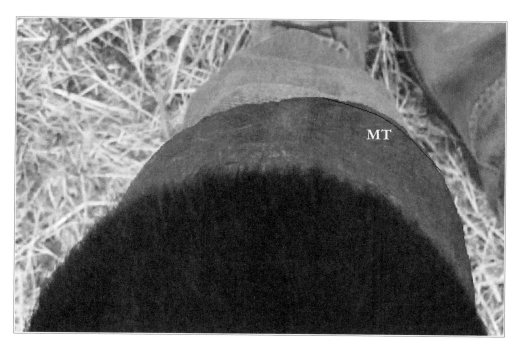

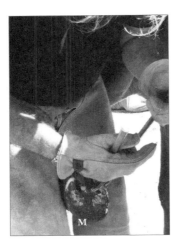

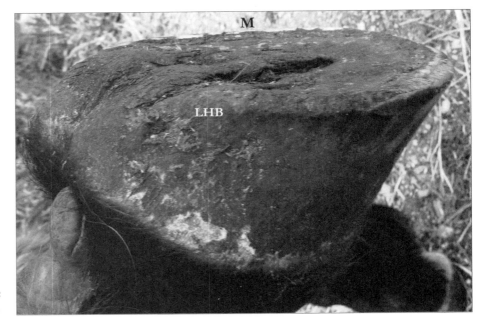

Apollo: Trim Active Wear Growth.

(Above) I've lowered the medial wall from the toe to the heel buttress with the nipper. The lateral heel buttress (LHB) is now in my sights and I will go after it next.

(Below) Another view to this first nipper run. Note that the water line still protrudes actively above the sole. I achieved this by keeping one blade of the nipper flat against the sole during the cut. In this way, the concave angle of the sole "aims" the angle of the nipper in the right direction to maintain an active water line.

Apollo: Trim Active Wear Growth.

(Above) Continuing, I've now switched to my flat rasp and begin to lower any active wear/growth above the hard sole plane (HSP) on the lateral side of the hoof. There's not much in the toe-to-quarter sector to remove, but I will lightly file it to distinguish the water line.

(Below) The lateral heel buttress has been lowered down to the HSP, like the medial heel buttress. Visible now is a thick, healthy and durable hoof wall the same thickness all the way around — just like the wild horse hoof. I've lightly abraded the surface of the sole all the way around, to reveal its smooth, hard character. This happened entirely through natural wear — not by my tools.

Note that I've also trimmed the frog — with the nipper, not the hoof knife. I seldom, if ever, deploy the hoof knife when trimming biodynamically balanced hooves. Such hooves simply wear their own soles.

Note also that the white line is very dark and wide. This is due to debris forced into and between its leaves — not separation of wall and sole.

Finally, note the very prominent water line. In the next step I will cut at its perimeter — where natural wear hasn't done it for me already — to form the mustang roll.

Keeping track of time, at this point I will have spent one minute to get this far.

Apollo: Cut Mustang Roll — Volar Profile.

These are important views, which explain how we can integrate the natural trim into existing natural wear patterns:

[1] I've rasped the mustang roll as there was not enough wall to remove to justify bringing out the nippers. Two things to focus on here: black arrow points to rim of water line standing above (distal to) the sole; white arrow points to rim of mustang roll established by Apollo's natural wear. When remnants of natural wear such as this are extant, incorporate them into the trim as much as possible. They are they the forgings of a biodynamically balanced foot and you are at the threshold of "wildness". Note, too, the perfectly straight toe wall in very close proximity of the MATW.

[2] Another view to the hoof above with markers in place. The frog lies passive to the mediolateral heel axis (MLHA) ; the MATW, central frog sulcus (CS), and MPVP are all aligned; the MLHA is at right angle (90°) to the MLHA. The hoof, therefore, is naturally balanced in this profile.

[3] Similar view as [2} but the hoof tilted up so that the entire perimeter of the hoof wall, from bar to bar, is visible. Black arrow points ridgeline of bar which descends from the heel buttress down to approximately half the length of the frog, where the bar terminates and blends into the sole.

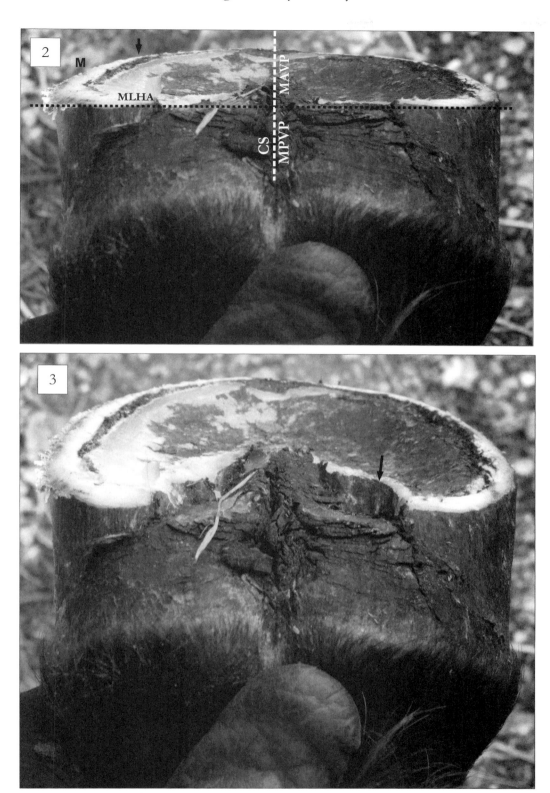

Apollo: Cut the Mustang Roll — Outer Wall.

We've reached the final step!

[1] First up is to get rid of any flare in the outer wall. What little there is has concentrated over the medial toe wall (p. 181). Flare in the outer wall must be removed with the flat file, as I'm doing here. By rasping the outer wall down to its natural thickness (p. 69), communication between the ground and the coronary corium's nerve bed then encourages "straight line" growth (p. 66, *above*).

Arrow points in the direction that I'm pushing the rasp, while holding it at the oblique angle you see here. The rasp is set against the wall below the coronary band, then pushed briskly downward at an angle across the grain of the hoof wall. Let the sharpness of rasp's mini-chisels do the cutting as you lightly push the rasp downward, rather than applying brute force against the hoof wall. My practice is to guide each stroke with the leading edge of the rasp, while pushing my palm against the rasp handle. I will skim the entire face of the outer wall with the lightest of action as I search out and remove excessive growth (flare).

[2,3] Once flare is removed from the outer wall, it is time to complete the mustang roll. Three tools are used: first, the Radius Rasp Pro with its coarse chisels for roughing in the roll; second, the Radius Rasp Original, with its fine, supper sharp blades for fine tuning the cut of the RRPro; and last, the Hoof Buffer for removing any residual epidermal fray and for simulating the very fine polishing effects of sand seen in the hooves of U.S. Great Basin wild, free-roaming horses. Experience has shown that the mustang roll is less likely to ravel when these particular tools are used in the sequences here. Check them all out in the appendix on pages 304-305. In this image, and in the two of the facing page (discussed below), I have deployed the RROrig over the medial toe wall where active wear had created flare.

[4] I have switched hands and am driving the RROrig towards the toe. Because the blade of this and the RRPro are curved, I am able to add a rotating motion to the rasp as I move it forward, an action that further rounds the roll. Again, the sharp slicing action across the tubular horn sharpens the medulla "transmission lines" of communication between the nerve bed in the coronary corium, the ground, and the horse's central nervous system (p. 62). The information derived through this network, which must negotiate and translate the contraposing forces of weight-bearing and concussional shock waves, is vital to the discrete distribution of active and passive wear points along the mustang roll.

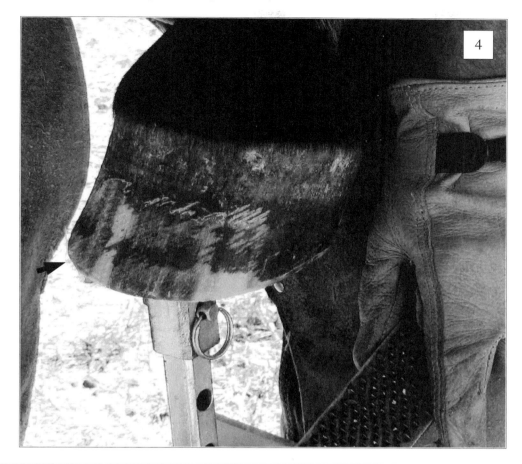

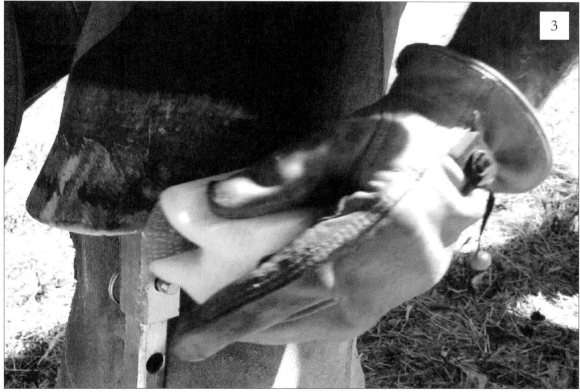

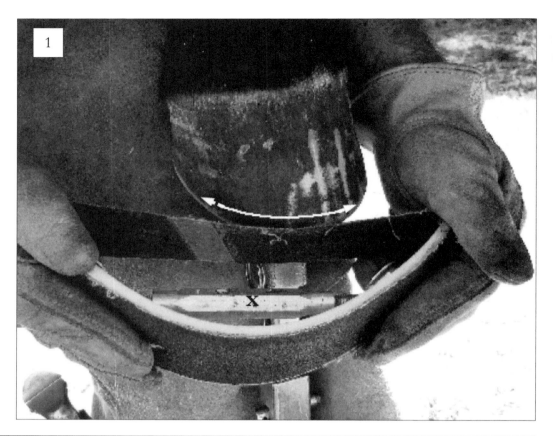

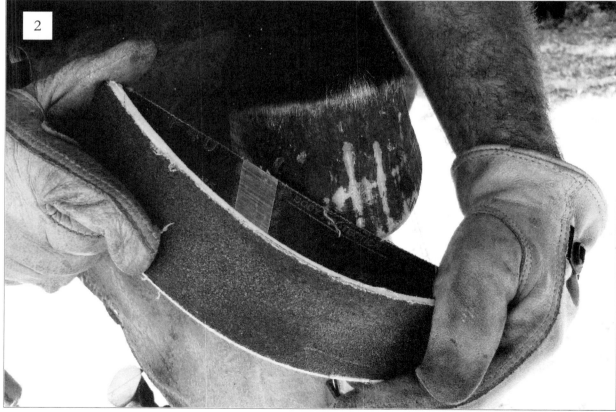

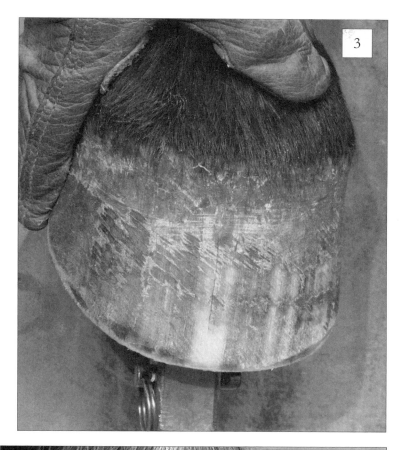

Apollo: Sand the Mustang Roll and Outer Wall.

This step completes the natural trim:

[1] To simulate natural wear, we must sand the entire face of the outer wall from the coronary band to the mustang roll. This is the job of the Bow Sander (pp. 304-305). Here I am moving the Bow Sander roughly parallel with the volar plane as I smooth the mustang roll.

[2] The Bow Sander should also be used over and around the mustang roll as demonstrated here. The tension bar on the Bow Sander can be adjusted to increase or decrease the force and fold of the sanding belt. I prefer a tighter tension for all work with the Bow Sander.

[3] The hoof is finished. Apollo truly has beautiful and sound feet because of the natural trim and his life "on track" in our Paddock Paradise.

[4] Medial view of the hoof with its perfect straight line growth over the MATW from the bull's-eye (⊙) to the turn of the mustang roll. Note that the mustang tapers from the MATW to the heel, where (at the white arrow marker) the turn of the wall of the heel-buttress naturally folds under to complete the roll with only minor use of the RROrig.

Jill Willis

1

Libor Černý

Frederique Molenaar

Supreme Importance of Natural Boarding to the Biodynamically Balanced Hoof.

I decided to take a quick break from discussing Apollo's trim and include these photos. We should never neglect for a moment the supreme importance of natural movement in the shaping of the biodynamically balanced hoof. Nature intends for the horse's hoof to work hard, day and night, over challenging terrain, if it is to be genuinely naturally shaped. It cannot come through trimming alone, or standing still and isolated in a stall or corral, or grazing in lush pastures. Paddock Paradise is an important way to create varied terrain that simulates the horse's adaptive environment and help us achieve our NHC goals.

[1] [2] These photos were taken within seconds of each other. Apollo is leading the band as they round the front gate (just north of the solar panel in our Paddock Paradise, p. 42) in close formation, all taking their left leads with near orchestrated precision, on their way to Feed Station #1. One can literally feel the ground rumble as they race by — very exciting! Their athletic movements — powerful, sound, and natural — represent the foundations for natural riding practices.

[3] Naturally shaped hooves are able to move over very extreme terrain, even in the moist, sandy flatlands of the Netherlands, where this photo was recently taken. Gravel was incorporated into segments of a Paddock Paradise track in Paarden. The effect is to toughen the hooves, no differently than with Apollo and his fellow band mate's hooves in our own naturally rocky Paddock Paradise.

Effects of Natural Wear on Apollo's Hooves in Our Paddock Paradise.

(Above) This is Apollo's LF hoof after a month on track following his natural trim. There is nothing apparent yet to trim as new growth has entered into a biodynamic equilibrium with natural wear in our Paddock Paradise. The smooth, "fresh trimmed" look of the natural trim is gone, replaced by the tough, rugged look that is characteristic of life on track. Apollo's hooves are never picked out, except at his trim session to protect my cutting tools.

His hooves, as of this writing, are at seven weeks and there is still virtually nothing to trim. Our plan is to step up environmental pressure and natural behavioral patterns to stimulate even more natural movement. Our objective: to eliminate all trimming.

(Below) Apollo's LH hoof taken at the same time as the LF above. Arrow points to the medial toe wall (MT) , which shares its active support duties with both heel buttresses. The darkness of the hoof here and above reflects both pigmentation and dirt literally ground into the outermost epidermal structures. Dirt also absorbs into the protective perioplic horn extruded over the coronary band, and is carried down the outer wall as the hoof grows. A quick measurement with the HMR reveals a toe length just under 3 in (< 7.6 cm). Because there are no fissures or exfoliating solar plates in the solar dome, we are assured that we are looking at the HSP. That's good, because these hooves are so hard, including the sole which cannot be penetrated with a hoof knife, we would just be dulling steel. I will check Apollo's hooves in another month to see if any trimming is needed at that point in time.

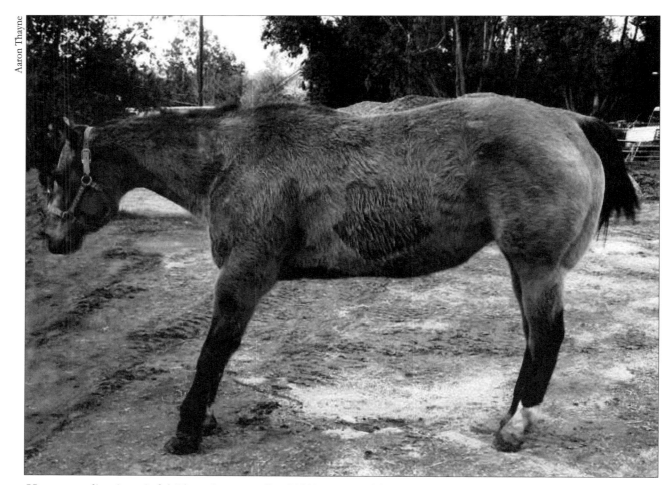

Horse standing in painful "founder stance" – 100% preventable!

Trimming the Laminitic Hoof

The NHC definition of laminitis is *separation of the hoof from the horse due to metabolic distress.* Known laminitis triggers include diets rich in sugars (e.g., feeds with molasses and beet pulp, and green grass or legume pastures), vaccinations, and chemical wormers. Any substance put into the horse that unbalances his intestinal bacteria puts him at risk of laminitis. Conventionally, laminitis is defined as inflammation of the laminae of the hoof, or failure of the lamellar attachment mechanism of the hoof. In my opinion, these definitions are too limited as they do not address causality. Moreover, inflammation clearly is not limited only to the dermal lamina as those definitions suggest, rather the entire dermis of the hoof — if not of the whole horse — is under inflammatory duress. The specter of the hoof falling off the horse gets peoples' attention, however, and, the fact is, that's what's happening. The pathophysiology of laminitis is complex, and I recommend strongly that it be approached from the standpoint of holistic preventive care. If this is ignored, the natural trim will in large measure be ineffective. What is really at work is that the horse's digestive system is upset, and it is expressing itself through symptoms in the horse's feet. Why and how this occurs is something I've written about for horse owners in another book, *Founder: Prevention and Cure the Natural Way*, and should be read in conjunction with these trimming guidelines.

Symptoms of what is actually laminitis occurring are often referred to by other colloquial names, including "seedy toe", "stretched white line", "white line disease (WLD)", and "founder". Founder is actually a more advanced case of laminitis wherein the bottommost bone in the hoof (P3) tips downward towards the sole, typically referred to as "P3-Rotation". Even more advanced cases than founder can happen: *P3 Penetration* occurs when the tip of the coffin bone appears through the bottom of the sole; *hoof slough* is the most extreme case of laminitis, as the hoof detaches completely from the horse. All extremes of laminitis are potentially life-threatening, and, once more, prevention is the best course of action.

According to Pollit, laminitis appears to be caused by an explosive and harmful proliferation of specialized enzymes[1] that are also involved with the healthy lamellar attachment mechanism (LAM). These enzymes are responsible for normal and healthy detachment of the hoof wall as it grows down from the coronary band (page 141); other mechanisms are at

---

[1]Called *matrix metalloproteinase* (MMP). See "Equine Laminitis", (AAEP presentation, 2003) Australian Laminitis Research Unit, Queensland University: Christopher C. Pollitt, BVSc, PhD; Myat Kyaw-Tanner, BSc, PhD; Kathryn R. French, BSc, PhD; Andrew W. van Eps, BVSc; Joan K. Hendrikz, BSc; Mousa Daradka, DVM, PhD

work simultaneously to restore the attachment. When this bonding mechanism fails, due to excessive enzymatic degradation (called *proteolysis*, meaning destruction of protein), the hoof begins to detach and grow forward and away from the horse, forming what is called a *slipper toe*. Pollit has shown that a cascade of highly complex metabolic failures actually precede the laminitic episode, beginning in the horse's digestive system. I concur, and, accordingly, treat laminitis as an immune system failure wrought by unnatural diets, or any substance fed to or injected into the horse, and which disrupts normal digestive bacterial balances and activity. Stress has been implicated to play a catalytic role as well. Laminitis can occur violently all at once, *acute laminitis*; subtly, with symptoms such as the white line widening or perfusing with blood, and the horse showing "on-off" again foot sensitivity, *subclinical laminitis*; or perpetually, *chronic laminitis*.

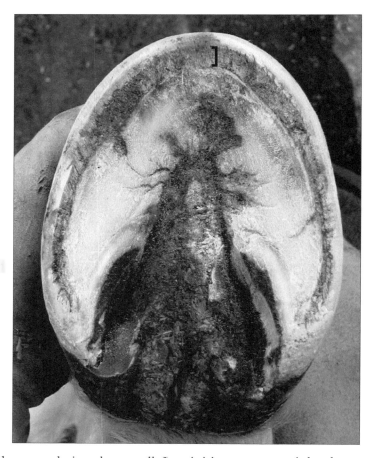

(*Across*) Bracket frames pathological elongation ("stretching") of white line as a result of laminitis.

The symptoms and consequences of laminitis may include one or all of the following:

- Pain and heat in the feet (front and/or hind).
- A palpable digital pulse above the medial and lateral cartilages (above the coronary band on both sides of the hoof).
- Inability to stand comfortably.
- Tendency to shift body weight either to the back of the front feet or towards the hind feet altogether, called the "founder stance" (page 194).
- Frequent laying down and standing up without relief from pain.
- Emergence of "lamellar stress rings" descending below the coronary band.
- Elongation of white line (*above*, "stretched white line").
- Palliative relief when standing the horse in cool or cold water.
- Hoof slough (the capsules disengages from the foot).
- Death.

Prevention is simple, inexpensive, and requires minimal or no veterinary intervention. By faithfully adhering to the following NHC recommendations, horses will be essentially "founder proof". Laminitis is epidemic around the world, however, and nothing to take lightly.

What to do if laminitis strikes!

All stages of laminitis should be treated as an emergency. First, the equine veterinarian should be consulted for a diagnosis to confirm the attack; in addition, he or she will probably be needed to provide pain medication. My recommendation is that a competent NHC practitioner should be present for this visit.

NHC principles and practices do not permit shoeing of any kind (nail or glue-on); surgical manipulation of the hoof capsule, tendons, or nerves; pharmaceutical manipulation of the vascular or digestive systems; or any trimming method except the "natural trim". If any of these procedures are advised by the vet (or anyone), the NHC practitioner should advocate to the contrary, encouraging the horse's owner to decline. Some vets and farriers will deploy the notorious "hoof tester" (*right*), a mechanical device that grips and squeezes the hoof to pinpoint pain within the hoof capsule. This procedure is unnecessary and could cause damage to the digit, dermis and capsule, resulting in permanent lameness of the horse. Beware!

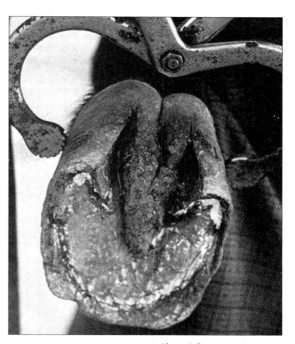

(*Above*) The notorious "hoof tester" at work. Let's get these medieval torture devices banned. Harmful, unnecessary, barbaric! The alternative? NHC!

[Photo credit: Leslie Emery]

The NHC practitioner may concur with the vet's recommendation to use a temporary NSAID (non-steroidal anti-inflammatory drug, such as "bute") to relieve pain. Beyond this -- and the diagnosis -- the vet's role in the care of the horse's feet should be limited.

In those instances where the vet is supportive of NHC practices, healing can begin immediately. First, and immediately so, the horse must undergo detoxification to bring the laminitic attack (proteolysis) under control; simultaneously, the laminitis trigger (cause) must be identified and removed. Both steps must occur together, or treatment is ineffectual. The NHC practitioner should help the horse's owner engage the following steps:

- Remove horse from pasture immediately to a dry lot or other safe environment.

- Stand horse in cold water, or run hose over lowers legs and hooves, or wrap all four feet in blue ice (acute attack). Pollitt has shown that destructive enzymes become sluggish and less operative when hooves are subjected to external cooling approaching freezing.[1]

- Have vet prescribe & administer proper dosage of an unsweetened NSAID.

[1]"Equine Laminitis: Cryotherapy reduces the severity of lesions evaluated 2 days after experimental induction with Ogliofructose." A.W. Van Eps and C.C. Pollitt, Australian Equine Laminitis Research Unit, School of Veterinary Science, Faculty of Natural Resources Agriculture and Veterinary Science, The University of 8 Queensland, St. Lucia, QLD 4072, Australia

- Begin naturalizing the diet immediately, even as horse is standing in cold water, as only the diet will alter the bacterial imbalances triggering the laminitic attack. It is advisable to cease feeding all supplements, treats, legume and grain hays.

- Do not force the horse to move, but do provide opportunity for free-choice movement.

- If the horse is in shoes, do not remove them until pain has sufficiently subsided that the horse can lift his feet for trimming after 3-7 days; the previous steps are of higher priority.

- If there is hoof slough, a vet should be involved as this constitutes a medical emergency. Confine the horse to a stall or other close quarters to prevent movement. Provide soft bedding to minimize dislocation of the coffin bone joint or fracture of the digit.[1] Detoxification is of paramount importance if the foot's basement membrane is to proliferate stable secondary epidermal lamella (SEL). *Feed the animal as he lay on the ground.* In lesser severe laminitic events, SEL disorganization forms the lamellar wedge, by means which the foot retains a viable connection to the inner hoof wall PEL). In slough, the best one can hope for is desiccation of the SEL across the face of P3, followed by reattachment of descending new growth to the PEL, with parallel healing occurring across the inner solar dome epidermal substrate. As soon as confirmed stable solar plates emerge, the horse will be able — and should be facilitated — to walk. This can happen in days. Hoof boots are suggested for exercise periods only, removed otherwise. NHC practitioners in the field report success following this model for recovery. Veterinary protocol should be to control wound sepsis and pain, or euthanasia if the owner makes the call.

As the laminitic episode begins to abate, the AANHCP practitioner should map out a rehabilitation and prevention program with the owner.[1] The owner should also be alerted to the possibility that as descending stress rings approach ground level, concussional forces may cleave segments of the hoof wall from the capsule along the peripheral axis of a particularly deep ring (*facing page*). These sorts of fractures should not be debilitating to the horse, as a dessicated stratum of secondary epidermal lamina will have been laid by the dermis underneath. Raveled strips of cleaved wall should be nippered off by the trimmer (or vet), and the horse booted for exercise in hand or riding if the amount of hoof wall lost is significant. Recovery time can be calculated by using the *hgc* rate of ¼ in. (1 cm)/month once the final measurement for H°TL has been determined.[2]

---

[1] *Founder* (Jackson), pp. 150-151.
[2] Ibid., "*hgc:* Hoof Growth Cycle", fn., p. 102.

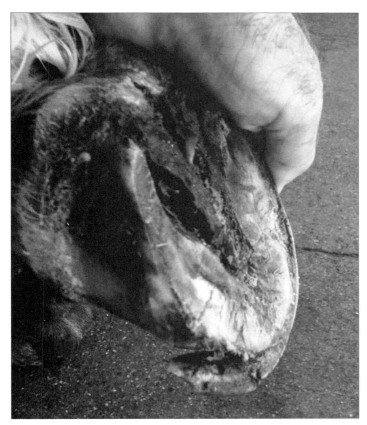

Stress rings emanate below the coronary band in the hoof wall, descending to the ground over a single *hgc* (hoof growth cycle[1]), approximately 9 months. They are caused by unnatural things we put into the horse (feeds, high NSC grasses, vaccinations, medications, chemicals), and are considered symptoms of sub-clinical, clinical, and chronic laminitis. Sometimes the rings form grooves that strike deep into the hoof wall, imperiling hoof integrity, particularly when they approach ground-bearing level such as the hoof above. In this case, the hoof had a series of stress rings arrive soon after a battery of pharmaceuticals following an injury requiring stitches.

(*Above, left*) A series of stress rings circumscribe the hoof wall, meaning horse owner management issues have not been resolved over many months.

(*Above, right*) The lower stress ring has reached the ground at the quarter, and shear forces strike deep into the inner hoof wall connection to the SEL.

(*Below*) Clear few of hoof wall separation, which must be clipped off by the practitioner. New wall will descend to take its place over several months; however, other descending stress rings have yet to be negotiated. Shoeing/nailing would only weaken the already compromised hoof wall; better management practices provide the correct path to prevent further damage.

[Photo credit: Erica Hopper]

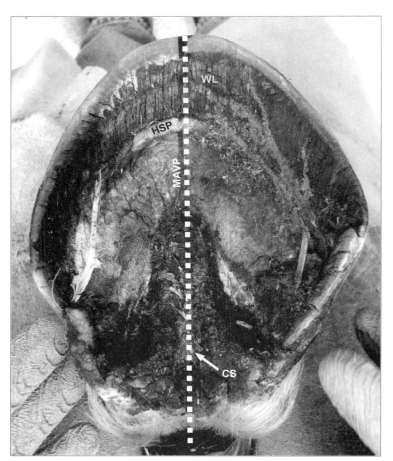

Laminitis: Pre-trim evaluation.

The trimming instructions that follow for laminitis apply to all hoof conformations deformed by this disease. The "key" to success lies in scrupulously accurate measuring, particularly H°TL. [All photos in this series by Jill Willis]

(Above) This is a left hind (cadaver) hoof. The horse had suffered from laminitis, eventually succumbing for the lack of NHC. The hoof is severely overgrown but showing surprisingly good structure and hind shape. This will become apparent later to the uninitiated eye. The distention of the white line evidences the disease's long term chronicity. After surveying the hoof in this profile, I've marked the MAVP with a Sharpie, from which I will extend the MATW in the next step.

(Below) Another view to the bottom of the hoof. Here one can appreciate the overgrown hoof wall protruding far above the hard sole plane (HSP) — and the work that lies ahead!

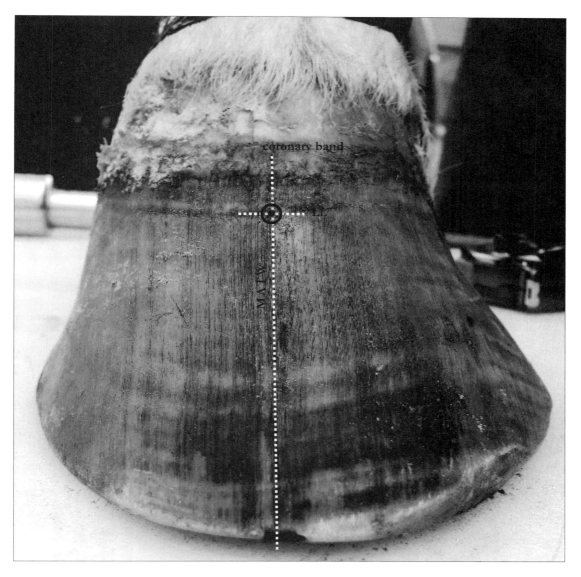

Laminitis: Pre-trim evaluation (cont'd).

    (Above) The MAVP drawn across the bottom of the foot is now extended up the face of the toe wall to the coronary band following the "grain" (horn tubules) of outer wall, delineating the MATW. Next I palpate this soft tissue band (located just below the hairline), feeling for the top edge of the toe wall. From here, I measure 1 cm (~¼ inch) down the MATW and draw a second horizontal line, the "limit line" (LL). The bull's-eye is positioned at their intersection.

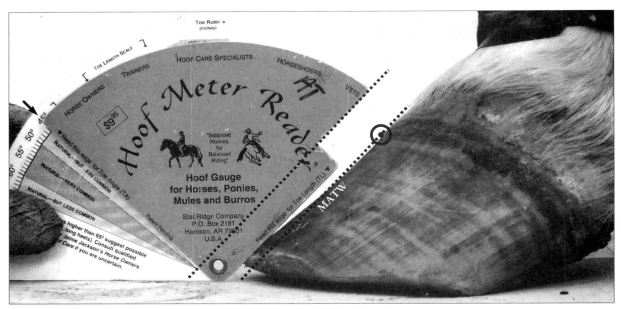

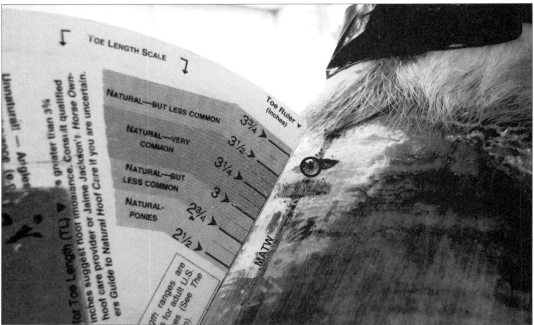

Laminitis: Pre-trim evaluation (cont'd).

This is a very important step in the natural trim using the Hoof Meter Reader, which enables the NHC practitioner to cross-link measurements for the domesticated hoof with the wild hoof.

(*Above*) The angle dial of the HMR is set parallel to the MPTW over the MATW. H° is measured at 46°. The noticeable "bend" in the toe wall near its end is called "flare" and is due to unnatural growth patterns caused by laminitis and unnatural hoof care. Over successive trimming sessions, flare can usually be entirely removed; however, it is too early in this process to know if all of it can be trimmed away in this initial trim. Note that the dashed line of the MATW is not a cut-line, but is simply included to illustrate how H° is gauged.

(*Below*) The HMR is set to the bull's-eye and H°TL is measured at just over 3¾ in. (9.7 cm). The scale indicates that this length is nearly off the "natural" grid. Our previous examination of the hoof suggested strongly that H°TL will require considerable shortening, and the HMR confirms this.

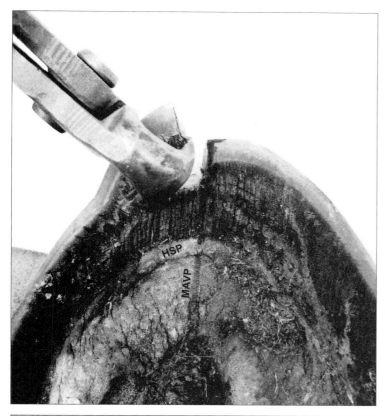

Laminitis: Shorten hoof wall to the hard sole plane (HSP).

The task immediately ahead is to lower the protruding hoof wall down to the visible HSP. Once there, the sole can be "teased" with the nippers to see if it is receptive to exfoliation. If so, then the door may be open to another run at lowering the hoof wall.

(Above) I'll begin at the MAVP and work back in both directions to the heels. As a farrier, I was taught to start at one heel, and then trim all the way around to the opposing heel. This is a practice I've abandoned as an NHC practitioner. The principle reason lies in over-trimming the heels, which are needed to sustain H° and also the capsule's mediolateral balance. Experience has shown me it less risky if one first lowers the toe wall to the HSP, then lowers and adjusts heel height as needed. Over-trimming the heels can also make them passive to the quarters — a violation of the wild horse model and can cause pathological changes in the capsule.

Note also that the protruding hoof wall is too long to trim in one run without obstructing the jaws of the nipper. Instead, I began half way down the MAVP and work my way back from there to the outside (lateral) heel.

(Below) Sufficient heel length has been left on the outside (lateral) heel, and I've nearly reached the inside (medial) heel after first returning to the MAVP. Looking ahead, I see a bit of work to do on the frog; but finding that it isn't in the way of the nipper at this stage, I will continue lowering the hoof wall forward of the heels until I reach the HSP.

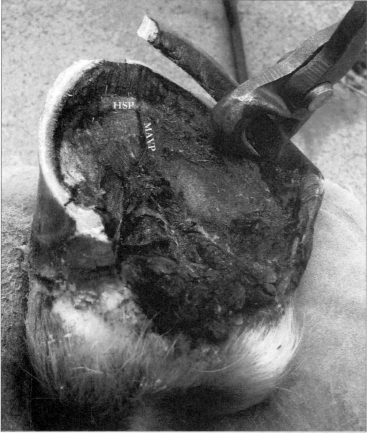

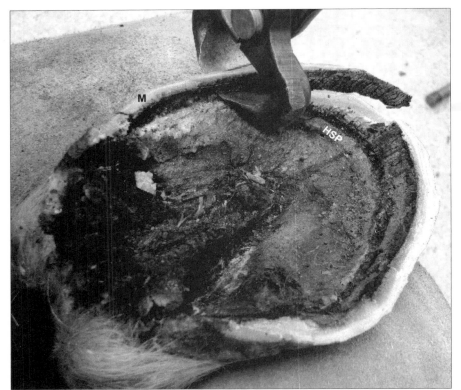

Laminitis: Shorten hoof wall to the hard sole plane (cont'd).

(Left) I've returned to the MATW and initiated the second nipper run down the inside (medial) wall (M). I will taper the cut-line to come out of the hoof wall in advance of the heel, which I will fine tune later.

(Below) This is an interesting view as I approach the HSP. The nipper cut-line is smooth and within several millimeters (~⅛ in.) of the HSP. The arrow points to a furrow of deformed white line, forming a visible gap between the sole and the hoof wall. This calls to attention the 4th Guiding Principle ("Ignore all pathology"): obsessive personality types with hypochondriacal tendencies will immediately eye this gap and feel the lure to dig into it and open he door to sepsis, infection, and chronic abscessing. Control this propensity by adhering to the principle of relative concavity and trim only to the axis of the HSP.

Laminitis: Shorten hoof wall to the hard sole plane (cont'd)

The second trim run around the hoof wall is now complete. The question before me is whether I have reached the HSP or a crust of "false sole". The solution is two-fold:

(Above) A quick check of the HMR reveals H°TL = 3⅛ in. (8 cm) — short and very central in the data range for "natural". There should be little to no excess sole to be removed. Note the shadowy area below the fore toe wall and quarter — a strong indicator of passive wear area in the finished hoof.

(Below) A light scraping of the sole near the toe with the hoof knife reveals little excess growth to remove. However, I suspect the sole in the vicinity of the heels is crusted with excessive growth. I'll make a determination in the next step.

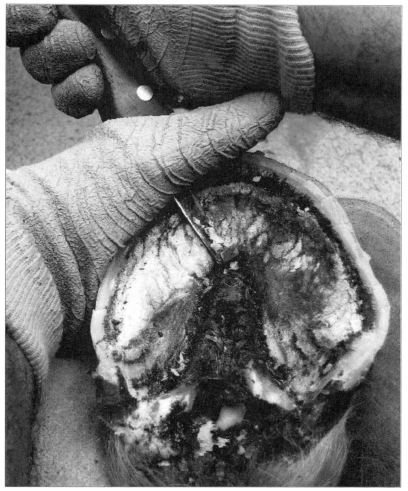

Laminitis: Shorten hoof wall to the hard sole plane cont'd).

(*Above, below*) To find out if sole is ready to go, I use a technique called "nipper dragging" — bracing one blade of the nipper against the outer wall, and carefully dragging loose sole away with the other. See *Sidebar* discussion about removing sole on the facing page. My suspicions are correct, excess sole abounds, and I will drag both heels to clear the way for lowering the heels.

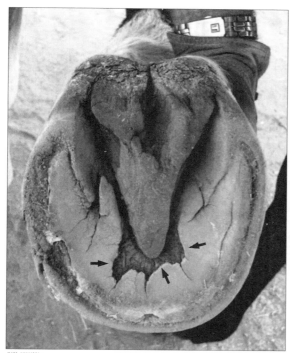

Jill Willis

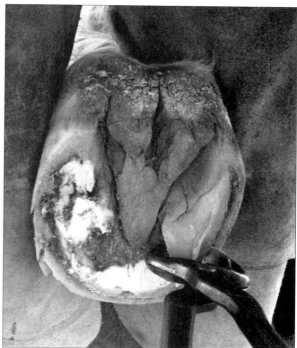

Jill Willis

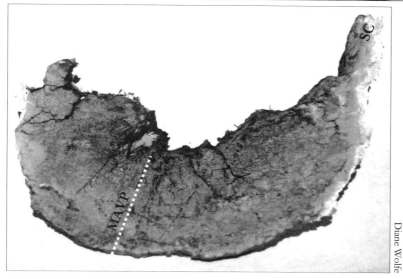

Diane Wolfe

Sidebar: About removing "solar plates".

   The sole is extruded by its dermis into thin laminated plates. When the hoof becomes over-grown from insufficient wear, these "solar plates" can be teased and tugged loose from one another as they approach ground level. This is done efficiently by means of "nipper dragging":

   (*Top, left*) The sole of this LF hoof is replete with solar plates ready to go. Arrows are aimed at points of entry I've targeted.

   (*Top, right*) I've removed most of the plates to the lateral side of the hoof. This is done by lightly lifting the edge of a plate, then slipping one nipper blade under it, and then either tugging or cutting it loose, or some combination.

   (*Below*) A "mega-plate" I removed from the paired RF hoof. Two navigational landmarks are denoted to give bearing: MATW and SC (seat-of-corn).

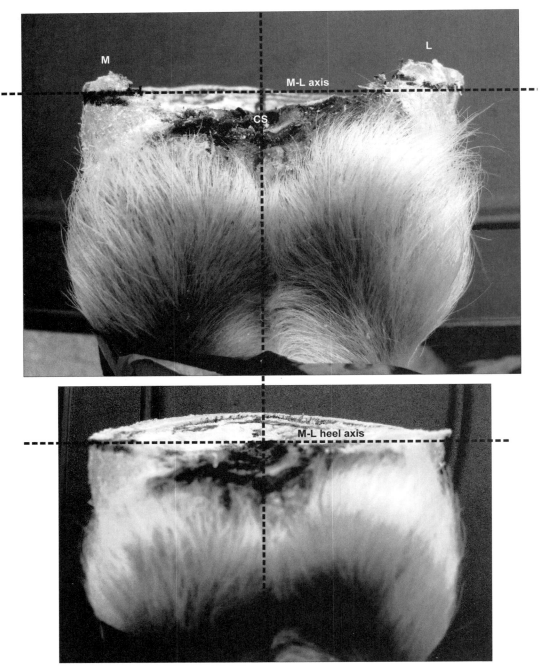

Laminitis: Lower and balance the heels.

Nipper dragging in the previous step has exposed the heels, preparing them to be lowered and balanced through precision trimming. Minor adjustments are done with the rasp, major with the nippers.

(Above, top) The hoof is sighted from behind, and the heels are aligned at 90° to the centerline (MAVP) drawn through the central frog sulcus (CS) in Step 1. When this is done, the heels are readily evaluated for reduction and balance.

(Below) Both heels are lowered evenly across the medial (M) to lateral (L) wall axis. When this is done, the angle-of-growth for the toe wall will be consistent with the wild horse model.

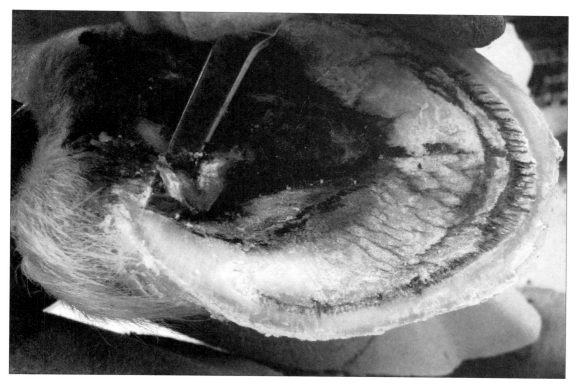

Laminitis: Trim the frog.

I've mentioned very little of the frog up to this point. Experience has taught me to leave it to natural wear as much as possible, and minimize trimming. Much of its mass is needed for the protection of its sensitive growth corium (dermis) and the digital cushion above it. Of all the hoof's weight-bearing structures, the frog is the most passive in the dome, has the highest moisture content, and is the easiest to trim away due to its high water-to-epidermis ratio. Lacking the extensive protective armor of the hoof wall and sole, the frog is more vulnerable to concussional trauma. Its relatively dense, tough, and apparent minimal presence in the wild horse foot during the summer months is somewhat of an illusion. In fact, it swells considerably during the rain and snow times of the year; hence, the mass is always there, but is simply desiccated to a fraction of its winter size during the more arid times of the year. There is a tendency of trimmers to thin down the frog to "neatify" it and prevent thrush. To the extent that this causes hypersensitivity, I think it is better to leave enough mass to fill the space between the heels, providing it does not exceed the heels in length. An exception to this rule would be the hoof where the heels have been over-trimmed, leaving a prolapsed frog. In this instance, the frog is left untrimmed and the heels allowed to grow until they are actively supporting the back of the hoof and the frog has retreated into its passive niche in the dome.

(Above) I've deployed the hoof knife to shave off clearly excessive, if not necrotic and infected tissue, a condition known as *thrush*. In life, I would simply shear the infected frog back until just passive to the heels (as described above), drench it with an anti-fungal medication, and stop — no matter how "raggedy" the rest of it looks. From there on, a reasonably natural diet and natural boarding conditions (such as Paddock Paradise) in conjunction with the natural trim are needed to complete the healing process.

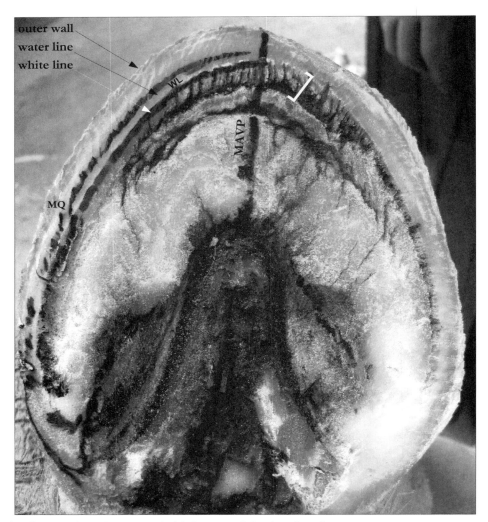

outer wall
water line
white line
WL
MAVP
MQ

Laminitis: Determine the natural thickness of the hoof wall

(Above) The natural thickness (width) of the hoof wall is measured from the outside of the white line to the outer wall. In spite of the white line's pathological width (white bracket), the hoof wall here is uniformly wide from heel to heel — characteristic of the naturally shaped hoof. Surprisingly, this is not uncommon in laminitic hooves, in spite of the pathologically elongated white line. Navigational landmarks: MQ = medial quarter; MAVP; WL = water line.

(Facing page, top) The previous step suggested strongly that the hoof wall is at its approximate natural thickness. The hoof is now taken upon the hoof stand and evaluated again in a new profile. Straight-line growth, the absence of any significant DTA, and only minor flare (marked by the arrow) near the tip of the toe wall along the MATW, provides us with credible confirmation that we are looking at the natural thickness of the hoof wall. The preponderance of flare we witnessed at the outset (page 200) was removed when the hoof wall was shortened to the HSP.

(Facing page, below) The entire outer wall is given a light filing over to simulate natural wear and cut off communication to grow in a pathological direction.

Note: Had there been obvious variation in the natural thickness of the hoof wall (i.e., flare), NHC practitioners sometimes use a vertical cut to establish the "average" peripheral boundary of the hoof wall's natural thickness. This is explained in the *Overleaf.*

~Laminitis trim discussion continued on page 214~

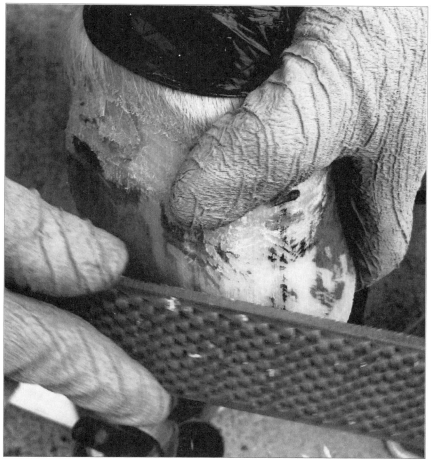

(Sidebar) *Overleaf*
Removing excess
growth from the
outer hoof wall.
[Photos in series from
*AANHCP Official Trim
Guidelines*, J. Jackson]

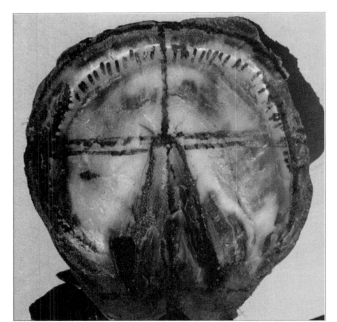

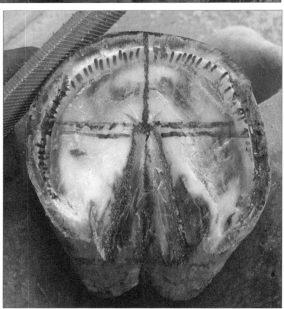

Sidebar: Measure & Cut Natural Thickness of Hoof Wall

(*Above, left*) With a Sharpie, or other indelible pen, mark the white line. Estimate the natural thickness of the hoof wall by using the quarters and toe wall as reference points. Measure from outside the white line in all cases, including laminitic capsules. Then, with Sharpie once more, draw a second line all around the entire hoof wall using your estimate of its natural thickness.

(*Above, right; below, left*) Using the nippers for a clean finish, and following the outer line just drawn, cut the hoof wall straight down at 90° to the hoof's volar profile.

(*Below, right*)) With the fine side of the rasp, smooth and round off the nipper cut line. The rasp edge should also be kept at 90° to the hoof's volar profile.

(*continued on facing page*)

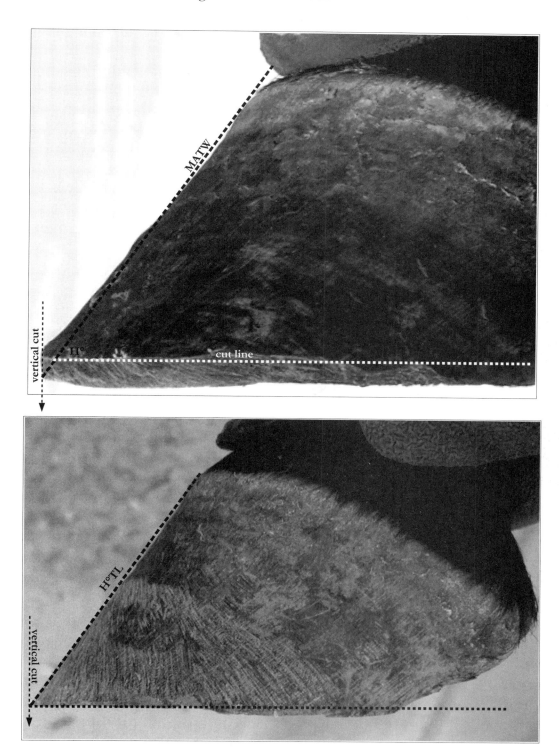

Sidebar: Measure & Cut Natural Thickness of Hoof Wall (cont'd from facing page).

(*Above*) Navigational landmarks grid the outer wall. Hoof wall laying outside the intersection of the vertical cut line and the projected MATW constitutes excess growth and can be rasped away.

(*Below*) Excess growth removed to natural thickness of the hoof wall. H°TL has been established and hoof wall is ready for mustang roll.

white line
water line
outer wall

sole

MH

MAVP

white line
water line
outer wall

x

y

Laminitis: Cut the "mustang roll" (cont'd from p. 200).

The principal objective of this step is to confirm an active water line relative to the white line, sole, and a well-rounded outer wall ("mustang roll"). The water line is the most distal structure in the naturally shaped hoof.

(Above, below) Trimming commences at the intersection of the toe wall with the MAVP and continues alternately back to each heel. The nipper blades cut at 45° to 50° degrees to the plane of the sole to bevel the wall as the first step in creating the mustang roll. Both edges of the cut line along the outer wall (*x* and *y*) will be somewhat acute and jagged. It is not time well-spent to make these cuts "elegant"; this will be done later with the Radius Rasp and Bow Sander-Buffer.

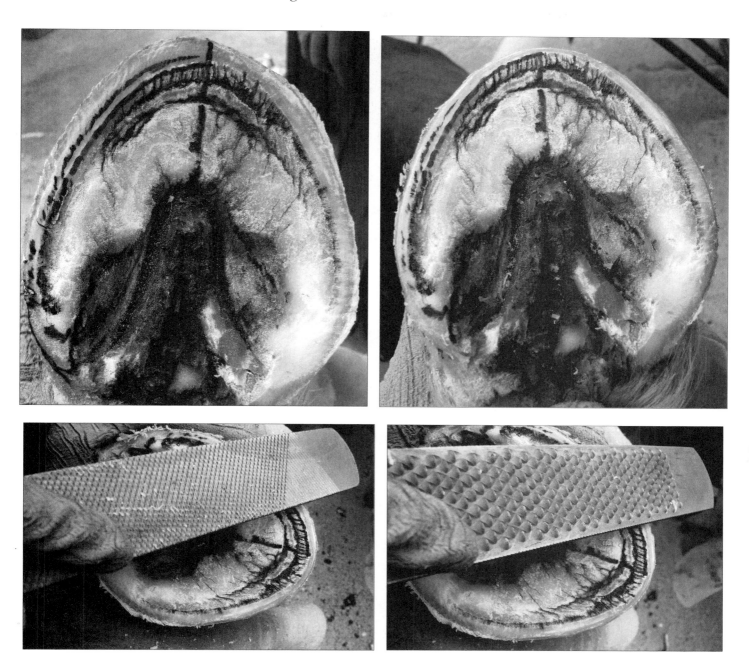

Laminitis: Cut the "mustang roll" (cont'd).

(Above, left/right) On the left is the view before the wall was reduced to its natural thickness and the mustang roll applied. On the right is the same view after mustang roll was applied. This is the view the master practitioner learns to see in their mind's eye before trimming commences, and then so trims straightaway to the final destination without marking the capsule with these navigational landmarks. However, the HMR is consistently deployed to pinpoint (or estimate) H° and measure H°TL.

(Below, left/right) The nipper cuts of the mustang roll are next smoothed out with the rasp: first with the coarse side *(left)* then with the fine side *(right)*.

Laminitis: Fine finish the "mustang roll".

We're almost done. On a hoof this overgrown, I might spend 3 to 5 minutes to reach this point in the process.

(Above) This is an important view for the NHC practitioner. The hoof is brought back up to the grip head of the hoof stand, rasped and filed to complete the mustang roll and fine finish the outer wall for wall symmetry (front) and asymmetry (hind). Notice that my hand is laid over the coronary band to protect it in case of a mishap with the rasp. At the same time, I am holding the body of the rasp with my hand rather than the handle — this gives be better control. Rasp chisels and the outer edge of the hoof wall (before the roll is finished) are both sharp. Wear gloves!

(Facing page, above) At the time this cadaver was trimmed, the Bow Sander-Buffer (as shown with Apollo) had not yet been invented. It has completely replaced hand held sandpaper as shown here. See Appendix: "Tools & Equipment".

(Facing page, below Bird's eye view of the finished outer wall, revealing exemplary natural hind hoof asymmetry across the centerline: the lateral side (L) of the hoof is wider than its medial side (M) at any point along the MATW.

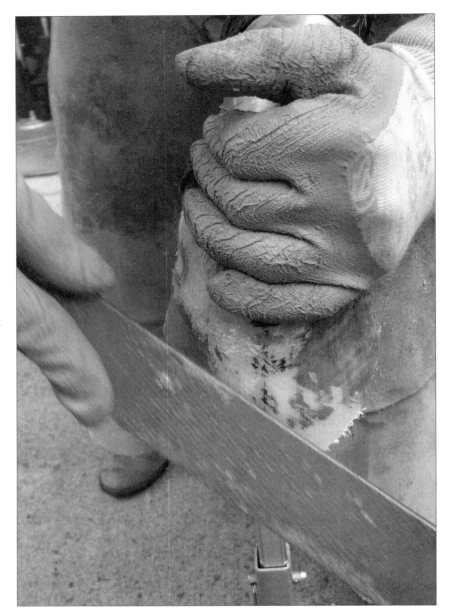

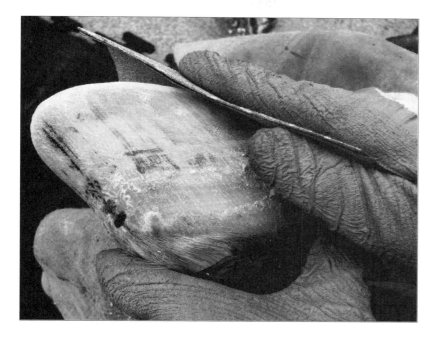

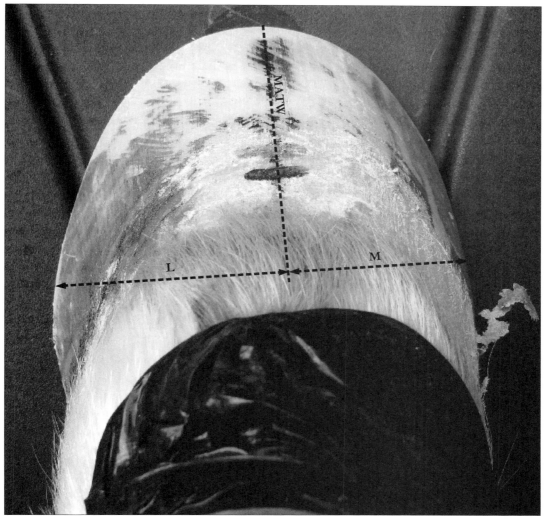

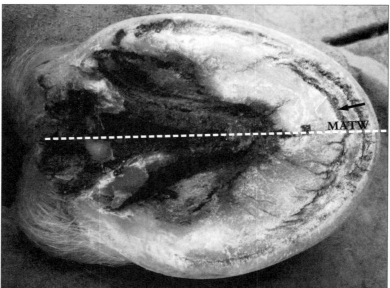

Laminitis: Finish bottom of hoof

With the hoof wall finished, I will turn my attentions to the bottom of the hoof one last time.

(Above) There's not much to do, but I'm using the Round Rasp to lightly smooth out the con-caved sole here and there. The reason for doing this is to promote more natural solar growth patterns — just like I did with the hoof wall to promote straight-line growth over the MATW. Sole rasping should always be minimal, however, and never tantamount to gouging and/or pene-trating the HSP.

(Below) The bottom of the hoof finished. Note small fissures here and there in the solar dome and the large crack pointed to by the arrow. These are all early indicators of solar plates that will be taken in future trim sessions when they are ready to shed — like the bark of a tree. All my measurements fall within the HMR data ranges for *natural,* so I see no need to penetrate further into the capsule. Time is on my side, and the outcome of this trim in terms of size, shape, and proportion, support this decision.

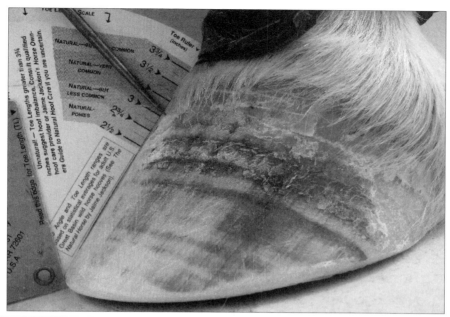

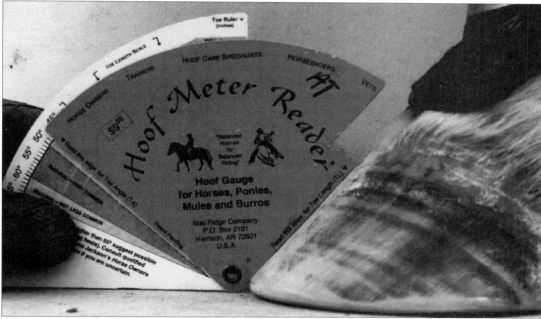

Laminitis: Post-trim evaluation

(Above) A quick check of the HMR reveals a toe length of just over 3 in (7.7 cm); that's down ¾ in. (1.9 cm) from 3¾ in. (9.7 cm), a 20 per cent reduction in toe length. Said another way, at ¾ in. (2 cm) of excess growth, there was a 25 percent increase in toe length beyond the hoof's natural toe length. By natural trim standards, that's way too much. NHC advocates recommend that toe lengths not exceed 8 percent, approximately ¼ in. (1 cm) of their natural toe length — measured over the MATW or MPTW (if DTA is present).

(Below) H° is gauged over the MATW at 48 degrees, a two degree angle elevation from when we started. *I did not sustain the intake measurement for H° because the hoof had not previously been trimmed to our guidelines, moreover, we do not want to maintain unnatural angles.* Had this horse lived, this angle would no doubt continue to increase over time as growth angles across the capsule (front to back) self-correct under the influence of the natural trim and allied NHC holistic practices. Under such a regimen, the toe angle would eventually stabilize and cease to change, providing the laminitis causality is checked.

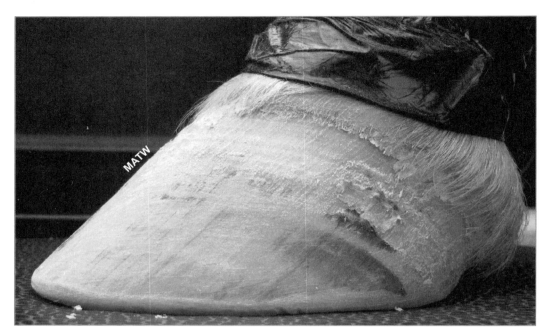

Laminitis: Post-trim evaluation

What strikes NHC practitioners like myself is how readily hooves suffering from such diseases as laminitis transform into very nice looking hooves when trimmed to the natural trim guidelines. This specimen is not an exception. There's little doubt the horse would have survived to walk and run on sound, healthy and handsome feet if NHC intervention had been brought to bear.

(Above) Side view of the finished hoof shows the outer wall growing down "straight as an arrow" along the MATW. There's not a split anywhere in the outer wall, and the mustang roll, although modest, is exemplary by NHC standards. Compare with the view at the outset on page 123.

§

(Facing page) The two images here are worth discussing as they speak to every hoof's predisposition to form active and passive wear in the hoof wall if given a chance, This includes those suffering from the worst deformities. In fact, when I trim any hoof I am on the lookout for active and passive wear, encouraging them at each successive trim session. This, in contrast to my earliest work as a farrier, whose hallmark of technical expertise is to produce a hoof wall as flat as the horseshoe that will be nailed to it.

(Facing page, above) Consistent with the wild horse model (pp. 50-51), this left hind hoof shows active wear over both heels and the medial toe wall. I've pushed the HMR against the active toe pillar, which is less than a ¼ in (1 cm) wide along the supporting water line base.

(Facing page, below) From this forward support pillar on back, there is no active wall support until the heel-buttresses are reached. The HMR could be passed under the hoof from one passive quarter to the other, without making contact.

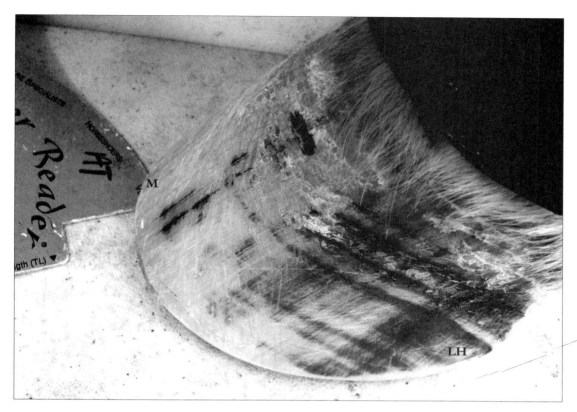

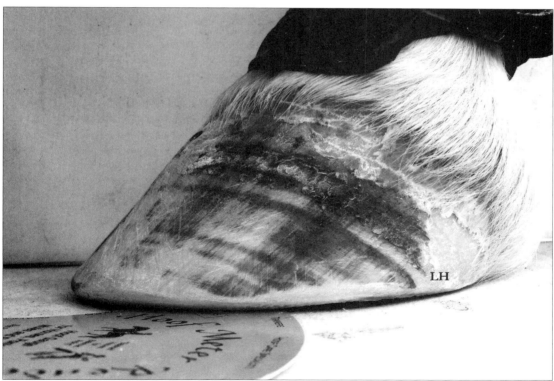

Hoof with apparent "dropped sole". But is it really?

CHAPTER 10

Trimming the Laminitic Hoof
with "Dropped" Sole

I've added this additional set of trimming instructions for a laminitic hoof with a "dropped sole" for two reasons. First, these instructions counter current conventional approaches to trimming and shoeing hooves with extreme P3 rotation with the heart bar shoe, which is truly unnecessary, counterproductive, and harmful, in my opinion. And, second, because it also counters a trend among some barefooters to trim hooves that prevents peripheral loading — which is a direct violation of nature's model. This particular cadaver specimen was trimmed this way (*facing page*), and it is clear from the NHC perspective that the horse's problems with laminitis were only compounded by the trim method. It is a supreme irony that the objective of the farrier, to stabilize P3 by bracing the descending sole (and frog) by mechanical means (the heart bar shoe), is diametrically opposite to the barefooter, who wishes to build in sole that the horse would stand on it to the exclusion of the hoof wall! In either case, the hoof wall is viewed as either useless or an obstacle to their methods. And both, as I explained in Chapter 7 (Form and Function), premise their respective positions with the same hoof mechanism model. I would ask, why would nature even create a hoof wall if it is such an obstacle to optimal hoof form and function under any circumstance?

Our objective in trimming such a hoof will be identical to trimming any other hoof, and, always, always, with the implicit understanding that it must be accompanied by the allied holistic care practices of NHC. Using H°, H°TL, and other familiar natural trim navigational landmarks, we will endeavor to see how much sole (or solar plates, page 207) we can get out of the solar dome without compromising capsule integrity or causing any hypersensitivity. This, and other facets of the natural trim, will trigger the foot's coria to respond in concert with the cycle of hoof form and function. Over time, the compacted sole will release its plates as its corium generates healthy replacement epidermis. No heart bar shoe is needed to support anything, and trimming away the hoof wall to carry the load is just as contraindicated. All photos in this series are by Jill Willis.

Laminitis with dropped sole: Pre-trim evaluation.

This is our starting point, and I'm ready to go in on the sole to set things in a healthy new direction.

(Above) A quick scan shows the hoof wall trimmed back, giving the horse no choice but to walk on a massive "sole pillar". The MAVP and MATW are gridded, and I've overlaid the bull's-eye. We're ready to measure and get going.

(Facing page, above) As I'm able to lay the HMR flat against the MATW, there is no apparent DTA that will require harmonizing later. One less thing to do! H° gauges at 44°, a tad off the low end of the natural angle range. Because there is no DTA, and because H° is so close to being on the natural grid, I won't reset the HMR to 54° to measure H°TL, but go with 44° instead with a cautious eye.

(Facing page, below) With the HMR's ruler set flush to the MATW, H°TL gauges at 3½ in. (8.9 cm) on the bull's-eye. Limit line is shown.

§

My thoughts at this point are that, with H°TL at 3½ in. (8.9 cm), it is very likely that we'll be able to safely remove some of that sole. We need to look closely at the sole with some nipper dragging to help us in this determination.

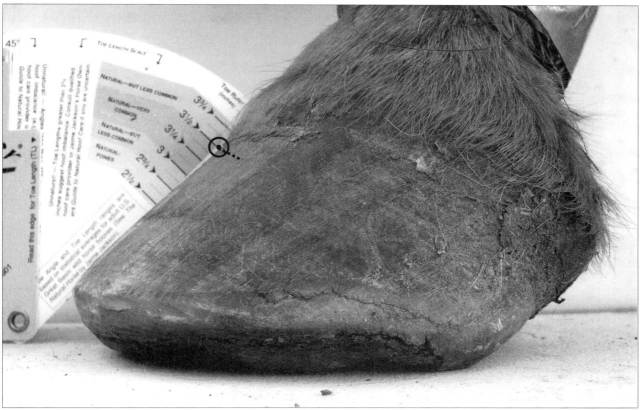

Laminitis with "dropped" sole: Pre-trim evaluation.

This will conclude the pre-trim evaluation and set the stage for precision trimming.

(Above) I was curious to see just how much of the hoof wall had been trimmed out of the way. Using a tape measure reveals the answer: 3½ in. (8.9 cm) - 2 in. = 1½ in. (3.8 cm). If we use 3¼ in. (8.3 cm) as an estimate of our final trim destination for H°TL, then 1¼ in. (3.2 cm) of toe wall was removed at the MATW. Arguably, there was little to no dropped sole to begin with in this case. But over an inch (2.54 cm) of toe wall had been trimmed away that should not have been touched. As we will see below, this hoof definitely suffered from laminitis, but its LAM was further compromised by the wall removal..

(Facing page, above and below) The astute eye of the NHC practitioner will avoid focusing on the obvious draw of the dropped sole and look for important clues to guide trimming. Two things are immediate apparent in both views and merit discussion. First, the heels are excessively long and run under (long bi-directional arrows). This is consistent with our mathematical deduction that H°TL is 3.5 in. (8.9 cm). Which means that to shorten the heels back to where they belong, much of the present sole would have to go just to bring HTL down to 3¼ in. (8.3 cm). Second, the long fissures in the solar dome on either side of the hoof (short arrows), are suggestive of either solar plates ready to go, or overgrown bars. Nipper dragging will lead the way to the answer.

§

The pre-evaluation is complete and I am confident of several things I didn't know before taking the vital measurements. First, most, if not all, of the dropped sole, can be attributed to the trimming method, not laminitis. And second, at 3¼ in./(8.3 cm)/*hgc,* 1¼ in./(3.2 cm) x 1 month/¼ in./(.6 cm) = approximately 5 months just to restore the hoof wall to its normal position in the volar dome's natural relative concavity. Therefore, this will be no quick fix, but we can at least get the ball rolling in the right direction.

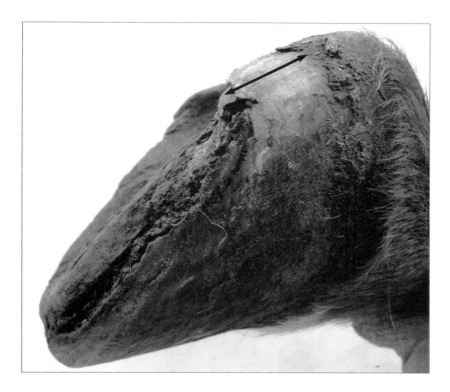

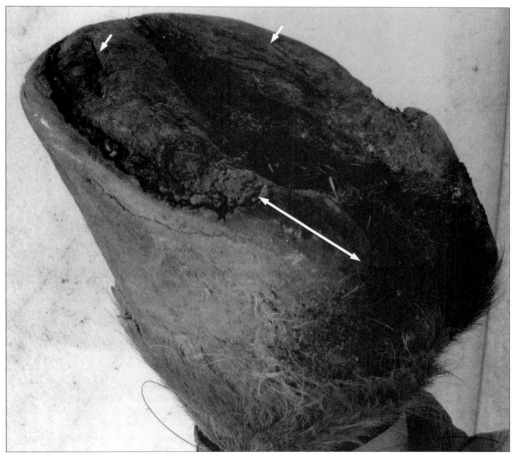

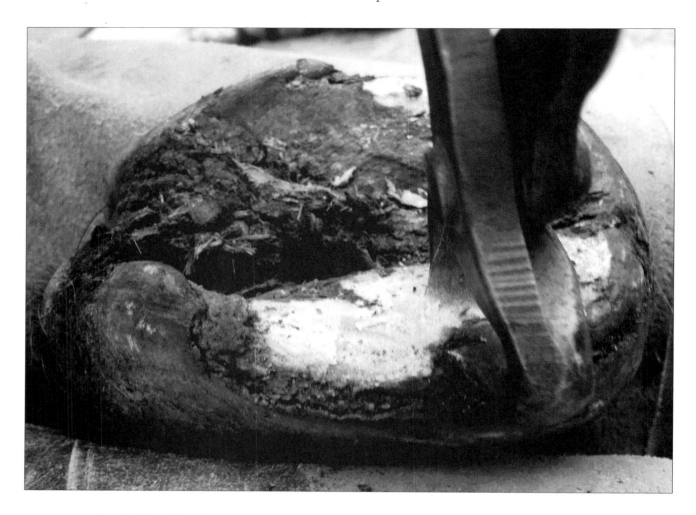

Laminitis with "dropped" sole: Shorten hoof wall and remove sole.

Armed with vital information garnered in the pre-trim evaluation, we are ready to trim.

(Above) Using the long fissures in the solar dome cited in the pre-trim evaluation, I've embedded the nipper and removed large chunks of compacted sole that readily come out with little resistance.

(Facing page, above) Half the solar dome has been cleared of compacted plates, and I've lowered one heel to half its original length. A perfectly natural solar domes is already beginning to make itself known. In addition to the MATW, the following gridlines are marked for orientation: x = base of heel where it emanates from its dermis (coronary corium); y = where I've lowered heel to; z = pre-trim length of heel.

(Facing page, below) Returning to the MATW, I've trimmed down the other side of the hoof. To get to this point, I've invested approximately 1 to 2 minutes of work. We'll be done in another minute once I bring the hoof to the grip head of the hoof stand.

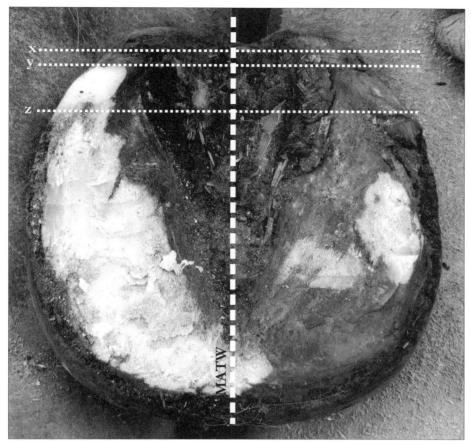

Laminitis with "dropped" sole: Finish sole.

Knowing in advance that there will be little to do around the outer wall, I will go right to fine finishing the volar dome.

(Above) As the solar dome was a bit uneven due to compaction and lack of natural wear for who knows how long, I've brought out the Round Rasp to smooth out its surfaces and to stimulate a more natural growth pattern.

(Facing page, above) I was pleased to find the medial wall (M) at the quarter nearly active in relation to its nearby sole. No so fortunate on the lateral side (L), where the arrow points to hoof wall far below.

(Facing page, below) This view, with bracket and arrow in place, also shows the gap of missing wall below the solar dome. But our focus, instead, is on the excellent structure of the sole itself. With the allied pillars of NHC in position, new wall will descend to its rightful berth adjacent, and just active, to this exemplary solar dome.

Laminitis with "dropped" sole: Finish outer wall and take final measurements.

We are done, and — in spite of the 5 month wait ahead for the wall to come down and take its position in the volar dome's relative concavity — it is quite the fine looking hoof.

(Above) I have taken the foot to the hoof stand and lightly rasped, filed, and sanded the outer wall for straight-line growth. Placing the hoof back on the ground, we find that the sole is still active to the hoof wall from quarter to quarter, but the solar dome is structurally in tact and will hold its own until the first segment of (medial) hoof wall (M) descends into position to relieve the sole. Both heels are active, however, and they will pick up some of the active support in the meantime. In another month the now still passive medial wall will become active and able to aid the sole with support duties until the remaining toe wall arrives.

(Facing page, above) H° has been sustained at 44°, in spite of the one inch (2.5 cm) or more of heel I removed. This testifies to the exponential relationship of heel length to toe length in relation to H°, even though no wall mass was present to shorten. Review page 105 to confirm your understanding of why more heel must be removed than toe/quarter to sustain H°.

(Facing page, below) Our estimate of H°TL = 3¼ in. (8.3 cm) was correct as the bull's-eye reveals here.

§

This concludes the trim — a four minute task at most after the pre-evaluation is completed.

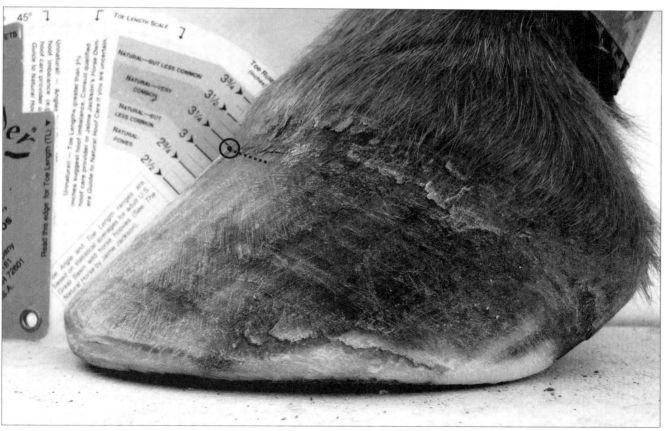

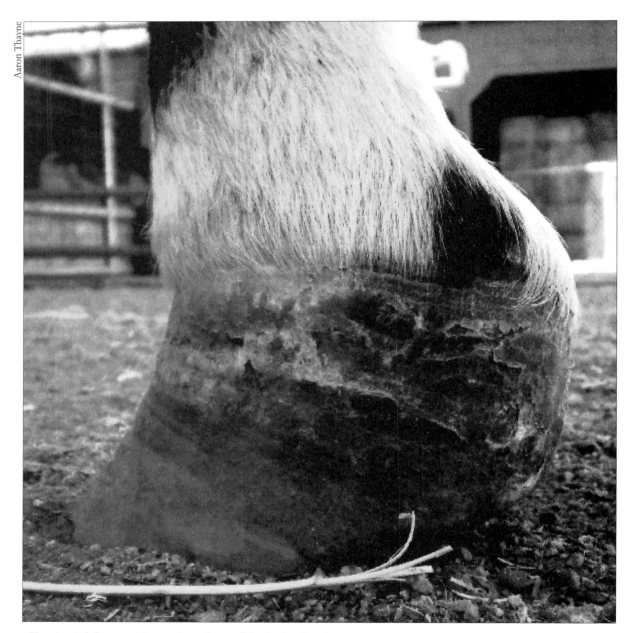

Classic clubfoot conformation due to Navicular Syndrome.

CHAPTER 11

Trimming the Clubfoot

Clubfoot is the third hoof type to discuss in our natural trim instruction series. The medical definition of clubfoot (human or animal) is "a deformity of the foot". Farriery and veterinary texts also classify clubfoot as a deformity — arising from heredity or genetic predisposition, a congenital defect, or a diet-related problem with bone development following birth. There is also some speculation that club foot is a genetic predisposition in some horse breeds, but researchers have not identified responsible genes. Typically, the clubfoot is described as happening to just one foot (left or right), with a noticeably higher angled pastern, and often a rotated coffin bone (P3). It is often associated with Navicular Syndrome, defined conventionally as "an inflammation or degeneration of the navicular bone and its surrounding tissues". Severity ranges from mild (light riding only) to severe (unsound for life). Treatment is traditionally limited to pain management, corrective (orthopedic) shoeing to help the horse move, and surgery.

It is interesting to note that, in two separate published studies, researchers did not find a single incidence of clubfoot among U.S. Great Basin wild, free-roaming horses based upon veterinary classifications.[1] This is consistent with the NHC perspective that clubfoot is man-made and not natural at all to *Equus ferus caballus*.

From the NHC perspective, clubfoot is viewed quite differently. It is defined as "a hoof whose healing angle (H°) is permanently three or more degrees higher than its left or right pair".[2] For example, if a left front hoof trimmed to NHC guidelines measures H° = 57°, and its right front pair measures H° = 52°, then the left front foot is defined as a clubfoot. It does not matter if the clubfoot measures within the natural angle ranges for front feet, only that there is a significant angle differential between it and its paired front foot. In addition, there is no pain associated with clubfoot itself, including the navicular bursa and nearby tissues. *Clubfoot is also not attributed to heredity, congenital defects, or complications of bone development due to diet.* Instead, its cause is linked directly to extreme riding practices that repetitively obstruct the horse's natural gaits, and so much so that there is traumatic, and often a

---

[1]Neither my U.S. Great Basin studies conducted during 1982-1986 (*The Natural Horse: Lessons From the Wild*, Jaime Jackson, Northland Publishing, 1992), nor Dr. Ric Redden's 2000 corroborative study in the same region (*The Wild Horse's Foot*, Bluegrass Laminitis Symposium Notes, written and presented January 2001 by R.F. Redden, DVM), witnessed a single instance of club foot.

[2]±2° margin of error between paired L and R hooves. So, if there is less than 3° difference, then it is likely not a club foot, or more data is needed to evidence it.

devastating, breakdown of the horse's body anywhere above the hoof. This is the NHC definition of Navicular Syndrome (NS). Clubfoot is also sometimes closely associated with hoof contraction, laminitis, and unnaturally trimmed or shod hooves; however, none of these in and of themselves cause clubfoot according to NHC principles. To understand club foot from the NHC perspective, then, we must distinguish its causality from the symptoms of hoof contraction, laminitis, and unnatural hoof care practices — all of which can contribute to the illusions and complications of club foot while not causing it in and of themselves.

Effects of hoof contraction

The NHC definition of hoof contraction is the degeneration of foot mass due to unnatural horse care practices, hence, there are many possible causes such as the effects of shoeing/nailing, invasive trimming practices, close confinement (life in a stall), and/or pain for whatever reason. Because the clubfoot appears narrower than its left or right pair, it is assumed that the hoof is so conformed due to the effects of contraction. But this is not the case, as hoof contraction does not cause clubfoot.

According to my NHC research, hoof contraction cannot be definitively diagnosed by merely looking at the hoof, in spite of what might appear to be — and probably is if the hoof is shod or has been invasively trimmed — obvious hoof contraction. Nor can it be determined by taking critical measurements *at the first trim session*. Instead, the hoof must be measured over time and the data evaluated accordingly. This protocol is necessary due to the complexities of mass changes over time (in the NHC vernacular, we call these "4D changes").

The graph on the facing page is a simplification of a study I conducted over four consecutive years on hoof de-contraction following the de-shoeing of client horses.[1] Each of the horses had been in shoes for at least three years. The graph depicts changes in hoof width (HW, page 124) for front hooves over time (a 4D change) following removal of the shoes. On average, HW increased ~⅜ in. (1 cm) over 2.5 *hgc*, which was the average length of time when measurements for HW stopped changing. In other words, it took nearly two years for the hooves to restore their optimal widths under NHC practices and strict adherence to natural trim guidelines. Note in the graph at the bull's-eye (◉) that one *hgc* was required for the foot to recover 50% of its width (HW). This demonstrated to me the long term egregious effects of shoeing, although even the most astute eye could not see the subtle 4D changes. Bear in mind also that contraction of *HW* due to shoeing, while diminishing the size of the hoof's volar profile, also corresponds to a loss in three-dimensional capsule mass. For this reason, gathering all the critical measurements discussed in Chapter 4

---

[1] J. Jackson, "Does Horseshoeing Cause Hoof Contraction?" SRP Bulletin #111 (5/1/2003), p.3.

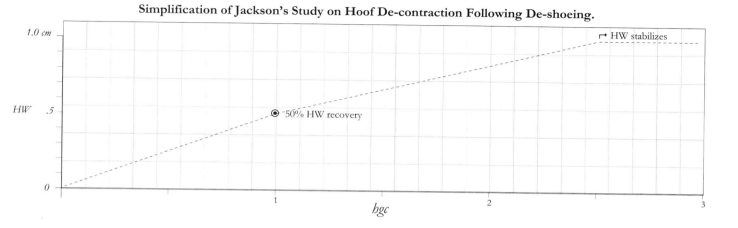

Simplification of Jackson's Study on Hoof De-contraction Following De-shoeing.

are imperative in evaluating hoof contraction, as they facilitate the evaluation of mass changes in all three dimensions over time. Incidentally, not one of the study horses suffered from clubfoot in my study, which I attributed to my client's excellent horsemanship and large paddock turnouts.

In conclusion, it is next to impossible to ascertain whether a clubfoot, or any hoof, is pathologically contracted, and, for sure, to what extent, without evaluating its critical measurements over time.

Effects of laminitis

The deforming effects of laminitis on the hoof capsule are quite varied — including the degree of failure of the LAM (e.g., elongated white line, slipper toe, and DTAs), how the hoof has been trimmed and if it was shod and how, if neglect was involved, and so forth. Distilling and differentiating the effects of laminitis from clubfoot, however, is straightforward: first, the symptoms of laminitis are diagnosed to confirm the disease (page 196). Second, the hooves must be trimmed to NHC standards. Third, H° must be contrasted for left/right paired feet. Fourth, once pain is brought under control through holistic management practices, the horse is evaluated at the trot as explained earlier. The possible concomitant effects of hoof contraction on the capsule can only be determined through 4D evaluation, but this will not stand in the way of a diagnosis based on the previous measures.

In conclusion, it is difficult to diagnose clubfoot with certainty in the laminitic horse as long as the feet are in pain due to inflammation of the LAM. However, as soon as pain is relieved, and the hooves have been trimmed to NHC guidelines, the tests for clubfoot can begin.

Effects of shoeing and unnatural trimming methods

While the effects of shoeing and different trimming methods on the hoof's size, shape, and proportion are as varied as cloud formations in the sky, and both are capable of rendering the horse unsound with contraction in all four feet, all their egregious effects immediately begin to abate once NHC practices are implemented, including the natural trim. H° is then measured and contrasted for the left/right paired hooves and the horse is evaluated at the trot as explained earlier.

Clubfoot, crookedness and Navicular Syndrome (NS)

Clubfoot is a symptom of Navicular Syndrome (NS). Logically, why it is symptomatic of NS lies in understanding NS itself. NS is widespread and rivals laminitis and colic as a reason for horses being disabled, euthanized, and/or retired because they are no longer ridable due to lameness. As stated earlier, NS is a generic term encompassing the breakdown of the horse anywhere above the hoof due to extreme riding practices with symptoms of laminitis. My observation has been that NS often begins with young horses, although it can happen to any horse at any age. Why young horses?

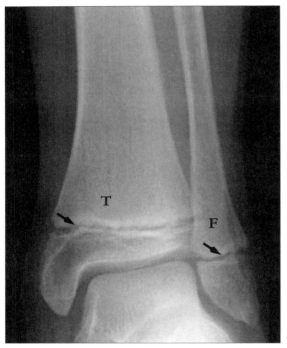

Epiphyseal plates at lower ends of tibia and fibula of 12 year old human.

I concur with the many experts who believe mounted training should begin no earlier than five years of age and as late as eight years. Work in hand can commence earlier, but always in keeping with the principles of natural horsemanship and the natural gait complex. Although it is the tradition of the horse world to start horses much earlier under saddle, horses that are ridden at these young ages are at considerable risk of enduring serious, potentially life-threatening, injuries and breakdown — NS. These principally concern fractures and joint disorders in the horse's *axial* (torso) and *appendicular* (extremity) skeletal bones (page 133). This is a time when *epiphyseal* (i.e., growth changes due to maturation) *plates* have not yet formed compact bone, and are susceptible to *physeal* fracture (*left*). Assuming the horse survives his youth as a hard worker, what might his fate be as an adult? My preference is to approach this question from the standpoint of natural horsemanship.

Two core principles of natural horsemanship lie at the very foundations of being a natural rider: for the adult horse to carry the weight of the rider, and not cause harm, he must be systematically trained to become what is called *straight* and *rounded* when being ridden. So gymnasticized, the "straight" horse is able to gather himself, called *collection*, and, so rounded and balanced, carry the rider with less risk of harming himself. Horses that have not been thusly prepared are said to be "crooked" and are at high risk of becoming victims of NS when subjected to extreme riding practices. This isn't to say that straight horses are not at risk — they are, only the risk is much less.

For the most part, riding a horse that isn't straight will not be a problem if the riding is

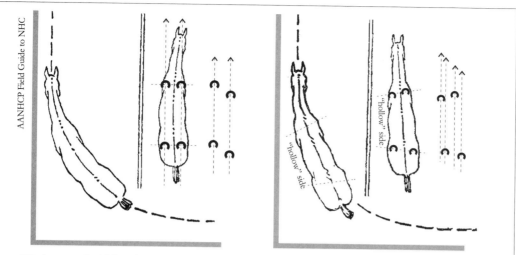

The horse on the left bends evenly through his body in the arc of the turn. In this case, he is moving to the right, but he is equally able to bend to the left and sustain the same arc of motion. Such a horse assumes rein contact equally on both sides. He is said to be "straight" in that he has no "hollow" and "stiff" sides, and is physically able to track forward bending to one side or the other. Both sides are equally strong and able to carry the weight of the rider in the extended and accelerated paces. Moving straight forward, his hooves form two trails of hoof tracks.

The horse on the right is unable to bend evenly through to body to his right. The side against the wall is his hollow side. He would bend readily in that direction but would be unable to accept rein contact. Such a horse is said to be "crooked", resulting in multi-tracks when moving straight forward. If not straightened through systemized gymnastic exercises or a natural lifestyle, he is at extreme risk of developing Navicular Syndrome and possible irreparable lameness.

casual and not extreme, such as light trail riding and light arena work. I call this "free forward riding". On the other hand, the same horse, if ridden repeatedly hard or competitively — and thus, vigorously and frequently with both mental and physical pressure applied (e.g., track racing, lengthy trail rides, hunter/jumper, reining, dressage, gymkhana, and endurance) — is at high risk of physical breakdown and succumbing to NS. There is some good news here, however! — NS is 100% preventable provided that the holistic practices of NHC, and natural horsemanship in particular, are followed. This means riding within the "safety zone" of the horse's natural gait complex.

What then is crookedness, exactly? First, most horses are born crooked rather than straight, and I'll offer my own speculations as to why in a moment. Crookedness is something that can be observed and felt by the rider. While moving forward and turning, the crooked horse cannot bend (arc) his body equally and symmetrically in both directions (left and right) from head to tail (*above*). Moreover, when moving straight forward, he is not able to move consistently in two tracks — that is, his hind feet are not following in the same path as the front. Nor is he able to take his leads with similar ease when turning to the left and right. Further, he cannot accept rein pressure evenly on his left and right sides. Colonel

Alois Podhajsky, a former Director of the Spanish Riding School and world renowned expert in classical horsemanship explained it this way:

> A horse may not accept the bit evenly on both sides. He will make himself stiff on one side and will follow the slightest action of the rein on the other by turning his head. He will take a firmer contact and only reluctantly follow the action of the rein on the side on which he is stiff. On the other side he will anticipate the action of the rein and bend this way; this to say, he becomes hollow on this side. When the reins are applied evenly the horse will bend his neck to the hollow side, on which he will not accept the rein. The rider will be able to recognize this as the rein will not touch the neck on this hollow side, whereas it lies close to the neck on the side on which the horse makes himself stiff.[1]

An explanation for this, in my opinion, is that, from birth, the muscles of the horse are naturally more compressed on one side of his body than the other; which is to say, he has a "short" or concaved side, and a complementary "long" or convex side. The term "crooked" is derived from this difference. There is some suggestion that crookedness could follow from the predisposition of the developing fetus in the womb, where it is typically "bent" to one side for months on end.[2]

Unless gymnasticized through a natural lifestyle or training, the muscles on the short side, which Podhajsky calls the "hollow side", remain shorter and less flexible than the muscles on the long or "stiff side". Moreover, the hind leg on the hollow side tends to be more flexed or "bent", yet less flexible (bendable), while weaker and less able to carry body weight than the hind leg on the stiff side. It is worth pointing out that nature remedies this in the wild through herd behavior and the threat of predation. This is something I observed. As an animal of prey, there is constant stimulation to bend and look in both directions for his survival (*facing page*). The hollow side, thus, is naturally developed to become flexible and as strong as the "stiff" side; whereas, the stiff side becomes as "bendable" as the hollow side. The wild horse, then, is said to be "straight", meaning he bends equally on both sides, and both sides are equally strong to help carry and propel his weight.

Crooked horses will also have hollow (concaved) rather than rounded (arched) backs.[3]

---

[1]Alois Podhajsky, *The Complete Training Of Horse and Rider* (Doubleday/1966), p. 43. Podhajsky was a Silver Medalist in the dressage competition at the 1936 Olympics in Berlin, Germany.

[2]*En utero* position of the horse has not been overlooked by some of the great equestrians of the past, including Alois Podhajsky, *The Complete Training Of Horse and Rider* (Doubleday/1966), p. 46.

[3]As an exercise to help distinguish "rounded" vs "hollow", get down on your hands and knees and alternately arch ("round") and sway ("hollow") your back. Notice that your abdominal muslces are brought into play when rounding your back, versus relaxing them when making it hollow. Think also of your rounded back — and the horse's — as an "arched structure."

The making of a straight horse nature's way. Wild horses in central Nevada ever on the alert to threat of predation.
[Photo: Luca Gandini.]

Consequently, they are unable to collect themselves naturally and bring their hind legs further under the body to provide enhanced support, thrust, and, ultimately, locomotive balance. As Podhajsky warns, "Balance can be obtained and collection possible only if the horse is straight." Horses ridden with hollow backs feel particularly jarring to the rider, especially at the trot and canter, as the horse is unable to collect, round his back, and extend his stride naturally in his paces (the key to a comfortable ride in any gait). Riders commonly resort to the *post* (at the trot and canter), being unable to sit comfortably or with stability at accelerated tempos sans stride extension.

Ironically, crookedness — to the limited extent that it is ever noticed or given any thought at all — is considered an inherent fault of the horse. Typically, it is ignored altogether, or coped with by the rider as an inevitable annoyance ("My horse hates taking his right lead."). The reality is that crookedness is a characteristic of horses that are not afforded natural lifestyles and/or appropriate training. The implications of riding a crooked horse, therefore, are of paramount importance to all caring horse owners. The NHC practitioner should, therefore, understand the relationship of NS and riding crooked horses to the incidence of clubfoot.

Clubfoot, per se, is not a foot disease or pathology, but a unique conformational adaptation tantamount to a "crutch" (or, "crutch foot") that arises to support serious injuries occurring above the hoof itself. This becomes evident when the horse sets his clubfoot and bears weight upon it like an upright crutch. Faltering occurs when the horse turns sharply at the trot. This appears to be a compensatory response — and there is still considerable debate as to whether pain is triggered during the clubfoot's support phase, or during the paired hoof's support phase with the clubfoot quickly taking action to provide "crutch-like" support. Whichever, the response is clearly amplified by the horse's center of gravity, which predisposes unnatural loading over the forehand due to crookedness and the horse's inability to collect himself naturally. My observation is that the clubfoot conformation is not painful to the horse, because it does not suggest any hypersensitivity during support such as one sees in feet obviously in pain (e.g., due to laminitis, hot nails, wall resections, and invasive trimming). But the mere presence of the clubfoot, along with the faltering, is enough to lead most horse owners, farriers, and vets to conclude that the pain is somewhere matrixed in clubfoot. And that's precisely when the arsenal of invasive trimming, corrective shoeing, surgery, and drugs, is brought out to do battle with nature.

Years ago, when I began to doubt not only the conventional hoof mechanism model, but the conventional diagnosis of Navicular Syndrome as well, I began to pay closer attention to what was ailing the horse above his feet. It just seemed that the hoof was being saddled as the culprit for about everything going wrong with the horse. At the same time, I begin to organize my data streaming out of wild horse country, formulating for the first time a model for gauging hoof size, shape, and proportion among my client horses relative to the wild horse foot. Out of this synthesis emerged the concept of $H°$. I dutifully tracked its changes over time under the influence of the natural trim in horses that I de-shod, seeing that nature was up to something, and usually something good as, in most cases, capsule structure — size, shape, and proportion — improved dramatically. Inevitably, I began to correlate changes in $H°$ to pathological changes occurring elsewhere in the horse's body: swelling or pain in or around the major joints of the front and hind legs (e.g., the knee, shoulder, hip, hock, stifle, and fetlock), bowed tendons, damage to the vertebra and intervertebral discs of the neck and back, and what soon became a major tell-tale symptom of NS — faltering at the trot in the turn. The more severe the damage that was done to the horse's body, the more pronounced the faltering and the more elevated did $H°$ assert itself in one front foot over the other. Rather than seeing the clubfoot as a dark and mysterious pathology to wage war against — conventionally the object of aggressive trimming, shoeing and surgery to "make it look like the other foot" — I came to see it as a healing aid — a crutch — for damaged horses. Instead, I began to defend and even facilitate the clubfoot, and lobby the owner for better horsemanship. That was twenty years ago, and I'm still of the same opinion and practice.

Prevention of NS lies strictly in NHC and natural horsemanship. This is what I advise. Become a better, more natural rider, and embrace the Four Pillars of NHC, rather than to create a broken horse. The competent NHC practitioner knows the breeding grounds for NS, is able to untangle and sort through potential concomitant symptoms that have nothing to do with NS but may be confusing the picture, and can advise the horse owner how to take immediate preventive action. Let's review the NS "red alerts" that all NHC practitioners should know by memory:

- There is an unusual elevation in H° in only one of the front feet.
- The horse is crooked: he multi-tracks, cannot or will not take both leads with equal ease, cannot or refuses to take up the reins evenly, cannot bend in the same even arc through his body when turning to the left and to the right.
- There are palpable and visible calcification "lumps" emerging along the spine.
- There is repeated swelling in the sheath of the DDFT (i.e., bowed tendon).
- There is repeated swelling in one or more of the three major joints of the hindquarters.
- The horse owner reports the horse is beginning more and more to falter at the trot when making a turn.

I have bad news to add to the picture, however. If the upper body damage is sufficiently severe and permanent, then I am unaware of any realistic prognosis for full recovery. NHC may help the horse to be more comfortable, but I would not make any promises. Healing in such extreme cases cannot be forced upon the horse through any shoeing, trim, or surgical procedure aimed at the clubfoot, because the nucleus of the problem isn't there. Most horse owners unfamiliar with NHC, face the choice of permanent pasture retirement or euthanasia when the gamut of corrective shoeing, surgery and invasive trimming leads nowhere.

§

This brings us to the trimming instructions for the clubfoot. The question the NHC practitioner must be prepared to answer when all is said and done, "Is this, in fact, a genuine clubfoot, or is it simply the result of unnatural management practices?" The solution, of course, lies in the critical measurements and a critically conducted comprehensive evaluation of the symptoms of NS. All photos in this series are by Jill Willis.

Clubfoot (cadaver): Pre-trim evaluation

Our first step is to scan this left front hoof in various profiles in search of clues revealing what the full extent of its problems are. Try this before reading my observations below, and think about what you would do or recommend as captain of our trim team.

(Above) Three things pop right out at us:

First, the outer wall is covered with stress rings, so we may find a distressed white line and confirmed laminitis as we go in.

Second, the heels are so excessively long, we actually have a run under hoof — in spite of what appears to be a clubfoot conformation! Confirmation lies in the gridlines: gray arrows point to the shrunken volar support base; black arrows frame the pitch of the heels; white arrow is significantly oblique to the MATW.

Third, although somewhat hard to see in the photo, the toe wall has been nippered and filed back, putting active weight-bearing responsibilities elsewhere. I'm already suspecting it's the work of the solar-loading barefoot faction, since the hoof was not shod. More evidence for this is forthcoming.

Without even bringing out the HMR, we can see the extent of neglect and incompetence. And that there's a lot of work to be done here.

(Below) Try to ignore the gnarly mess of overgrown frog and heels. My nippers are quivering to get at it right now, but let's continue with our pre-trim evaluation on the facing page.

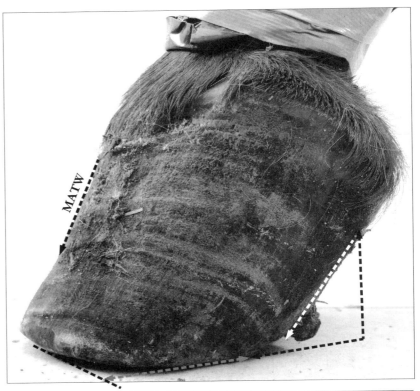

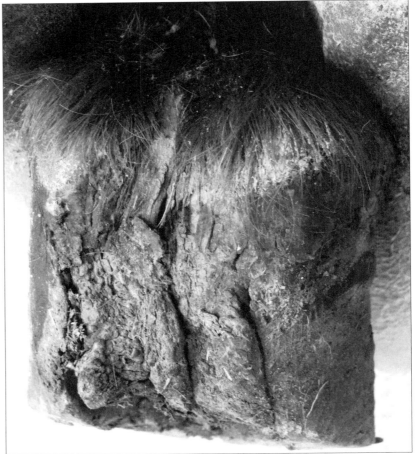

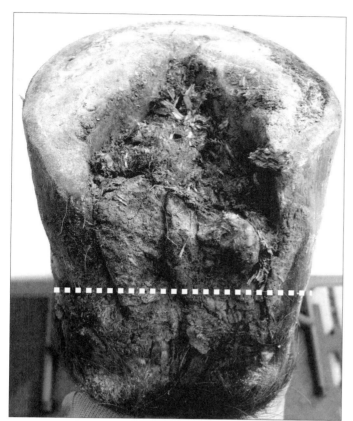

Clubfoot (cadaver): Pre-trim evaluation

I've tilted the hoof to give a bird's eye view of the volar dome.

(Left, above) We are drawn immediately to the massive bed of solar horn on both sides of the frog. Major excavation ahead! Gridline is my estimate of the M-L heel axis, the navigational landmark I will likely lower the heels to by the time I'm finished.

(Left, below) Arrows point to cracks in the solar dome forward of the point of frog — and our way in.

Clubfoot (cadaver): Pre-trim evaluation

The MAVP and MATW have been determined and a probe points to the crest of the coronary groove. Measuring can begin.

(Right, above) The bull's-eye has been set at the limit line and H°TL gauges in at just over 3¼ in. (8.3 cm). In spite of the illusion (due to heel length) of very long toe length with this hoof, this reading falls well within the average range for natural lengths on the HMR scale. Careful examination of solar plates as we approach the HSP in the volar profile will be critical in the decision to shorten H°TL any further.

(Right, below) H° gauges at 65°, pushing the upper limits of the HMR, inviting the unwitting to confirm we are dealing with a clubfoot. At this point, we have insufficient information to confirm this.

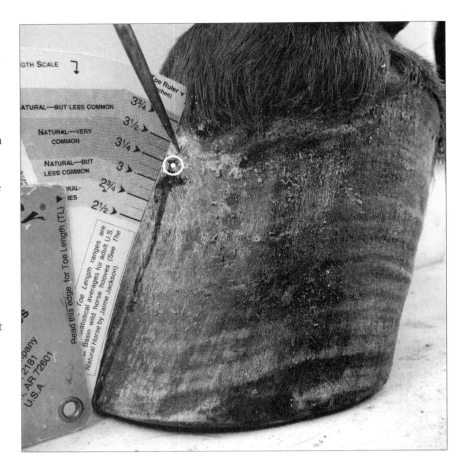

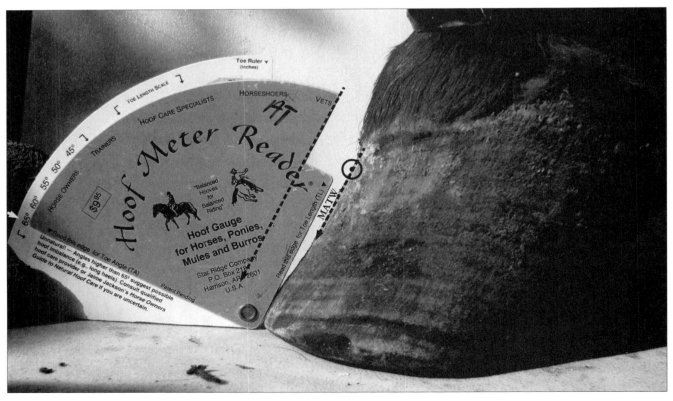

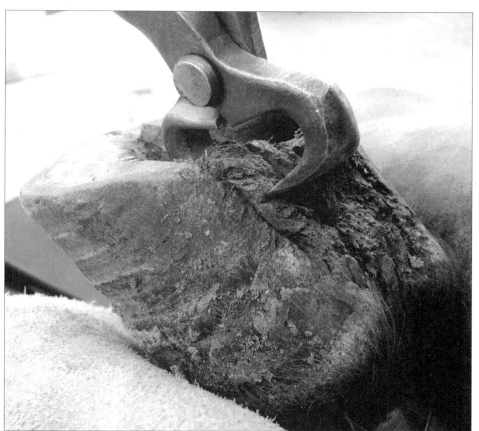

Clubfoot (cadaver): Trim the frog and sole

Before we can do anything else anywhere to this hoof with reliability, the overgrowth of the frog has to be dispensed of in order to better see what can and cannot be safely removed.

(Above) When my fellow AANHCP CPs and I pulled this specimen out to be trimmed for a photo shoot, we immediately noticed the compacted sole and compacted frog. What struck us was the relatively neat trimming that had been done, but that the trimmer allowed the sole and frog to overgrow. I suspect it was another application of the solar loading method discussed in Chapter 4, misunderstood and out of control.

(Below) We shot this view up close to show how I slipped one nipper blade under a solar plate, and braced with the other blade before making the cut.

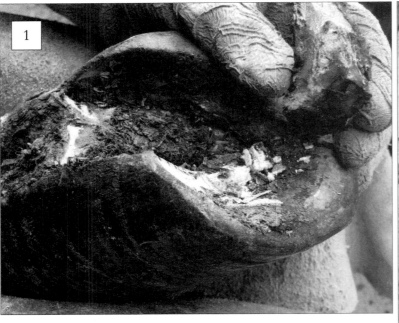

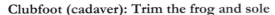

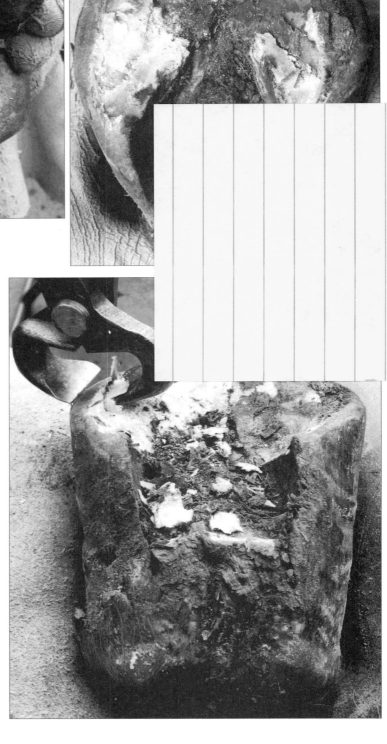

Clubfoot (cadaver): Trim the frog and sole

This is a very critical part of the trim, as we are having to sort through a bungle of hand-me-down gross negligence and hoof care incompetence to restore order

[1] I feel like I've hit the jackpot with a chunk of 1 in. (2.5 cm) thick solar plate! This much sole likely cuts off sensitivity to the foot as much as a metal shoe. The outrageous length that the heels were allowed to grow surely must have translated to instability and duress in the mind of the horse. We're talking about athletic animals by nature, and this type of foot is clearly inhumane. Asking a horse to ambulate in it at all it is, in my mind, tantamount to asking an Olympic sprinter to do so wearing spiked high heels.

[2] I've pried both major solar plates out of the dome and the HSP is now becoming visible. The crescent of sole near the marked MATW is in my sights now. Because H°TL is at 3¼ in. (8.3 cm), I will have to nipper drag to see if it goes or stays.

[3] Nipper dragging reveals that the crescent of sole, which extends around to both quarters, all goes. This is a straight-forward application of trimming to the hoof's relative concavity, in spite of the previous hoof care neglect and recklessness.

Clubfoot (cadaver): Lower the hoof wall

We are ready to go after the hoof wall, finally, and those lengthy heels in particular.

(Above) While I was able to establish concavity in the dome at the MATW, I decided that I had also reached the HSP and would leave HTL at 3¼ in. (8.3 cm). In real life, I would wait for the plates to fissure before removing them after much teasing with nipper dragging. For now, I will begin shortening the toe wall at the arrows on either side of the MATW, working back to each heel along the cut lines I've marked with the Sharpie. Since my cut lines run deep into the solar dome, this will entail some cautionary nipper dragging along the way to confirm that the compacted sole is ready to go

(Below) Completing the first nipper run. I've marked the cut line along the bar as well to emphasize the destiny. In my teaching clinics, I have students mark this, and all other cut lines, before they put a cutting tool to the hoof. My motto is, "Know precisely where you are going before you start your journey." With experience, you will envision this in your mind's eye, but always use the HMR to cross-reference.

Clubfoot (cadaver): Finish volar dome

With the hoof wall taken down, we are almost done. Text below is keyed to a medley of images on this and the facing page.

(This page.)

[1] This is the last nipper bite of heel. H° TL is as low as I'm going to take it in this trim session.

[2] The entire hoof wall is down. Sight the hoof for balance along the M-L heel axis by peering across both heels at 90° (right angle) to the MPVP as shown. One or both segments of the toe wall (arrows) on either side of the MAVP will align with both heels. The quarters will lie even with or below this plane.

(Facing page.)

[3] Bird's-eye view of volar dome hints of hoof contraction across the heels, but this must be ascertained and corrected in the 4D. Black arrow points to segment of flare, which I will remove shortly. White arrow points to rim of water line. Follow this critical navigational landmark around the solar dome, as we will try to accentuate it in the next step.

[4] Flare has been nippered away as I cut the mustang roll. The volar dome is really beginning to take shape now.
Arrow points to segment of sole-wall separation. Is this an important focus for our attention? Of course not! "Ignore all pathology". It will take care of itself in the 4D.

[5] I've fine finished mustang roll with rasp/file. Arrow points to thin rim of water line, which I've kept active. The white line is clearly distressed here and elsewhere around the dome, confirmation that the horse was suffering from laminitis. It's not clear to me if he was put down because the owner thought he was suffering from clubfoot or laminitis, or both. We'll never know.

[6] I'm now finished in the volar dome.

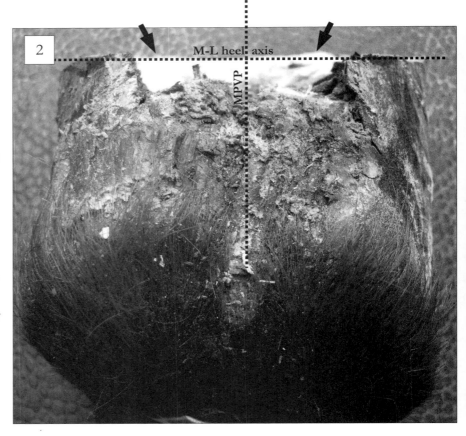

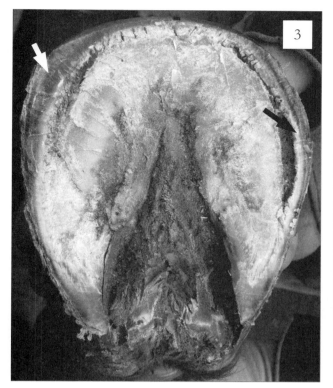

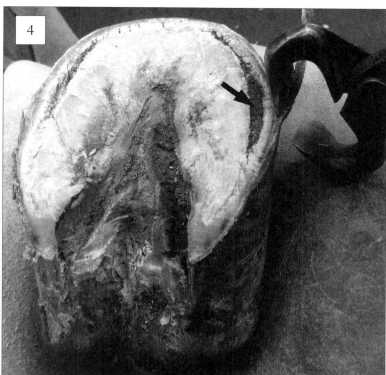

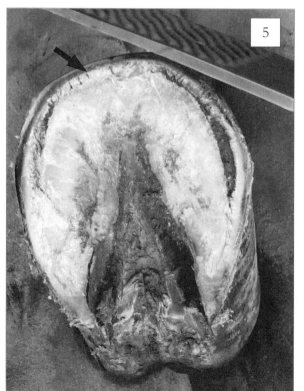

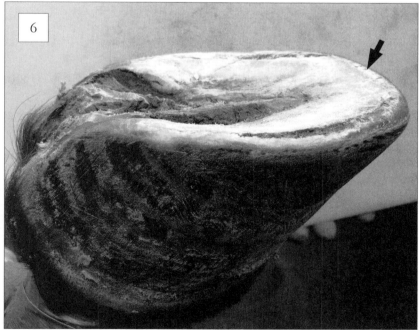

Clubfoot (cadaver): Finished outer wall.

We're ending up with a fine looking hoof, but the scars of laminitis are reminders that the horse suffered terribly for lack of a reasonably natural diet.

(Above) To foster more natural growth, I've rasped/filed the entire outer wall from just below the coronary band on down. It is not possible here to rasp away the stress rings entirely, or I would have to invade the natural thickness of the hoof wall — a violation of natural trim protocol. But shaving down these laminitic ridges to the hoof's natural thickness, whatever amount that might be, short circuits the miscommunication to the coronary corium. More straight-line growth then follows.

(Below) I am done and the bull's-eye marked at the outset with the Sharpie is the only vestige left from our original gridlines. Arrow points to a fairly severe stress ring, which, in life, I would red flag as a possible – but unlikely – fracture site as it approaches ground level.[1] Overall, the hoof's size, shape and proportion looks really good, and the mustang roll is nearly exemplary. Under strict NHC management for 6 months, I have little doubt that this hoof would be as fine an example of a naturally shaped hoof as the domestic horse world has to offer. Let's look at the post trim numbers next to see where things are exactly.

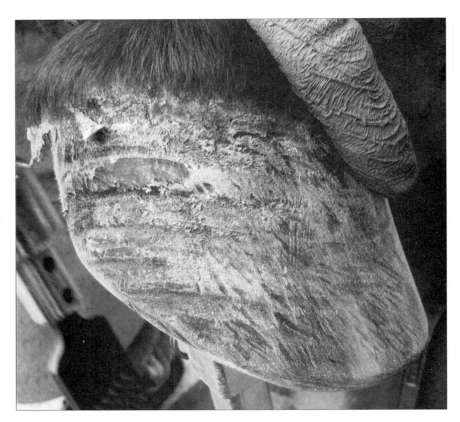

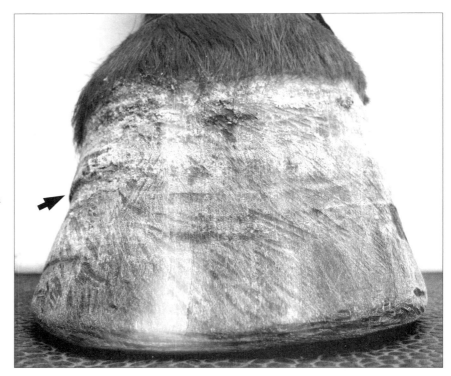

[1]Recall discussion of wall fractures due to stress rings on page 197.

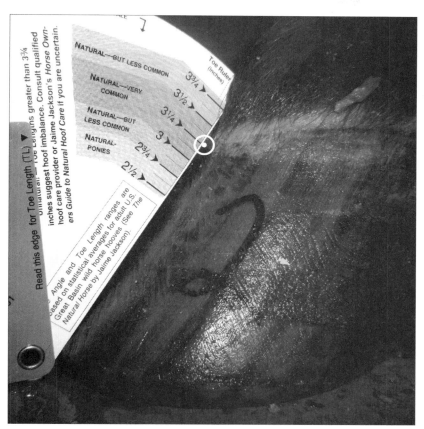

Clubfoot (cadaver): Final assessment.

I've washed and numbered the hoof for long term keeping in my freezer. This hoof will be dissected and used in future training clinics.

(Above) H°TL was sustained at 3¼ in. (8.3 cm) at the bull's-eye. The severity at which this hoof was run-under — in spite of its clubfoot-like conformation — suggests to me that H°TL will probably shorten somewhat in the 4D as the growth coria regain their bearing under full NHC management..

(Below) In the end, H° measured over ten degrees lower than where we started. This is very central in the angle range for natural toe angles, and, in life, would represent our starting point for sustaining H°. At 54°, I am dubious that this was a genuine clubfoot, but am certain this was a tragic case of laminitis with complications from mismanaged trimming. We will never know for sure if clubfoot and NS were also at work here, not having the paired hoof to compare.

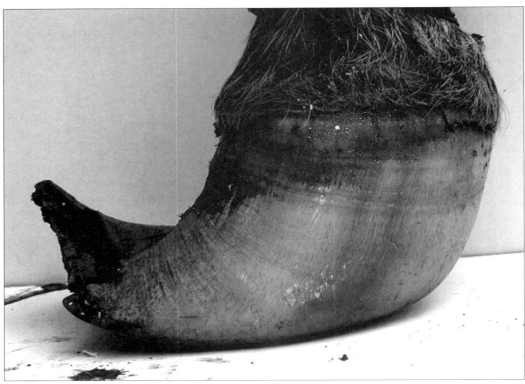

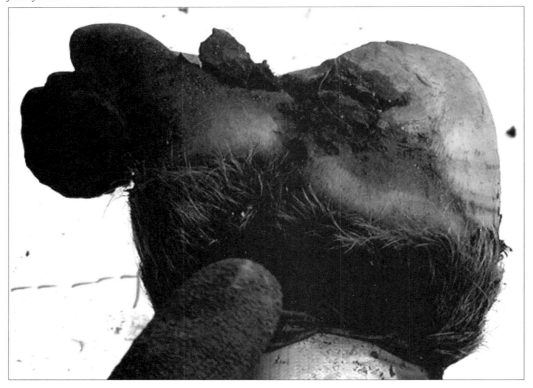

This is a "wry foot", with obviously very troubled growth patterns. Natural trim guidelines provide a straight-forward path to restore healthy, balanced new growth.

CHAPTER 12
Trimming the Wry Foot

W*ry foot* refers to a capsule that is, quite literally, "lopsided". Typically, the toe rather "veers" off to one side, while the opposing heel and quarter folds over in the same direction, covering parts of their own hoof wall, solar dome, and frog — in some instances, shrouding the entire volar dome! Just like the hoof on the facing page. Traditionally a nightmare to correct in farrier circles, the wry foot readily yields to a strict, consistent regimen of natural hoof care over many *hoof growth cycles* (hgc).

First, we'll tackle the cadaver hoof at left to demonstrate how the principles of the natural trim apply to it. This will be an orientation, with abbreviated trimming instructions. Armed with this foundation, however, we will tackle another hoof step-by-step — one seemingly a bit more complicated at first look, but which will yield to the natural trim as readily as the most naturally shaped hoof with less than a centimeter of hoof wall to trim.

Before beginning, I want to say that the wry foot, like the most severe laminitic slipper foot, is one that requires much patience and encouragement over time (4D). As I explain to students, it took a bit of time for it to get like this, let's be reasonable and allow it *enough* time to get out of it. The hoof will let you know. However, change comes slow in such cases and the NHC practitioner should be diligent in taking critical measurements to reflect those changes. Leave nothing to chance, because the owner's uneducated eye may grow impatient if numbers aren't provided to substantiate what's actually happening in the 4D.

Wry Hoof
An Orientation

Wry Foot (cadaver): Orientation.

Our initial objective is, first, to get our bearing, then locate our navigational landmarks, and, finally, establish our cut-lines with which to work our way in.

(*Above*) The entire hoof wall is twisted such that the horse is walking on the back of the medial heel (MH) as seen in this view. On the other side, not visible here (but is in the image below), the quarter is so flared that the horse isn't even walking on hoof wall forward of the heels! The toe wall, as you can see, is twisted upwards and then back towards the MATW. H° measures in the 70°s, well off of the HMR grid. A real mess!

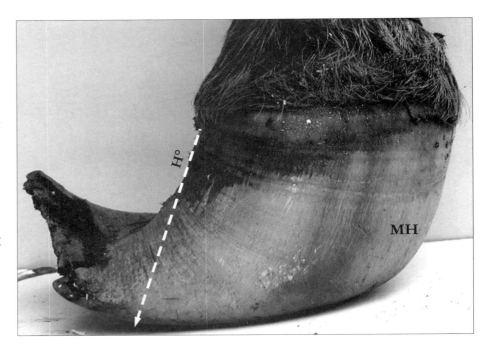

(*Below*) Continuing, much of what is wrong is revealed in this view. Clearly the horse is walking nowhere on his hoof wall, which is completely folded over. Hence, he is bearing all weight on the back side of his medial heel (MH) and lateral bar (LB). As can be seen and readily surmised, this type of imbalance across the M-L heel axis dooms the medial side of the hoof to grow over the lateral side. Arrows point to the direction of growth. The lateral bar has no choice but to flare to the side. I've seen such severe cases of this that the entire volar dome is sealed off by the run under wall. (In one such case, a toe wall so twisted actually grew around and embedded itself in the fetlock joint and had to be surgically removed.)

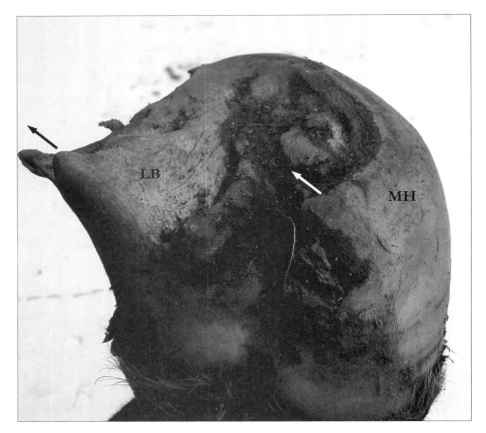

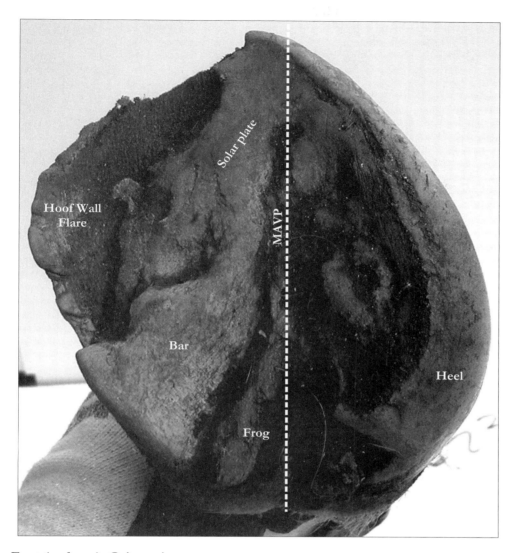

Solar plate

MAVP

Hoof Wall
Flare

Bar

Heel

Frog

Wry Foot (cadaver): Orientation.

The volar profile of the wry foot can challenge even the most advanced trimmer's astute eye. Wall flare, compacted sole, along with folded-over bars, quarters, and heels, all conspire to obscure the true volar dome beneath. Typical of these kinds of hooves, and as is the case above, the deeply ensconced and shrouded frog is infected (thrush) and pathologically compressed.

(*Above*) I've marked the principle structures we need to go after to reach the volar dome beneath. The nipper must be slid under the heel and bar to cut them back. Similarly, work the nipper under the massive solar plate extending to either side of the MAVP forward of the frog.
With H°TL markers in place, trim away all compacted sole down to hard sole [8].
Trim "flared" hoof wall and bars down to hard sole, making sure water line is distal to the white line (so that hoof wall is active, sole passive). Once these steps are taken care of, it will be a straightforward matter of taking the wall flare out, as well as other hoof wall made accessible. This isn't the case here, as will be revealed on the following pages, but if the heel were discovered to have grown over and into the frog epidermis, it must be cut out; however, if it has entered the underlying dermis, the procedure should be done under the supervision of a veterinarian and treated as an open wound.

Wry Foot (cadaver): Orientation.

Properly lowering and balancing the heels of the wry foot is probably one of the most challenging trimming tasks in modern hoof care. As with all hooves, the key to success lies in sighting the volar plane relative to the MPVP) and setting the M-L heel axis parallel to it. When this is accomplished, the hoof is set at its most advantageous and natural support position for 4D healing changes to take place.

(*Above*) Don't be surprised if the positions of the heel bulbs, *x* and *y*, relative to the MPVP axis are staggered as is the case here. Ignore, as they will self-correct to where they need to be in the 4D. A major lure is to shorten each heel to the same length relative to their respective heel bulbs. Don't do that! Another temptation is to sight the M-L heel axis parallel to the z-axis instead of at right angle (90°) to the MPVP. Don't do that either!

The gridlines a^1, a^2, and a^3 will serve as guides for our cut-lines. Our destination is the M-L heel axis. Nipper away as follows:
Step 1: Shorten the longer heel (a^1) down to the level of the shorter heel (a^2).
Step 2: Now shorten both heels down to the M-L heel axis (a^3).

(*Below*) This is as far down as we go for this first trim. The reason (*facing page*) is that we've reached the HSP at the quarters, and any attempt to lower the heels further at this point in time, will render them passive to the quarters — a violation of our natural trim guidelines.

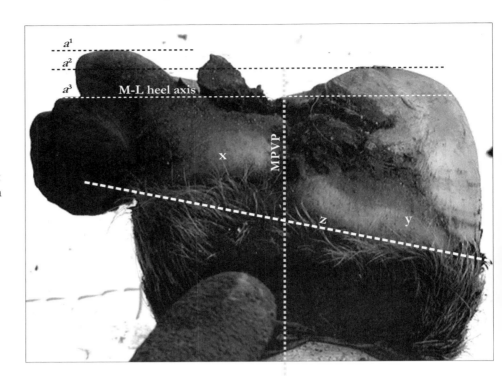

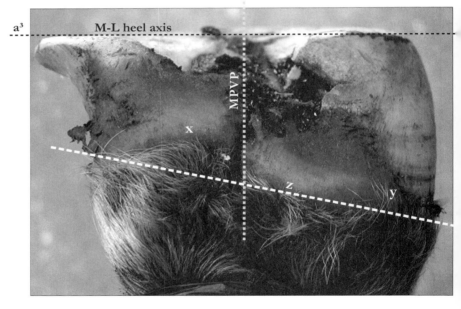

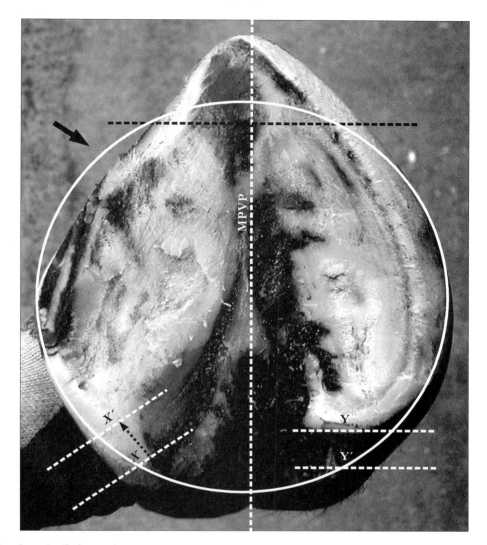

Wry Foot (cadaver): Orientation.

(*Above*) At first glance, one might assume that this hoof has been over-trimmed, given the apparent absence of wall and sole pointed at by the arrow. But this is largely an illusion as the capsule mass forward of the black dashed line has simply pathologically migrated there — the signature of a "run under" hoof (p. 113, *middle*). In the 4D, this will self-correct. Much of the mass forward of this line will atrophy and rebuild as new sole and toe wall near the arrow. The heel-buttress at y will also migrate through mass accretion to y´. The white circle is the approximate location of the rehabilitated capsule following 4D changes over the next six months.

There is a temptation to trim the heel-buttress back to x´ from x, which I will ignore and sustain things where they are here. The position of this heel-buttress is providing much needed support at the back of the hoof — both to contain the capsule's flare away from the MAVP, and to provide a foundation for more natural growth under the horse. On the other side, at y, however, is the opposite problem, with heel growth impinging on the nearby frog's turf I (*facing page, above*). For this reason, I nippered it back. In summary, 4D changes discussed above on the y-side will counterbalance simultaneous changes occurring on the x-side, as dermal structures within respond and take charge under the invitation of NHC.

Let's move to the next page for some additional views and confirmation that we are on the right path.

Wry Foot (cadaver): Orientation.

(*Above*) Same lateral view as the one on page 256 (*above*). Capsule mass between B°TL and H°TL reflects the pathological forward migration of the toe wall. Arrow points to the lone DTA.

(*Below*) Sagittal section revealing relationship of B°TL to H°TL and run under conformation of capsule.

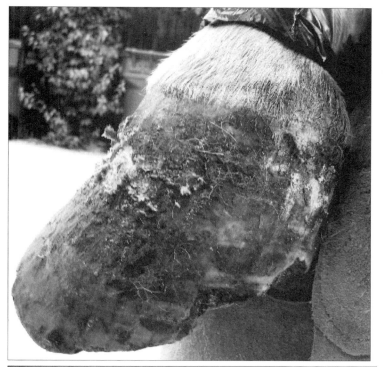

Wry Foot (cadaver): Pre-evaluation.

This cadaver hoof is so excessively overgrown at 6 in. (15.2 cm) that it presents us with two immediate challenges: first, not letting its wryness confuse where our navigational landmarks should be positioned, and, second, not getting lost in the massive amounts of waste epidermis we must bore through to reach the HSP. Let's go!

(*Above*) In spite of its great length, try in your mind's eye to see where the final cutlines will be. The master NHC practitioner learns to do this by integrating intuition and experience. When I look at this I see where I am going and I see the finished hoof. Can you?

(*Below*) Down below in the volar profile, the untrained eye immediately becomes ensnared in the emotional response of immoral neglect and the outflow of disorganized epidermis. Where is what? The trained eye of the NHC practitioner goes immediately to the navigational landmarks, which lead us straight in and through the chaos. Can you identify the structures here and the location of the MAVP?

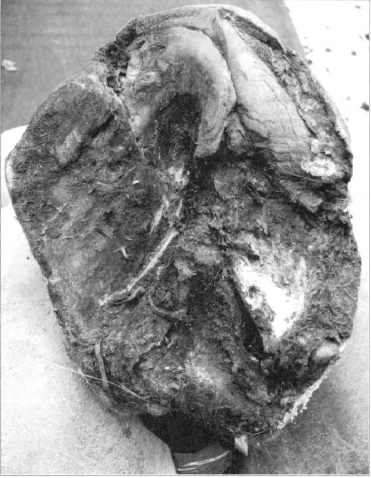

Wry Foot (cadaver): Pre-evaluation.

(This page).

(*Above*) This is the practitioner's bird's-eye view of the toe wall when the hoof is resting atop the hoof stand. I've marked the MATW, following the grain of the wall.

(*Below*) Moving to the mediolateral view, the arc of the MATW is equally apparent. The arrow points to massive separation of the wall and sole. The hoof wall here is jagged and passive to the solar dome below.

(Facing page).

(*Above, left*) The sheer length of the toe wall has rendered the HMR useless at this stage. We will deploy it later to spot check our cut-lines as we move through the debris.

(*Above, right*) Because of the curvature, the measuring tape replaces the HMR to get us started. Starting from the bull's-eye, I measure down 3¼ in. (8.3 cm) and mark the toe wall over the MATW. This is an estimate for H°TL, and I will shorten the toe wall to here unless solar plate resistance in the dome tells me to leave a longer toe. Notice that I continue marking the hoof wall at this length from the MATW back to each heel, keeping the tape parallel to the angle of growth. In this way, I will be paralleling the capsule's angle of growth and should end up very close to the M-L axis of the heels. Solar plate resistance will be my safety net, just as H°TL provides the safety net when the sole is mushy.

(*Below, left*) My cut-lines are completed and I'm now ready to move to the volar profile and begin work there.

(*Below, right*) This is a rendering of the finished hoof I see in my mind's eye.

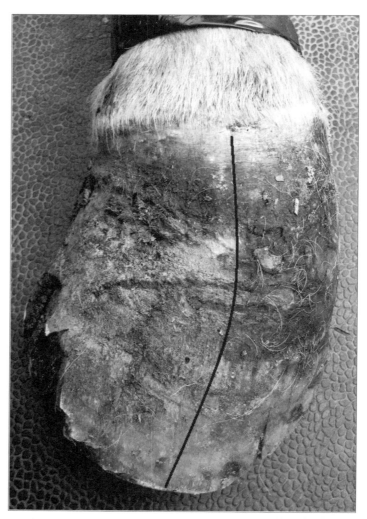

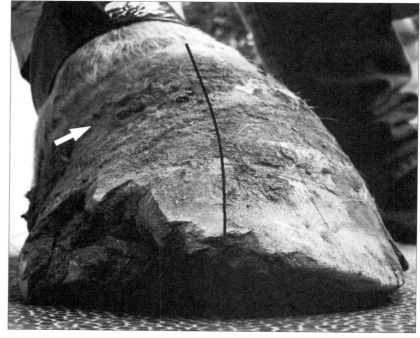

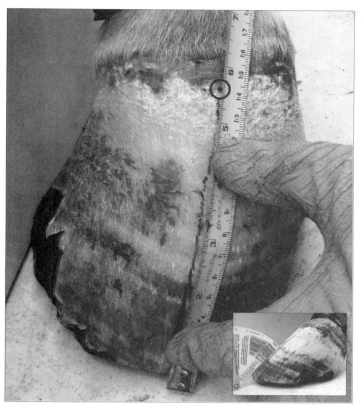

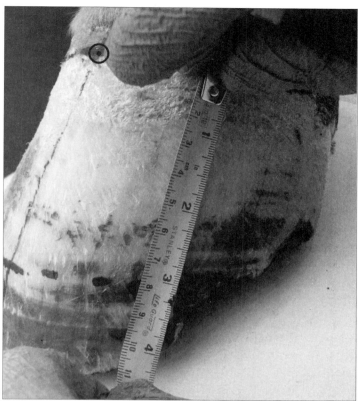

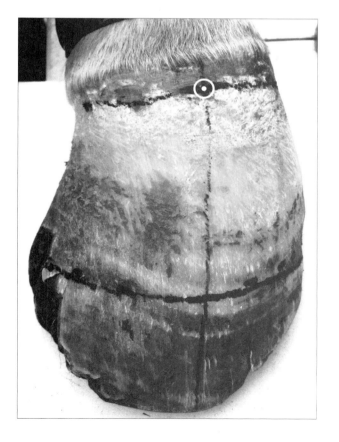

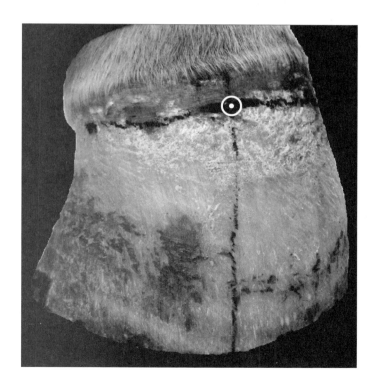

Wry Foot (cadaver): Finding Our Way In.

Keeping in mind my cut-line drawn across the face of the outer wall, I'm ready to open the volar dome.

(This page).

(*Above*) With a little poking around with my hoof pick, I've located the central sulcus of the frog and marked the MAVP. The first things that next caught my attention were the extraordinary length of bar (black arrow) and giant flap of solar plate (SP) "begging to come out". It's a toss up, but I'm going after the bar first, just in case it opens the door to a clean sweep of many plates in the dome.

(*Below*) I've sunk the nipper broadly under the end of the bar. The white arrow points to our approximate final destination, where the end (ground bearing surface) of the bar should be. As we approach the bottom, the heel-buttress will begin to form.

(Facing page).

(*Above*) I'm still working the bar down here, but, as you can see, I couldn't resist going after newly exposed solar plates, most of which have been pulverized into dust just below an outer crust of formed plates — albeit gnarly ones. The approximate location of the frog's central sulcus is marked (F). Clearly, the dome is now opening up, and the hoof wall is also now begging our attention.

(*Below*) Although it can't be seen in this view, but half the bar has been lowered to its baseline, and the solar dome has been exfoliated of much of its epidermal scruff. In life, I would be brushing this waste away as fast as it tries to accumulate and get in my way — precision trimming requires this. If a rest break is needed, I also sweep the area so that debris doesn't find its way back in the dome. The further down we go, however, the tidier our working environment becomes as we approach the HSP.

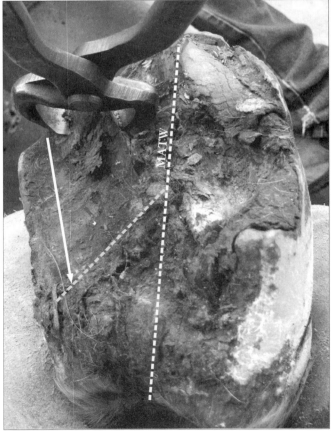

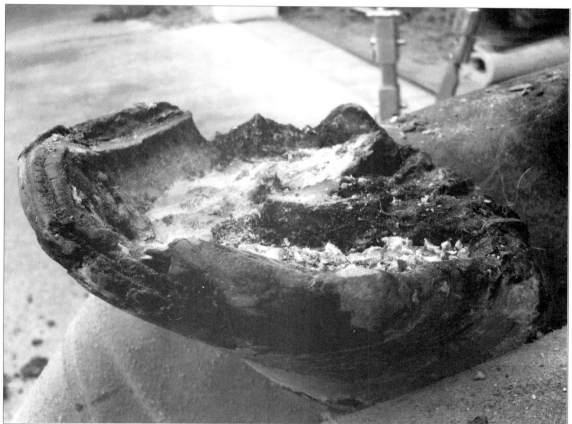

Wry Foot (cadaver): Finding the Hard Sole Plane (HSP).

We've a ways to go yet, but our navigational landmarks have guided us straight in without ambiguity.

(*Above*) The long, sweeping, white Left Right (LR) arrow marking the MATW speaks to the still lengthy and untouched toe, as we continue our way into the solar dome. The point-of-frog, exposed by sole exfoliation, reveals an extraordinary "ledge". We'll tend to that shortly. The black LR arrow is the targeted cutline for that bar. The short white arrow is the end of the bar, under which I will slip the nipper to expose the heel wall.

(*Below*) We are very near the HSP, so I've marked its periphery with the Sharpie to indicate our next destination. The point-of-frog has been nippered, and I've marked the MAVP along it and the awaiting hoof wall to restore our bearing.

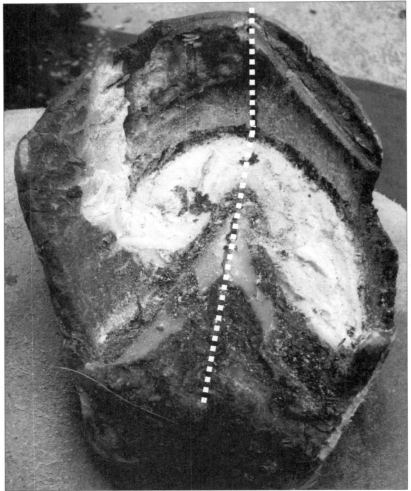

Wry Foot (cadaver): Lower Hoof Wall.

We've a ways to go yet, but our navigational landmarks have guided us straight in without ambiguity.

(*Above*) The frog is now my target, and the time has come to trim it down to firm tissue. I also need it out of the way so that I can complete my reduction of the heels and their bars. As an aside, the nippers here appear gargantuan against the hoof; this is due to the parallax effect of the camera.

(*Below*) An interesting and revealing contrast with the same view on this page (*lower*). The seat-of-corn (SC) is beginning to form atop the bar (B). I've made two nipper runs so far just to knock down this much of the hoof wall behind the bar. Note that I haven't even touched the quarter and heel walls on the opposing side as these were already broken out. [You can see this in the pre-evaluation photo on page 265 (*lower*)]. The two dashed lines mark the approximate destinations for lowering the bars.

Wry Foot (cadaver): Continue to Lower Hoof Wall; Confirm the HSP.

At long last, we've removed the wry hoof wall extending from the toe to the bar and are at or near the HSP.

(This page).
(*Above*) On the near side, the hoof wall is very near the HSP, but we need to confirm we are at rock bottom solar dome before removing any more wall on this side. Last stanchion of hoof wall is marked at its base with the Sharpie. It will require 2 to 3 nipper runs to take it down.

(*Below*) This view shows the cut-line I made at the beginning with the measuring tape. The wild horse data ranges are spot on, and the proximity of the nearby solar dome is another positive indicator we are very near the HSP.

(Facing page).
(*Above*) Black marker line spans a high spot on the quarter wall, which, if ignored, would render the quarter active to the toe and heels — a violation of the hoof's relative concavity (i.e., quarters should be passive to the toe and heels).

(*Below*) Same view as above with correction made. The cut-lines of the bars still need to be addressed. This will entail shortening the bars roughly along the lines drawn.

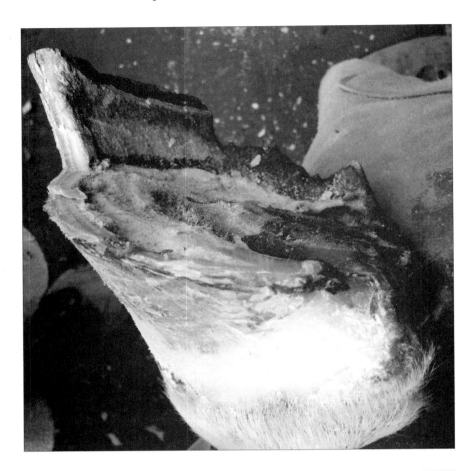

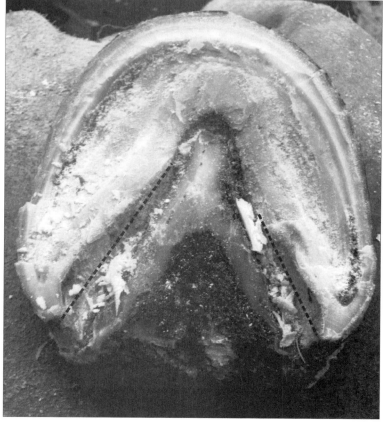

Wry Foot (cadaver): Final Nippering of Hoof Wall and Bars.

(*Above*) I am using the nipper to lower the bars one step closer to their final position. Although minimal bar is being removed, it is still more efficient to use the powerful nipper instead of the hoof knife for this purpose, providing there is sufficient room to fit the nipper blades. At this point, virtually all excavation work in the volar dome has been done by the nippers. I tell students, "Use the hoof knife for fine finishing and that's it."

(*Below*) The nippers are again deployed, this time to the heel, giving it a smooth, even cut-line, off of which to render the Mustang Roll in the next step. This is possible by "walking the nippers": keeping one blade slightly pressed against the sole at all times, making the cut, and then sliding the nipper along the sole "half the nipper blade width at a time" still keeping the blade in contact with the sole. In this way, cutting is more efficient and the hoof wall will not be marred by "step-like" notches that will only have to be cleaned up later anyway. I tell students, "Be stingy when it comes to doing anything that isn't necessary."

Wry Foot (cadaver): Cut the Mustang Roll.

(*Above*) Cutting the mustang roll. Black arrow points to water line, white arrow to white line.

(*Below*) The mustang roll is finished, the sole lightly abraded with the Round Rasp to test for and smooth the HSP, and all raggedy pieces of frog removed with the hoof knife, which I've brought out for the first time. In contrast to its earlier gnarly state, the volar dome now possesses a somewhat elegant finish. The frog is actually passive to the hoof wall, although it may not be apparent from the image.

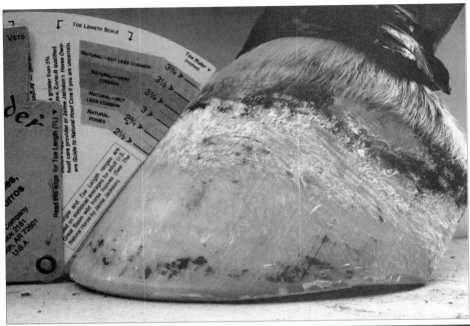

Wry Foot (cadaver): Post-trim Evaluation.

The hoof is finished as shown here and on the facing page.

(*Above*) The HMR reveals some 3 in. (7.6 cm) of excess toe wall has been removed. Now at less than 3½ inches,
H°TL falls well within the "natural" range. In life, as further growth changes supplant its wryness, this hoof would undoubtedly heal and also shorten at least another ¼ in. (1 cm).

(*Below*) H° also measures very centrally in the natural range at 53°. There is scant evidence of DTA.

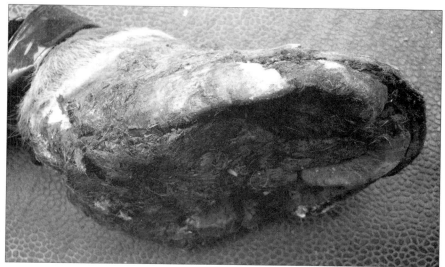

Wry Foot (cadaver): Post-trim Evaluation (Cont'd).

(*Above*) Bleak reminder of where we started.

(*Center*) Looking good!

(*Below*) Wry growth is evident in the curved grain of the toe wall and the MATW, which runs obliquely to the MPVW. Under a strict regimen of NHC new growth will supplant the wry growth over 2 to 3 hoof growth cycles (hgc).[1]

[1] "*hgc*: Hoof Growth Cycle". SRP Bulletin #100 (4/28/2003).

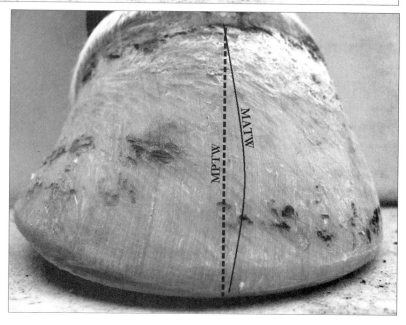

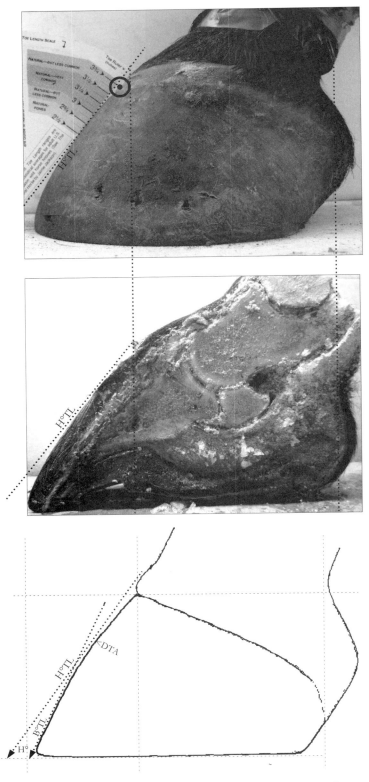

A bull-nosed hoof. The toe wall at the MATW is bent into an arc. H°TL > B°TL.

CHAPTER 13

Trimming the "Bull-nosed" Hoof

The term "bull nose" for such a hoof so conformed comes from the toe wall's resemblance to the rounded nose of a bull, or so farrier convention has it. It's a serious pathological conformation, in my opinion. Nearly half of all cadaver hooves coming through my training clinics are bull-nosed. Why is this? And what is the effect upon the hoof and the horse?

There seems to be several causes, which are easily correlated to front and hind feet. With hind hooves, the bull-nose seems to arise from horses that habitually drag their feet either from indifference and boredom or the inability to collect themselves ("crookedness"); it is also caused by invasive shoeing and trimming methods. In the front, it is caused solely by the same deleterious shoeing and trimming methods that have the effect of "backing up the hoof", purportedly to correct or prevent overreaching. In any case, the long term effect of bull-nosing is to create a DTA, wherein B°TL is shorter than H°TL (*facing page*) — a direct violation of the wild horse model.

Bull-nosing, regardless of cause, also has the effect of displacing mass behind H°, which is to say that the hoof's (volar) support base is rendered too far back. And as a consequence of this, the hoof's entire support base shrinks when the MATW is no longer aligned with H° TL. Very likely, the foot's nerve receptors in the growth coria are hypersensitive to this loss of mass, and, to protect the foot's sensitive and vascular contents, alters the wall's growth pattern by a "mass retreat". In sum, such pathological changes can only obstruct the natural gaits as horses with bull-nosed hooves simply cannot and do not move naturally. Tripping, interference, and outright pain are just some of the most obvious consequences.

Reversing the bull-nosed hoof conformation takes time and patience. Once NHC practices are implemented, the foot will need its own time to respond — typically 1 *hgc* or less. I think of this as "coaxing the foot to come out from hiding". NHC practitioners are often amazed the first time they witness this miraculous change wherein the foot release enormous amounts of healing growth after having been "locked up" and in a retreating disposition. As far as work at the hoof is concerned, the natural trim is all that is needed. Keep a log of critical measurements and photographs to track the 4D changes.

All photos in this series are by Jill Willis.

Bull-nosed Foot (cadaver):
Pre-trim evaluation.

In addition to the images on this and the facing page, study those on the chapter frontispiece (p. 280) as part of our pre-trim evaluation.

(*Above*) The MAVP has been marked and the rasp has served as a straight-edge to mark the MATW. Note the extreme convexity of the toe wall.

(*Below*) The bull's-eye is marked on the MATW. H° is unreadable due to the convex nature of the toe wall, hence, in keeping with natural trim protocol, it is set at 54° for this front foot. H°TL (calibrated to 54°) gauges at 3¾ in (9.5 cm), suggesting the toe wall can be shortened. We are now ready to go to work.

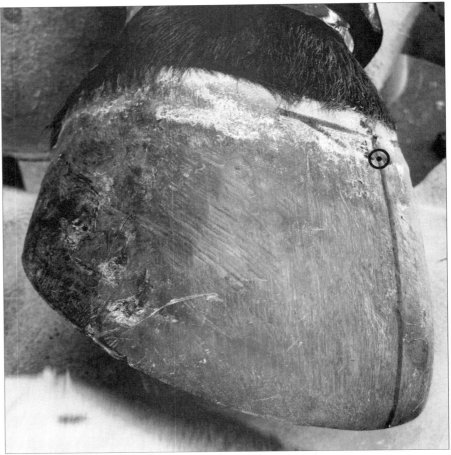

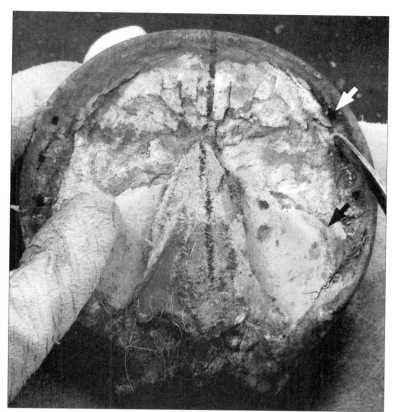

Bull-nosed Foot (cadaver): Find HSP and Shorten Hoof Wall.

This hoof had been shod, but the shoes were pulled prior to this photo series.

(*Above*) 6 nail holes ring the solar dome periphery. White arrow points to forward nail that was set inside the white line, always risky due to close proximity of the sole dermis and LAM. Solar plates forward of the point-of-frog are inviting of nipper dragging. Black arrow points to end of overgrown bar, ditto for bar on other side partially hidden by my thumb.

(*Below*) Nipper dragging exposes hoof wall, which I am now trimming starting at the MATW.

**Bull-nosed Foot (cadaver):
Shorten Hoof Wall (Cont'd).**

(This page)

(*Above*) Removing the wall at the quarter during our first nipper run.

(*Below*) Nippering out the bar. At this stage, the hoof knife has not yet been deployed.

(Facing page).

(*Above*) I was midway nippering the hoof wall on the opposite of the one just finished, when the frog caught my eye. "Take it" crossed by mind, and so I did. I'm one to move around the hoof at will when nippering, if I think breaking sequence (e.g., a nipper run along the hoof wall) will make my work more efficient later.

(*Below*) Back to the hoof wall, and I see the bar is begging for some action. It'll be gone as quick as I can slip a nipper blade underneath and squeeze.

**Bull-nosed Foot (cadaver):
Pre-trim evaluation.**

We are half way through the trim. Time wise, not more than a minute for a hoof of this size, shape, and proportion.

(This page)
(*Above*) I've slipped the nipper under the overgrown bar and begun cutting.

(*Center*) Bar nippered to its baseline just above the sole at and near the seat-of-corn.

(*Below*) One last precision cut at the heel to bring the hoof back underneath the horse and to balance the hoof in its mediolateral profile.

(Facing page).
(*Above*) Overview of volar dome at this point. I've dragged the sole with the nippers once more and concluded that I've arrived at or near the HSP. The HMR, in a moment, will give me final confirmation. In life, I would wait for more solar plates to separate, driven by movement and the effects of the natural trim, to lead me in further — assuming the HMR tells me otherwise. Time is on my side, and the principles of NHC have taught me to be patient.

(*Below*) I've set to cutting the mustang roll, always with the goal of getting the waterline to be the most distal structure, no matter how thing/narrow it appears to be. White arrow points to the roll just cut; black arrow to the direction I'm heading towards.

Bull-nosed Foot (cadaver):
Post-trim Evaluation.

We are done trimming, and the time has come to confirm the critical measurements for our records.

(*Above*) This image, we recall, was taken at the outset. H°TL is necessarily measured "through the bull-nose" along the MPTW rather than along the MATW. The HMR is calibrated to 54°, and H°TL gauges at 3¾ in (9.5 cm)

(*Below*) The HMR (again calibrated to 54°) is set once more to the MPTW and H°TL gauges at just over 3¼ in. (~8.4 cm), a drop in length of ½ in. (1.3 cm). That's very central in the "natural" range for H°TL, so I'll put the brakes on all trimming at this point. We are done.

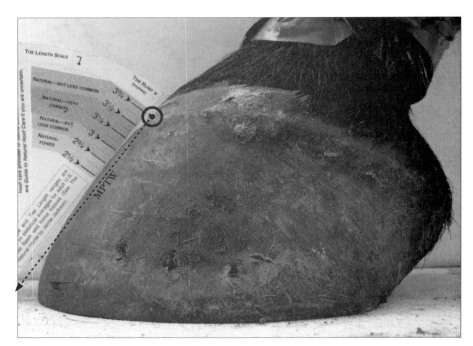

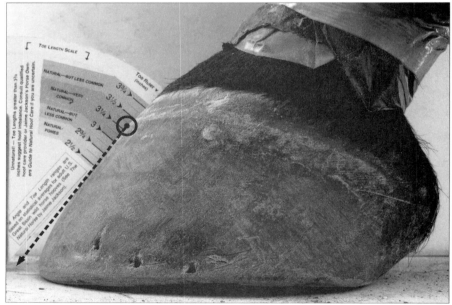

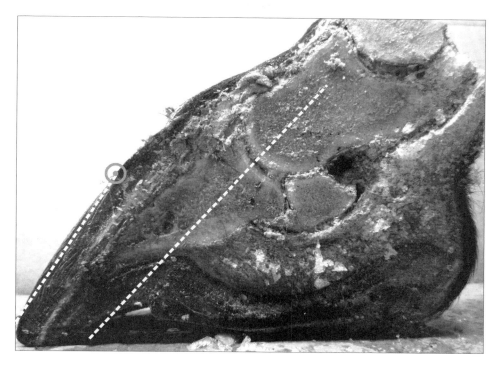

**Bull-nosed Foot (cadaver):
Post-trim Evaluation.**

(*Above*) The hoof is bisected along the MPVP-MPTW plane. I'm showing this view so you can see how the toe wall wraps around P3 in an arc, and that the digital axis and the MPTW eventually intersect. The only radiograph I possess of a Great Basin wild horse hoof suggests they should be parallel and not intersect. But I am not prepared to raise this to a standard in the absence of a larger statistical sample. Note too the rather acute angle that the solar dome makes with the ground forward of the frog at the MATW. As solar plates yield, in life, this will change as heel growth and toe wall growth modulate in the 4D to sustain H°. I have tracked such healthful changes in the 4D, and they truly are the stuff of miracles.

Band of wild burros in the American southwest.

CHAPTER 14
Trimming the Donkey (Burro) and Mule

Comprehensive research has not yet been conducted to establish NHC data ranges for donkeys and mules. During the winter of 1983, the BLM captured a 10 year old, 1,100 lb. female mule running with a wild horse band (*right*); she came through the BLM's Litchfield corrals during one of my data gathering sessions, and I was able to photograph and measure her feet. Her hooves were as stunning as her equine relatives and I reported my findings later in the American Farriers Journal.[1] Significantly, her measurements fell very centrally within the data ranges for *Equus ferus caballus*.

Only once did I accidentally come upon a "pack" of wild donkeys in the southern reaches of Nevada, and from what I could see in the brief moments before they darted away into the deep, rocky canyon below, they possessed the typical tough, short immaculate feet of the wild horse while retaining the characteristic features of a burro foot described on the following pages. What I have learned from experience over the years, is that the hoof of the donkey (*Equus africanus asinus*), and mule, trim precisely to the same guidelines as his equine counterpart, *Equus ferus caballus*. Both are also vulnerable to the same hoof pathologies that plague the horse. The principal difference in the hooves between the two species, however, lies in the conformation of the heels, and — relative to the donkey — angle-of-growth along the MPTW. The mule, depending on the interplay of dominant-recessive genes of his respective lineages, may show more of the horse or donkey foot.

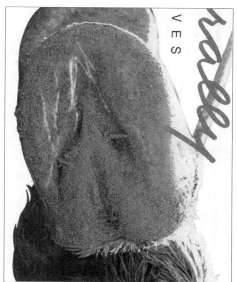

[1]Jackson, J. "What You Can Learn From Mule Hooves In The Outback" American Farriers Journal, July/August, 1993.

Donkey (cadaver):
Orientation evaluation.

Since the donkey and mule trim precisely to the same natural trim guidelines as the horse, I'm only going to conduct an orientation evaluation. Although there is no measurement data based on studies by which to gauge this donkey hoof, it is nevertheless gridded like all other hooves

(This page)
(*Above*) The MAVP is marked. Notice the full, well-rounded hoof wall. I've also outlined the periphery of the bar and heel on one side to accentuate the natural donkey heel-buttress conformation. The arrow points at the bend in the heel wall that gives rise to this shape. I've noticed this same bend in wild horse feet, but it is so faint that unless one is looking for it, it is sure to be missed.

(*Below*) The very upright conformation of the toe wall along the MATW is apparent here in profile. Yet the hoof is not clubbed. Arrow points to the aforementioned bend in the heel wall. Also visible are stress rings, more noticeable toward the heel.

(Facing page).
(*Above, left*) Mediolateral profile reveals steep quarter walls, and numerous stress rings cascading down the outer wall.

(*Above, right*) The wall from toe to heel was lightly rasped down. I've also lightly abraded the solar dome with the Round Rasp facilitate more natural growth therein. The water line is marked with the Sharpie to show where the mustang roll is turned.

(*Below*) I've tilted the hoof just enough to highlight the one errant area of active wear along the lateral quarter (white arrow); an astute eye can see the dip in the solar dome below the hoof wall, inviting nipper dragging and a generous cut. Black arrows point in the direction of the bars, below and behind which lies the frog mass.

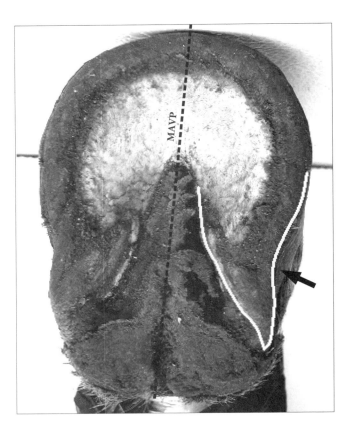

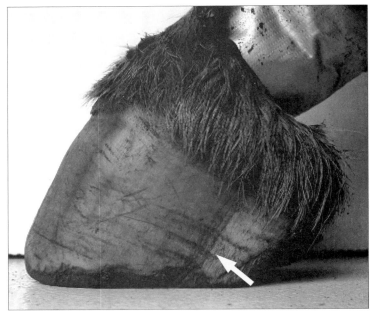

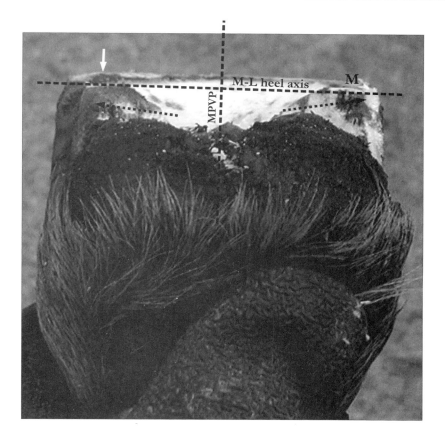

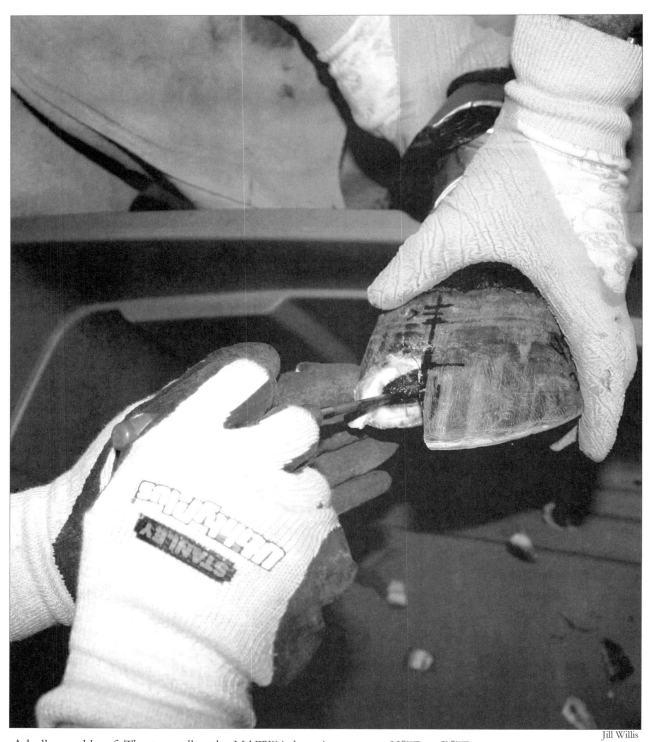

A bull-nosed hoof. The toe wall at the MATW is bent into an arc. H°TL > B°TL.

Notching the Hoof

A common concern among conscientious NHC practitioners is whether or not they are going to over trim the hoof and render it hypersensitive, if not bleeding. In my training clinics, I help students overcome this apprehension, or appreciate the risks of over trimming, by dissecting each cadaver hoof after it is trimmed. In this way, a method I call "notching the hoof", they learn to understand the relationship of each epidermal structure to its dermal counterpart (i.e., growth corium). In each instance, they take the critical measurements of the hoof before and after it is trimmed. Then, I ask them to predict before each dissection if they have left enough hoof (or too much) and how much. It doesn't take long before they gain a very strong and accurate sense of where things are at inside the hoof. In addition, they also contrast their dissections with the wild horse hoof cadavers I show them, which gives them even more confidence that what they are doing is in sync with nature. Later, during their hands-on training with live horses, they appreciate how notching is truly helpful in giving them confidence. In this chapter, we will go step-by-step with notching. You will then need to practice on cadavers yourself to gain the ever important hands-on experience.

Notching the Hoof.

(This page)

(Above) Using the edge of your rasp or other straight-edge, mark the MAVP with a Sharpie. Then, at 90° to the MAVP, and starting at the toe, draw a series of parallel lines ¼ in. (1 cm) apart from each other. These lines should extend accumulatively at least half the distance from the toe to the point-of-frog, typically 3 to 4 parallel lines in total, sometimes more.

(Below) Draw a second series of parallel lines over one heel-buttress, each also perpendicular (90°) to the MAVP. Collectively, these lines drawn across the volar profile are called *gridlines*. Where they intersect the MAVP gridlines form *sectors*. For example, I have whited out one toe and one heel sector. Sectors are notched out (hence, "notching the hoof") one by one with the nippers until the inner dermis is cut through. Arrows point in the direction sectors are removed.

(Facing page).

(Above, left) The objective is to notch out one sector at a time on one side of the MAVP until the dermis is reached. When notching, keep the nipper blades angled at 90° to the volar profile as shown here.

To aid students in predicting at which point they will reach the dermis, I have them initial which sector they think this is going to happen. The initials are placed opposite the sectors that will be nippered as I've done here with my own. This encourages students to pay closer attention to such factors as H, HTL, integrity of solar plates, and underrundedness.

(Above, right) Cutting through the hoof isn't easy, and certainly isn't a one person job. Highly recommended is that one person (sitting) positions the nippers on the gridlines, while an assistant (standing) provides the main clenching force on the nipper handles as shown. Trying to do this alone inevitably ends up with sloppy sectors and sore wrists.

(Below) Two sectors removed. Continue notching sector by sector until the dermis and P3 are reached.

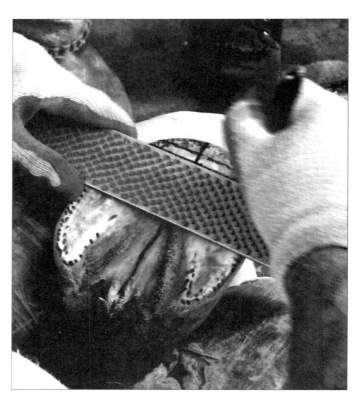

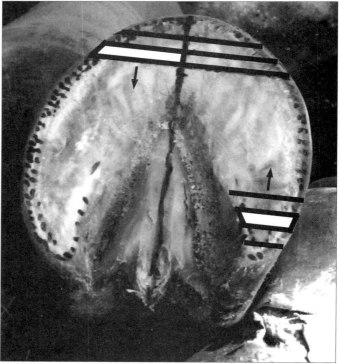

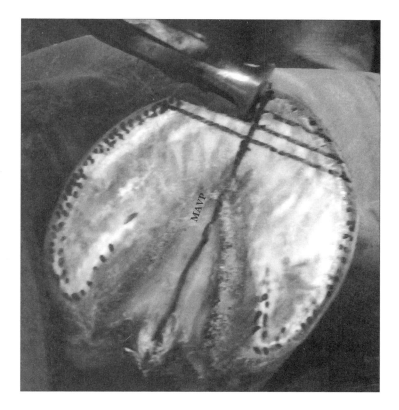

Notching the Hoof.

This discussion represents the main objectives of notching: first, to gain a sense of where the foot's growth coria lie in relation to their respective epidermal structures; and, second, to gain insight into how much epidermis can be removed without rendering the coria hypersensitive. As always, the wild horse model is the reference standard for interpreting the results of notching.

(This page)

(Above) Use the Vernier caliper to measure sole thickness. To calibrate to the wild horse model,[1] measure sole thickness along the length of its juncture with the white line, from the dermis to the ground, as shown here (arrow). The sole should measure anywhere from ¼ in. (1 cm) to 1 in. (2.5 cm) thick, which is the case here.

(Below) After notching the toe, notch and measure one or both heel-buttresses as shown. The sole should be as thick at the heel as the toe.

(Facing page).

(Above) Insert a narrow probe (I recommend the round-tapered Buck hoof knife sharpener, used for sharpening the knife's crook) into the solar and lamellar coria. You want to feel the space between the hoof wall and P3, and between the sole and P3.

When evaluating the lamellar attachments, ask yourself are these structures strong enough to sustain the weight of the horse during support? Are they difficult or impossible to tear when pressured by your probe? Near the sole, could they possibly survive laceration by the sharp distal periphery of P3 if thousands of pounds of pressure were applied to them? If the hoof is laminitic that you are evaluating, do the lamellar attachments appeared sheared from a weight-bearing force? Then review my discussion of the NHC hoof mechanism and see if you agree with me that the answer to each questions is logically "no".

(Below) Close-up view of structures to be evaluated during notching.

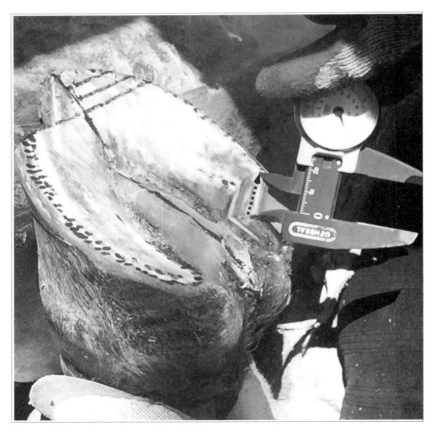

[1]*The Natural Horse* (Jackson), pp. 118-119.

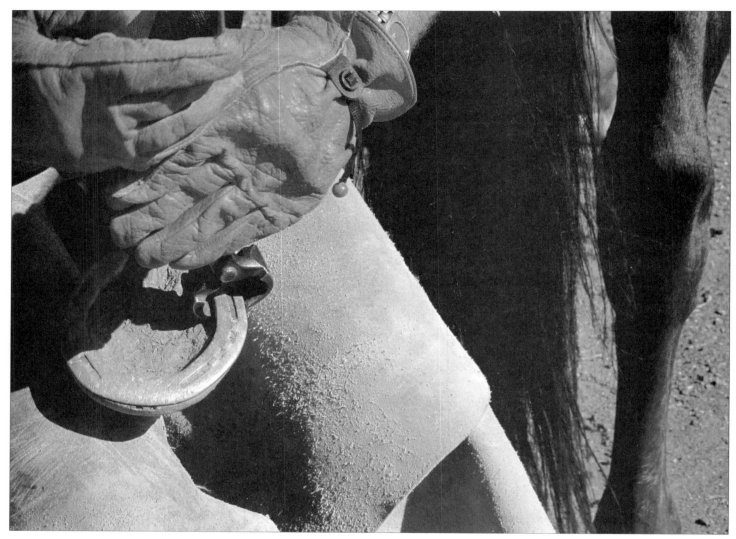

Removing a shoe is surprisingly easy . . . with good technique!

Shoe Pulling

Regretfully, removing shoes often comes with the territory of being an NHC practitioner. While "de-shoeing" is something I do teach in my training clinics, I always tell students that it is perfectly acceptable to ask the horse's owner have the farrier to remove them instead, but not trim the hooves afterwards. If you are an NHC cross-over farrier, like myself, then pulling shoes isn't an issue. But it can be tough on NHC practitioners who didn't come through the horseshoeing circuit, since removing shoes will be a rarity in their practices as barefoot trimmers. I've been told more than once, words to the effect, "On Monday I pulled the LF, on Tuesday the RF, and then on Wednesday I gave up on ever getting the hinds off, so we called the farrier." Such is the physical hardship of removing shoes. Fortunately, it doesn't have to be that way, but the NHC practitioner must understand the principles of efficient shoe removal, while, of course, being in good physical shape to do the work.

In the following pages, I will explain what I do in most instances. We'll be using the bull-nosed cadaver hoof discussed in Chapter 13 to demonstrate the techniques I use. What the beginner must try to process mentally is that using "brute force" is not what is needed, even though this is what seems logical and what many hoof care professionals — farriers and barefooters alike — resort to using. If you are very strong and "macho", well, go for it. But I happen to be pretty strong and muscular myself, and I still would prefer to do things the "easy way".

To begin, having a horse standing on his correct diagonal as explained in the introduction (Part II) is of paramount importance. This enables him to balance himself for the tugging that's going to take place. My experience has been that horses are more than receptive to getting their shoes off and will help by providing opposing forces that will help to get them off. This presupposes, however, that the practitioner is in communication with the horse through sequencing and RD. Horses are extremely intelligent and capable of helping when things are explained to them, or resisting at anything when you take them for granted, treat them harshly, or don't explain things. So having the horse balanced and receptive to helping, just leaves effective technique that gets the job done efficiently without exhausting the practitioner, or the horse, and that offsets the propensity for just trying to use brute force to get the shoe off.

All photos in this series by Jill Willis.

De-shoeing (cadaver).

Experienced farriers can remove a shoe in seconds by understanding how (nail) clinches secure it to the foot. There are ways to weaken the clinches with using no more than a shoe puller, and that is discussed here. As a former farrier, I'm well versed in other ways to help make it easier for beginners to remove shoes, and offer some of the tricks of the trade here as well. As I think about it, and you should too as an NHC student, the objective is to loosen the clinches as quick as possible, and get the shoe off as quick as the dislodged nails allow. This will require "feel". Clearly, de-shoeing is one of the hardest things for beginners to master, but once the "feel" is established, you can pop off a set of shoes in minutes, not "one shoe a day".

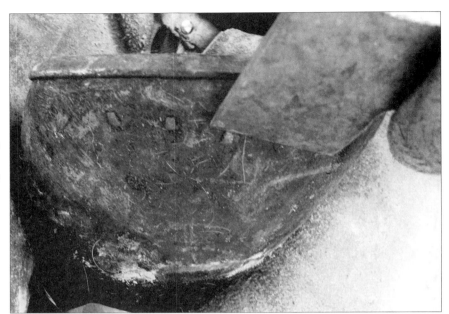

(This page)
(*Above*) Set the clinch cutter under the nail clinch protruding from the outer wall. This and other de-shoeing tools are listed in the Tools/Equipment appendix.

(*Below*) If the nail is flush with the wall, then edge the corner of the clinch cutter under the nail clinch.

(Facing page).
(*Above*) With a hammer, strike the clinch firmly with the shoer's hammer. Don't be bashful — really hit it firmly, and the clinch will loosen and open.

(*Below*) Black arrow points in the direction of the opened clinch. Area framed is called the "nailing zone". Generally speaking, until all the nail holes grow out, the nailing zone is an area of the hoof wall subject to ravel and splits. This is perfectly normal and protective measures are unnecessary. Natural wear will build in strong new growth. Measure from the nail (or nail hole once the shoe is removed), to the ground in the direction of the outer wall's grain to estimate how long it will take for the nailing zone to heal: calculate using ¼ in. (1 cm) per month per *hgc*.

De-shoeing (cadaver).

(This page)
(*Above*) Arrow points in the direction of the nail clinch just opened.

(*Below*) Other nails now opened. I've done the same thing on the opposite side of the hoof. So, with all the clinches opened, we are now ready to take the shoe off.

(Facing page).
(*Above*) This is an important step, in fact, critical to easy shoe removal. Beginning at the very end of the shoe branch on one side, squeeze the blades of the shoe puller together. In most instances, this will begin to loosen the nails in the hoof wall, but will be hardly perceptible.

(*Below*) Close up view. Opposing arrows point in the direction of the closing jaws of the shoe puller. Again, just squeeze the handles together and nothing more. Vertical arrow points to nail head of rearmost set nail. You want to make sure that the blades of the shoe puller are always set behind this nail. Advancing the puller further forward than here at this stage will make it too hard to lift the shoe. Moreover, the blades can also cut the nail in two, leaving part of the nail in the shoe, the other embedded in the hoof wall. This is not the end of the world, but just makes for more unnecessary work later to get the nail out of the hoof wall.

De-shoeing (cadaver).

(This page)

(*Above*) Next, go to the opposite heel branch of the shoe and repeat. Then, immediately go back to the branch you started on, and repeat there too. Do this several times, going back and forth between the branches. As you do, however, shimmy the blades of the puller slightly forward towards that rearmost nail, no more than ¼ in. (1 cm) at a time. In most cases the shoe will have lifted a little as you squeeze and advance towards the back nail. When this happens, remove the pullers from under the shoe and use it to hammer down both branches of the shoe with the serrated edge of the pullers (white arrow) until the shoe is flush against the hoof wall again. In many instances, one or more nail heads set in the grooves (called the "fuller) of the shoe will pop up above the shoe.

(*Below*) This head of this nail protruded above the shoe and I was able to grasp it with the blades of the shoe puller (never use your nippers to do this or to remove shoes!). Note that I've grabbed the nail head on one side of the blades, while bracing the other against the shoe. This provides leverage for pulling the nail out. One can also use the nail puller (not shown, but in the appendix) to do this, but I find I can do the same things with the puller, and that's one less tool to carry around.

(Facing page).

(*Above*) I've lifted the nail part way out, then grabbed it again but lower down its shaft. One more yank and its out. Once it's out, there is that much less resistance to overcome when using the shoe puller. In many instances, I don't pull all the nails out, but just pull the shoe off with the nails intact. It just depends on the grip of the clinches.

(*Below*) Notice here the position and action of my hands bracing the shoe puller. Note too that the direction I'm lifting and pushing in always in the direction of the hoof wall (marked by the path of white arrows). Never crank the nippers toward and/or away from the solar dome.

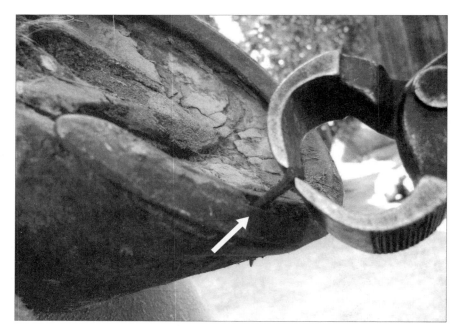

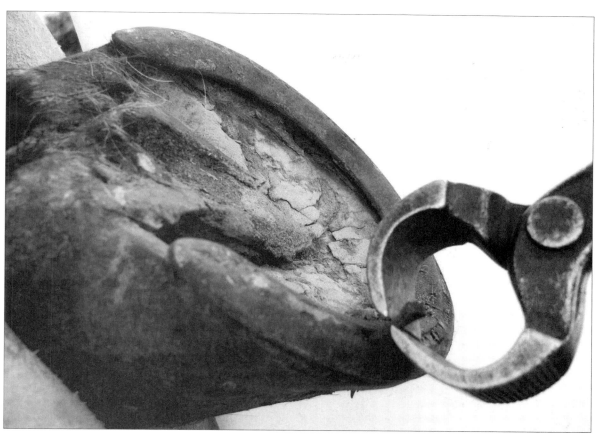

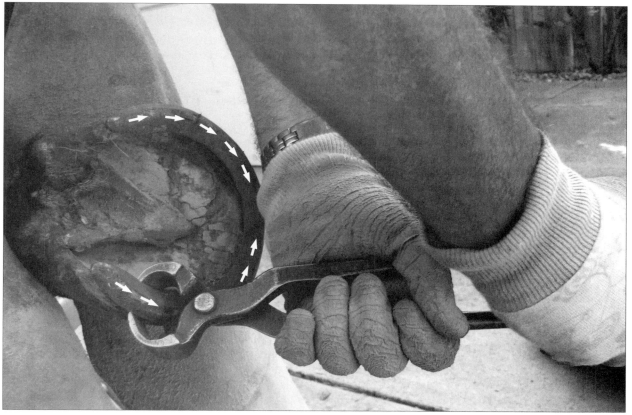

De-shoeing (cadaver).

(This page)

(*Above*) The shoe is now very loose everywhere and ready to come off with a slight jerking action. The idea is not to "pull" the shoe off, so much as to "snap" it off. The reason is that pulling tends to take the entire foot right along with the shoe, whereas snapping tends to leave the foot behind. This requires "feeling" and in my training clinics I have students put their hands over mine to learn to "feel" the snapping action. Accompanying the "snap" is a slight "cracking" sound as the nails snap loose and the jaws of the puller wrench the shoe. I teach students to listen closely for this sound, as it is a cue that the shoe is about ready to pop off. If the shoe will not give enough to snap off, then return to the previous step to further loosen the clinches. Once more, follow the direction of the hoof wall when snapping the shoe loose (p. 301, *below*).

(*Below*) As you move the pullers forward along the hoof wall, you will eventually run into the nails. Avoid cutting them, by lightly squeezing the puller blades against or close to the nail shaft. You can then pry the shoe without disturbing the nail itself or causing more damage.

(Facing page).

(*Above*) Some shoes are very resistant to come off from light snapping action. When this is the case, I take both hands in the same direction and push. This way I have the combined fire power of my hands, wrists, forearms, biceps and shoulders to weigh in! Follow direction of hoof wall with no side-to-side prying action.

(*Below*) The shoe is off. Note one hole is missing a nail. Where is it? It's always a good idea to take a nail count before you begin, and then make sure that you can account for all the nails at the end. Leaving an errant nail in the wall can be catastrophic to your nippers. If a nail is left in the wall, remove it by striking a nail punch into the nail hole at the bottom of the hoof. This will drive the nail up through its own clinch hole in the outer wall, where you can grab and remove it with the shoe puller blades.

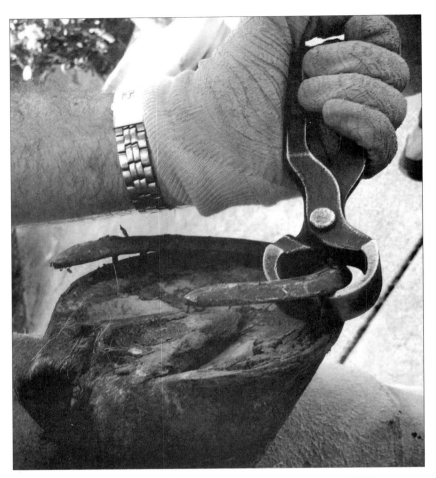

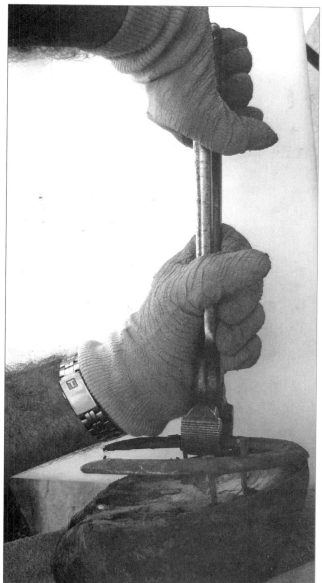

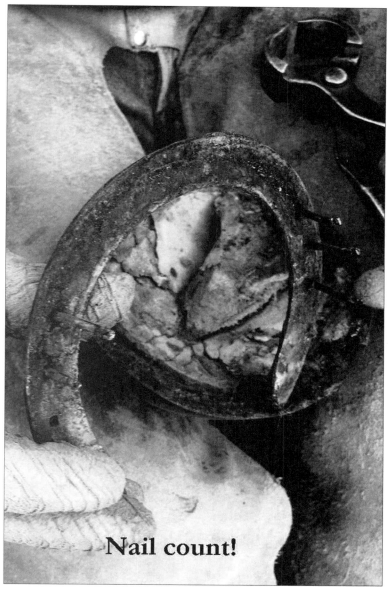

Nail count!

Recommended NHC Tools and Equipment

NHC practitioners should be equipped with suitable protective clothing, tools, and equipment. Below are the tools and equipment I personally use. Most everything is now available at Internet stores including my own (www.jaimejackson.com) or Star Ridge Company (www.star-ridge.com).

Trimmer's Apparel

Apron - Many types are available. I use leather version which extends down to my shins as seen in the trimming sequences in this book (e.g., p. 170). My design is sold at my online store.

Gloves - I use heavy duty leather work type with adjustable wrist straps.

Footwear - I use heavy duty leather work boots. I prefer to avoid metals toes as it is possible your foot could get crimped inside by the force of an errant foot.

Hand Tools

Hoof pick - I use an 8 inch professional model with finger grips. I don't like smaller hoof picks, and flimsy types with brushes at one end.

Hoof brush - I use a heavy duty hoof brush with non-metallic bristles.

Hoof knife - Many types available. Avoid loop knives, knives with two cutting edges, and knives with either very flat or very pronounced curved blades. Use either a left or right handled knife but not both — using two knives is not necessary and is less efficient. I use F. Dick and Halverson brands with narrow blades. Looped knives are popular but can easily take too much.

Rasps - I use a 15 inch F. Dick flat rasp, and the Concaving Sole Rasp and Radius Rasps by Evolutionary Hoof Care Tools (*facing page*).

Hoof sander - I use the Hoof Buffer by Evolutionary Hoof Care Tools (*facing page*).

14 or 15 inch (38 cm) Hoof nipper - The larger nippers are more efficient than smaller models. I use the Diamond 15 inch and Nordic Brand 14 inch. Don't be fooled into thinking the 12 inch rasp is easier to wield for women or small hands; it's just more work!

Shoe puller, Nail puller, Clinch cutter, and farrier's driving hammer - If you are going to remove shoes, then you will need these. These are available at farrier supply houses.

Equipment

Hoof Stand - I use the tripod type with rotating tool caddy by Evolutionary Hoof Care Tools.

Hoof Meter Reader - The 2012 model reads on both sides in inches and in centimeters.

Measuring tape - Measuring tape should read in both Metric and U.S. measurement units.

Hoof knife sharpeners - There are two types, round and flat, and both are needed to do the job. I use the round Buck brand sharpener and the Istor Swiss Sharpener.

Vernier caliper - This tool is indispensable for taking accurate hoof measurements. I prefer the plastic models over the metal ones:

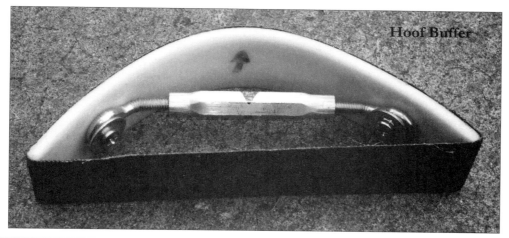

Hoof Buffer

Radius Rasp Pro

Radius Rasp Original

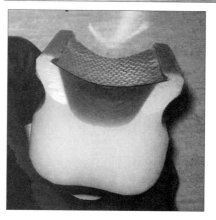

Concaving
Sole Rasp

BIBLIOGRAPHY

Emery, Leslie; Jim Miller and Nyles Van Hoosen, DVM. *Horseshoeing Theory and hoof Care.* Philadelphia: Lea & Fiber, 1977.

Handler, Hans. *The Spanish Riding School.* New York: McGraw Hill, 1972.

Jackson, Jaime. *Founder: Prevention and Cure the Natural Way.* Fayetteville: Star Ridge Publishing, 2000.

Jackson, Jaime. *Paddock Paradise: A Guide to Natural Horse Boarding.* Fayetteville: Star Ridge Publishing, 2006.

Jackson, Jaime. *The Natural Horse: Lessons from the Wild.* Flagstaff: Northland Publishing, 1992.

Jackson, Jaime. *AANHCP Field Guide to Natural Hoof Care.* Fayetteville: Star Ridge Publishing, 2010.

Jackson, Jaime. *AANHCP Field Guide to Sequencing.* Fayetteville: Star Ridge Publishing, 2010.

Podhajsky, Alois. *The Complete Training of Horse and Rider.* New York: Doubleday, 1967.

Pollitt, Christopher C. *Color Atlas of The Horse's Foot.* London: Mosby-Wolfe, 1995.

Seunig, Waldemar. *Horsemanship.* New York: Doubleday, 1956.

Xenophon. *The Art of Horsemanship.* M.H. Morgan, trans. London: J.A. Allen & Co., 1962.

GLOSSARY AND INDEX OF NHC TERMS

Note: This unique glossary of NHC terminology is indexed to definitions and their nearby foundational discussions in the text. It is not a comprehensive index, however. You are encouraged to build your own personal index by penciling in other page references pertinent to your study of NHC.

active wear: Areas of hoof's greatest abrasion and callusing relative to its volar concavity. *In naturally shaped hooves, the hoof wall endures more active wear, the sole and frog endure more passive wear.* 70

active support: Areas of the capsule that actively support the weight of the horse relative to the hoof's volar concavity. *In naturally shaped hooves, areas of active wear in the hoof's volar profile actively support of the weight of the horse, the sole and frog passively support the weight of the horse.* 71

adaptation: Evolutionary process whereby an organism becomes suited to its habitat. 31

adaptative environment: biomes to which *Equus ferus ferus* adapted 1.4 million years ago. 35

alpha: Position of relative dominance in horse's social hierarchy. 161

angle-of-adaptation (A°): A° is the underlying angle-of-adaptation among wild, free-roaming horses living in their adaptative environment, which, in life, is measurable as N°. 92

angle-of-growth: Angle at which the hoof wall grows down below the coronary band. 66

anteroposterior: From the front to the back of the hoof.

appendicular skeleton: Bones of the horse's fore and hind limbs. See *axial skeleton.* 238

arteriovenousanastamoses (AVA): Shunts connecting branches of the arteries and veins in advance of the foot's capillary beds. 151

axial skeleton: Bones of the horse's skull, vertebral column, sternum, and ribs. See *appendicular skeleton.* 238

backing up the toe: Inhumane trimming method that intentionally renders the toe wall thinner than its natural thickness, resulting in a bull-nosed hoof, obstruction of the natural gaits, and hypersensitivity. 103

bars: Extensions of the hoof wall passive to the volar plane and forming the collateral sulci of the frog. 56

barefoot hoof: An un-shod hoof.

barefoot trim: Generic term for any trim that does not including fixed shoeing. *A natural trim is a barefoot trim, but not all barefoot trims are natural trims.* 83

basement angle (B°): Any angle of the toe wall below a DTA aligned with the MPTW. 120

basement membrane of horse's foot (BM): Thin sheet of fibers that underlie the epidermis of the hoof. *The BM is connected to the lamellar dermis upon which SELs are anchored.* See *epidermis, lamina,* and *SEL.* 140

basement toe length (B°TL): Length of toe wall over MATW from the bull's-eye to the end of the wall when H°TL is bent by a DTA. 120

beta: Position of relative sub-dominance in horse's social hierarchy. 161

biodynamic hoof balance: Equilibrium between the living hoof and the environment characterized by natural shape, size, and proportion; and optimal healthfulness. 177

biomes: Climatically and geographically similar areas of the Earth with respect to communities of plants, animals, and soil organisms. Also referred to as ecosystems. 36

breakover: Cessation of the weight bearing (compressional) force. 152

bull's-eye (◉): Intersection of the limit line (LL) with the MATW. 116

bull-nosed hoof: (Pathology) Capsule with one or more DTAs and where the MATW has bent behind H°TL. 275

callus: Generally, the hardened state of the capsule resulting from natural wear, particularly over areas of active wear. 70

capsule: All of the epidermal structures comprising the horse's foot, including the wall, sole, frog, heel bulbs, periople, and coronary band. 60

cartilages: Large pads of tough, flexible connective tissue attached to the proximal borders of the wings of the coffin bone. The digital cushion is situated between the cartilages. See *digital cushion* and *palmer processes of coffin bone.* 57

clubfoot: (Pathology) Any left or right hoof whose Healing Angle (H°) is 3 or more degrees higher than its paired hoof. Typically, the clubfoot will also measure less across HL and HW. 235

coffin bone: Lowermost bone in the horse's foot, also known as P3, pedal bone, and distal phalanx. 55

coffin bone "rotation": see *P3 rotation.*

collection: Ability of a straight horse to round his back and bring his hind legs further under his body to execute extraordinary variations of his natural gaits. 238

common digital extensor tendon (CDET): Major tendon responsible for extending the digit and foot forward. 59

compressional force: Pressure within the capsule during support caused by descending body weight. 150

concussional forces: Shockwaves caused by the hoof's collision with the ground. 135

contraction: (Pathology) Atrophied state of the foot due to shoeing, invasive trimming, hoof pain, and unnatural boarding practices. 235

corium: Dermis responsible for growing its own epidermal structure (e.g., sole). 60

coronary band (coronet): Epidermal skin covering the coronary corium. 55

coronary corium: Dermis behind the coronary band that produces the hoof wall. 60

coronary groove: Tapered inner surface of the upper hoof wall in which the coronary corium is seated. 62

coronary width (CW): Widest expanse of the coronary band behind the pastern. A critical measurement used in booting horses and in determining hoof contraction. 124

crookedness: Curved predisposition of the horse's body from birth to the left or right. Horse is unable to move forward in two tracks. See *straightness.* 238

deep digital flexor tendon (DDFT): Major tendon responsible for flexing the digit and foot rearward. 59

dermis: Vascular (containing blood vessels) and sensitive (having nerves) layer of skin beneath the epidermis. 60

de-shoe: Removal of the horseshoe. 295

dermal lamina (DL): See *lamina (dermal).*

digit: Bones of the horse's foot including P1 (long pastern bone), P2 (short pastern bone), P3 (coffin bone), and NB (navicular bone). 55

divergent toe angle (DTA): Point or points along the MATW where there is a change in the wall's angle of growth. 103

digital cushion: Fibro-fatty tissue with the foot occupying the space between the cartilages, coffin bone, and heel-bulbs below the DDFT; below it also fills the grooves of the frog. 56

dropped sole: (Pathology) Sole that is convex or more active in the volar plane than the hoof wall, a symptom of laminitis and/or invasive trimming ("white line strategy"). 223

ecosystem: see *biome.*

epidermis: Outer aneural (lacking nerves) and avascular (lacking blood vessels) skin of the horse's foot. See *capsule.*

Equus ferus caballus: Domesticated horse genetically indistinguishable from *E. ferus ferus.* 31

Equus ferus ferus: Wild horse. A horse never domesticated. 32

farrier principle: Presumption that the horse's foot needs protection and support if the animal is to serve us in a civilized world. 83

feral horse: Horse living in the wild who came from domesticated stock. 33

flare: Hoof wall that has grown wider than its natural thickness. 183

flight phase: Airborne phase of the hoof during a stride. 136

foot: All the structures comprising the horse's foot, including the capsule and its contents. 53

founder: (Pathology) Separation of the coffin bone from the hoof wall. See *laminitis.*

Four Guiding Principles (of the natural trim): Humane and ethical guidelines for conducting the natural trim. 86

Four Pillars of NHC: Practices of natural hoof care including natural boarding, a reasonably natural diet, natural horsemanship, and the natural trim. 39

Fourth-dimensional (4D) changes: In NHC, changes in hoof mass relative to size, shape, and proportion over time due to the effects of the natural trim and other holistic practices based on the wild horse model. 90

frog pressure theory: Pressure upon the frog from the ground upwards during support, purportedly acting as a "blood pump" to the heart. Rejected by the NHC hoof mechanism model as bogus science. See *hoof mechanism.*

H°: See *Healing Angle (H°).*

hairline: Lower edge of hair growth above the capsule. 55

hard sole plane (HSP): Ground bearing surface of the epidermal sole when trimmed to its natural thickness in accordance with the principles of the natural trim. See *live sole plane (LSP).* 72

healing angle (H°): Angle of growth of the toe wall below the coronary band, measured in alignment with the MPTW. 100

healing toe length (H°TL): Length of the toe wall along the MATW from the bull's-eye to the volar plane. 102

heel: Segment of the hoof wall between the quarter and the bar. 56

heel bulbs: Posterior, bulb-like projections of the foot above the heels formed by the epidermal cleft of the frog. 56

heel-buttress: Turn of the hoof wall comprised of the heel, bar and seat of corn. 56

hoof: The epidermis of the foot. See *Capsule.*

hoof balance: See *biodynamic hoof balance.*

hoof capsule: See *capsule.*

hoof color: Pigmentation in the hoof wall. 74

hoof contraction: See *contraction.*

hoof growth cycle (*hgc*): Time that it takes the foot to produce a new capsule; in NHC, 1 *hgc* occurs at the rate of ¼ in (1 cm) per month. 90

hoof length (HL): Length of the underside of the hoof measured along the MAVP. 124

hoof mechanism: Physical changes the capsule undergoes between flight and support. 135

Hoof Meter Reader (MHR): Hoof gauge for measuring H°TL and H° relative to the volar plane. 112

hoof slough: (Pathology) Complete separation of the capsule from the foot due to laminitis. 138

hoof wall: Portion of the capsule produced by the coronary corium, comprising the toe, quarters, and bars. 56

hoof width (HW): Widest expanse of the hoof, measured at right angle (90°) to the MAVP. 124

HSP: See *hard sole plane (HSP).*

H°TL: See *healing toe length (H°TL).*

horse boot: As opposed to a therapeutic boot, a boot that horses wear temporarily for riding purposes. 85

Information Age: Also commonly known as the Computer Age or Digital Age, is an idea that the current age will be characterized by the ability of individuals to transfer information freely, and to have instant access to information that would have been difficult or impossible to find previously.

invasive trim: Trim method which intentionally penetrates the dermis or thins the capsule rendering the foot painfully hypersensitive; designated as inhumane and a violation of NHC principles and ethics. 87

interdigitation of the lamina: Intermeshing of the dermal and epidermal lamina, forming the LAM between the capsule and foot. 139

lameness: (Pathology) Inability of a horse to move soundly and naturally. See *natural gaits.*

lamellar attachment (suspensory) mechanism (LAM): The dermal "bridge" connecting P3 to the PEL of the inner hoof wall. See also *PEL* and *SEL-BM-DL matrix.* 140

lamina (epidermal): Inner most stratum of the hoof wall comprised of parallel vertical leaves. Also called the primary epidermal leaves, PEL. The PEL are part of the hoof wall and grow continuously down with it. 62

lamina (dermal): Dermal leaves that interdigitate (intermesh) with the epidermal leaves of the inner hoof wall. 62

laminitis: (Pathology) Inflammation of the foot's dermis resulting in the separation of the hoof from the horse. 195

lateral side of hoof: Away from the horse's midline. 109

limit line (LL): Approximate location of the lower shoulder of the coronary groove transposed to the MATW, approximately ½ in. (range ¼ in. to ¾ in) [1 to 2 cm] below the coronary band. Intersection of LL and MATW is the location of the bull's-eye (☉). 116

live sole plane (LSP): Dermis of the sole. 72

LL: See *limit line (LL)*.

longitudinal midline: An imaginary axis and plane passing through and in alignment with the horse's spine. 109

long toe: A toe wall which is longer than measurement ranges for "natural" defined by the wild horse model. See *Healing Toe Length (H° TL)*.

MATW: Median Axis of the Toe Wall. An imaginary vertical line running down the center of the toe wall that intersects the MAVP. 108

MAVP: Median Axis of the Volar Profile. An imaginary line that passes through the central sulcus of the frog bisecting the bottom of the hoof and that intersects the MATW. 110

medial side of hoof: Towards the horse's longitudinal midline. 109

mediolateral: In a direction away from the horse's longitudinal midline. From the medial side of the hoof to the lateral side of the hoof. 109

mediolateral (M-L) heel axis: Imaginary line at right angle (90°) to the MPVP, and aligned with the volar plane, used to sight and balance the heels. 186

mediolateral hoof balance: Orientation of the MATW at right angle (90°) to the volar plane when the capsule is viewed from the front. 110

MPTW: Median Plane of the Toe Wall. An imaginary plane passing through the bull's eye (☉) of the MATW. See also *plane*. 110

MPVP: Median Plane of the Volar Profile. An imaginary plane that passes through and is aligned with the MAVP. See also *plane*. 110

medicinal boot: A non-riding therapeutic type horse boot intended for treating hoof wounds and infections. See *hoof boot*.

medullae: Inner most layer of a horn tubule. 60

mustang roll: A term I created for the radius or curvature of the hoof wall along its ground wearing surfaces, commencing outside the water line. 23

natural boarding: Living conditions that simulate the adaptive type environment of *Equus ferus caballus*, such as the U.S. Great Basin. *Paddock Paradise is a natural boarding concept.* 40

natural diet: Diet of wild horses living in their adaptive type environment such as the U.S. Great Basin. 48

natural gaits: Physical manner in which horses of the U.S. Great Basin naturally move in accordance with their natural gait complex (NGC). This includes the walk, trot, and canter, and their extraordinary variations (e.g., trot in place), as well as movements above the ground (e.g., jumps). 134

natural gait complex (NGC): Natural manner in which wild, free-roaming horses of the U. S. Great Basin and similar adaptive biomes move as a result of herd behavior. 128

natural healing: The body's innate wisdom to heal (Hippocrates: "healing powers of nature"). 85

natural horsemanship: A system of training and riding horses based on their natural gait complex (NGC). 133

naturally shaped hoof: Adaptive hoof of *Equus ferus caballus*, such as we see among wild, free-roaming horses of the U.S. Great Basin and similar biomes. 34

natural hoof care (NHC): Holistic care of the horse based on the wild horse model, including, natural boarding, a reasonably natural diet, natural horsemanship, and the natural trim. 13

natural hoof care practitioner: A person or professional who trims horses in accordance with the practices and practices of NHC. 88

natural selection: Gradual, nonrandom process by which biological traits (physical characteristics) become either more or less common in a population. 34

natural toe angle (N°): The natural angle of growth at the toe, measured over the MATW, as documented for wild, free-roaming horses of the U.S. Great Basin. See also *angle of adaptation (A°)*. 92

natural trim: Trim method that mimics the natural wear patterns of wild, free-roaming horses of the U.S. Great Basin and other similar adaptive biomes. 14

natural wear: Wear resulting in natural hoof shape as exemplified by the hooves of wild, free-roaming horses of the U.S. Great Basin or similar adaptive biomes. 65

navicular: See *Navicular Syndrome.*

navicular syndrome (NS): (Pathology) Any severe trauma injury to the horse's body above the hoof, resulting in a clubfoot in one of the front feet, and a limp over the clubfoot when moving in a turn at the trot. 238

notching: Specialized NHC dissection for training students, emphasizing the location of the capsule's epidermal structures relative to their respective growth coria. 289

outer wall: The hoof wall anywhere below the coronary band and lying outside the water line. 58

P3: See *coffin bone.*

P3 penetration: (Pathology) Piercing of the epidermal sole by the coffin bone, caused by chronic laminitis. 138

P3 rotation: (Pathology) Separation of the capsule from the coffin bone, caused by laminitis. 138

Paddock Paradise: Natural boarding model based on the lifestyle of U.S. Great Basin wild, free-roaming horses. See *natural boarding.* 42

palmer processes of coffin bone: Wing-like posterior projections of the coffin bone; the cartilages are attached to their proximal borders. 57

papillae: Small nipple-like projections of the dermis into the epidermis which play a pivotal role in the formation of the capsule. 62

passive wear: Abrasion of the hoof capsule caused by indirect contact with the ground. *In naturally shaped hooves, the sole undergoes passive contact with the ground, while the hoof wall endures active wear.* 70

passive support: The portions of the naturally shaped hoof capsule which passively support the weight of the horse. *The frog passively supports the weight of the horse, the hoof wall actively supports the horse's weight.* 70

path: Pathways worn into the ground that horses make and use, usually in single file manner, in the wild or within the tracks in Paddock Paradise. See also *tracks.* 48

pecking order: Relative positions of dominance and sub-dominance among alphas and betas, respectively, in the horse's natural social hierarchy. 160

peripheral loading: Weight borne principally upon the hoof wall. 143

plane: A flat, two-dimensional surface. See *volar plane.*

primary epidermal lamina (PEL): See *lamina (epidermal).* 140

relative concavity: The natural positions of the hoof's weight bearing structures in the volar dome relative to the volar plane. *The sole is passive to the hoof wall in the hoof's volar dome; the water line is active to the white line.* See also *volar dome, volar profile, and volar plane.* 58

relative dominance (RD): Position of the trimmer and horse with respect to pecking order. 160

resection: Surgical or invasive trimming away of the hoof wall or others structures of the capsule to the dermis. Considered unnecessary and inhumane by NHC standards. 87

run-under heels: (Pathology) Condition of the hoof capsule in which the position of the heel-buttresses is too far forward under the hoof, caused by excessive growth and/or unnatural trimming and shoeing procedures. 104

seat of corn: Wedge of sole surrounded by the hoof wall and bars forming the heel buttresses. 56

secondary epidermal leaves (SEL): Epidermal leaves, or SEL, that interdigitate (intermesh) with the PEL. The SEL are not part of the descending hoof wall and are stationary, anchored to the basement membrane of the dermal leaf. 140

seedy toe: (Pathology) Misnomer for a symptom of chronic laminitis. See *laminitis*.

SEL-BM-DL matrix: Fibrous bridge connecting the inner hoof wall to P3 comprised of the SEL, BM, and DL. 140

sequencing: NHC approach to trimming the horse based on efficient tool/equipment management; communication with the horse through RD; and optimal positioning of trimmer, handler and horse. 166

slipper toe hoof: (Pathology) Capsule with one or more DTAs and where the MATW has bent forward of H°TL. 114

solar loading: See *white line strategy*.

solar plate: Sheet of epidermal sole that is biodynamically ready to separate from the HSP. 207

straightness, a horse that is straight: The ability of the horse to bend his body evenly in the arc of a turn in either direction, and to move forward on two tracks in his natural gaits. A straight horse is one that is not crooked and is able to collect himself naturally. See also *crookedness* and *collection*. 238

stress ring: (Pathology) Parallel ridges or grooves circumscribing the outer hoof wall as a result of dietary distress and/or chemical toxicity. 50

stretched white line: (Pathology) Disorganized LAM due to laminitis. Symptom of laminitis, visible as a white line that is wider than what is natural ("stretched"). 196

support phase: Weight bearing phase of the hoof during a stride. 136

thrush: (Pathology) Infection of the frog due to diet, exacerbated by unnatural boarding conditions. See *laminitis* and *natural boarding*.

toe angle: (Generic) Angle of the toe wall relative to the ground or the bottom of the hoof. See *Healing Angle (H°)*.

toe length: (Generic) The length of the toe wall from the hairline down the center of the hoof wall to the ground. See *Healing Toe Length (H° TL)*.

track (natural gaits): Orientation of footfalls on the ground during a stride; e.g., a horse is moving in two tracks when the LF and LH make one track, and the RF and RH make a second track. 239

tracks (Paddock Paradise): A system of fenced passageways containing paths for horses to move about from one activity (e.g., feeding area) to another (e.g., water hole) in Paddock Paradise. See also *path*. 118

tubule: Hair-like strand and component of the capsule produced by its own papillae. 60

volar dome: Generally, the concaved conformation of the naturally shaped hoof's volar profile. See also *relative concavity*. 58

volar plane: Imaginary plane that supports the active wear surfaces of the capsule. See also *plane*. 58

volar profile: Weight bearing structures of the capsule. 58

water line: Unpigmented stratum of the inner hoof wall. Aka, stratum internum. *The water line is the most distal structure in the naturally shaped hoof.* 58

white line: Juncture of the hoof wall and sole.

white line strategy: Inhumane trim method with objective of rendering the hoof wall passive to the sole (called "solar loading") in the volar plane. 143

white line disease (WLD): (Pathology) Misnomer for chronic laminitis. See *laminitis*.

wild horse model: NHC model based on wild, free-roaming horses living in the U.S. Great Basin or similar adaptive biome. See *NHC*.

wild horse trim: See *natural trim*.

wry foot: (Pathology) A deformed hoof that has grown lopsided due to unnatural hoof care. 255